The Kochia Chronicles

Systemic Challenges and the
Foundations of Social Innovation

Khanjan Mehta

The Kochia Chronicles:
Systemic Challenges and the Foundations of Social Innovation

Copyright © 2013 by Khanjan Mehta
All rights reserved.

Illustration Artist: Issa Jabez Mohammed
Copyeditor: Everleigh Stokes
Cover Design: Jan Sunday

This is a work of fiction. Names, characters, businesses, places, events and incidents are either the products of the author's imagination or used in a fictitious manner. Any resemblance to actual persons, living or dead, or actual events is purely coincidental.

Published in the United States of America

Library of Congress Control Number: 2013913982
ISBN-10: 1-4909-7791-0
ISBN-13: 978-1-4909-7791-1

Printed by CreateSpace, An Amazon.com Company

Contents

Preface

There is growing consciousness and boundless enthusiasm, especially among the younger generation, to make a positive difference in the lives of people in developing communities. There are several different forms of engagement to "change the world." Thousands of excited volunteers travel every year to developing countries to teach in schools, paint orphanages, conduct HIV/AIDS workshops, build toilets and homes, conduct health camps and dispense medication, or provide microloans to start new businesses. Academic programs, student clubs, and professional bodies have emerged to engage in the design, field-testing and commercialization of technology solutions for developing communities. Such ventures range from infrastructure projects like constructing renewable energy and wastewater treatment systems to social enterprises like those focused on solar lanterns, affordable greenhouses, and point-of-use diagnostic devices. Collectively, such endeavors have the potential to make a significant contribution towards making the world a freer, fairer, friendlier, and more sustainable planet.

However, good intentions and passion are not enough. While such projects are usually well-meaning, creatively designed, and enthusiastically deployed, they do not necessarily result in sustainable impact for the partnering communities. Projects fail, or do not realize their full potential, when local knowledge, perspectives and frameworks are not integrated into the venture. Whether naïve or deliberate, this lack of respect for the cultural and socio-economic context inhibits multi-sectoral innovation that is crucial for project success. The majority of the challenges on development projects can be attributed to the cultural, social, economic, ethical, and business development aspects. Key challenges include designing, implementing and evaluating appropriate systems (as opposed to individual products or interventions); ensuring equity from, and between, all stakeholders; scaling ventures; engaging marginalized stakeholders in the project; understanding and managing power dynamics and privilege systems; and identifying and incentivizing champions. To successfully navigate such issues, innovators need to understand the resources, challenges, social and behavioral norms, and innovation frameworks of the context that they will be working in.

For example, individuals planning to work in Sub-Saharan Africa need to understand how HIV implicates every single person and impacts every facet of life. Volunteers at the thousands of orphanages across East Africa or Southeast Asia need to be aware of the inner workings of the orphanage business, and realize that their involvement can actually hurt the children and compromise the livelihoods of the caregivers. Innovators need to realize that the "teach a man to fish" adage is actually impractical in many parts of the world where highly-skilled fishermen cannot access the millions of fish in their vicinity due to a variety of cultural, economic or political reasons. Entrepreneurs need to understand the short-term and long-term implications of donating or subsidizing products in resource-constrained settings. Such knowledge, and the empathetic mindset that emerges from it, can be transformative for the individuals, the partnering communities, and their collaborative development ventures.

While facts and figures about countries and cultures can be found with ease, deeper knowledge of "how things work" in developing communities is relatively difficult to attain. There is a growing collection of books that discuss development challenges, advocate a certain development philosophy, or tell stories of heroes and their projects. Such books, typically written by experts from a macro perspective, are inspiring reads that set the stage for deeper engagement. Chinua Achebe asks us, "If lions write their own history, will they glorify the hunter?" While the experts' view is important, it is critical to capture the people's own stories about their lives, development, challenges and practical solutions to address them. A dialog on development requires us to conceptualize and operationalize poverty and innovation as defined, or validated, by the people.

The Kochia Chronicles are a series of fictional stories about the inhabitants of Kochia, a rural area in western Kenya. These stories offer readers a glimpse of life, problems and innovations in developing communities in the backdrop of the rapidly evolving political, social, economic, technological and global context. They immerse readers in the intricacies and dynamic relationships between development, technology, business and everyday life while showcasing and celebrating the people's ingenuity, innovation and resilience. The stories weave a systemic web of concepts, approaches, facts, statistics, norms, musings, and emotions to help readers truly internalize and empathize with the people, their context, and their choices. The objective is to enable readers to step into a world radically different than their own and appreciate the paradoxical simplicity and complexity of development challenges.

The Kochia Chronicles are rooted in rigorous primary research and the vast academic literature on development. Every story owes its genesis to personal experiences gained while leading social ventures in East Africa over the past decade. The stories incorporate perspectives gleaned from conversations with thousands of people across the forty countries that I have traveled across. The stories are ultimately works of fiction and have the primary objective of informing and inspiring innovation that leads to self-determined improvement of lives and livelihoods.

The stories are based in Kochia, in Western Kenya, because that's where my first venture was located. I have been very fortunate to meet some amazing people in this beautiful little part of the world. They have taught me so much and impacted my life in so many ways. Kochia will always have a special place in my heart. While Kochia actually exists, and the issues discussed in this book are very real, the characters, organizations and events in the stories are figments of my imagination. At the same time, my friends from Kochia, replete with their little quirks, problems and ingenious solutions, come into being, put both their hands in the air, and wave at me everywhere I go.

I have the privilege of working with some of the absolute best students at Penn State. However, they have rigid schedules and short attention spans. My expectations from them, in terms of their entrepreneurial ventures and research endeavors, are absolutely insane. The Kochia Chronicles were conceptualized as a teaching tool, alongside formal coursework, to cut down on the number of books and research publications they need to read before they can start working on their ventures. "Don't cheat us by packing all the research papers you want us to read in the stories," my students warned me. I had to comply. In order to weave coherent and engaging stories, some issues were dramatized, some oversimplified, and some avoided altogether.

The challenges and solutions presented in this book are extremely context-specific. It would be downright stupid to blindly copy-paste solutions in other settings, or even in Kochia itself. Stories were chosen as the medium for this project because they provide readers a natural and meaningful learning context by transcending language, culture and disciplines. Stories can 'bring to life' complex concepts and let readers draw their own lessons and inferences that fit their unique project context and design challenges.

Chimamanda Adichie, the Nigerian raconteur, reminds us of the 'danger of a single story,' alluding to the notion that our lives and cultures are composed of several overlapping stories. We risk a critical misunderstanding if we listen to a single story about another person or country. By integrating several overlapping stories into a coherent yet pliable medium, the Kochia Chronicles aim to bring forth a wide range of issues and perspectives that are unlikely to be studied due to the high cost of conducting rigorous hypothesis-driven studies and are often too broad for specialized peer-reviewed journals. Sensitive issues like the abuse of religion, use of contraceptives for AIDS prevention, and perceptions of naïve foreigners are dealt with in an honest and humorous way. The language and sentence structures of the characters are typically Kenyan. Specific costs of various goods and services are provided to help readers put the facts into perspective. The stories have been critiqued by several Kenyan and American individuals with expertise in technological, business, medical and social issues to ensure that they are balanced and inadvertently do not convey wrong notions or stereotypes.

This book presents the first set of nine stories that focus on systemic challenges and the foundations of social innovation. The second set of stories, estimated to be completed in December 2013, focus on engineering design, business strategy, implementation strategy, access to capital, partnerships and allied topics. The third, and final set of stories, are related to community health challenges, mHealth, and practical implementation issues with Community Health Worker (CHW) programs and telemedicine ventures. The Kochia Chronicles can be easily integrated into pre-travel reading regimens, formal coursework, extra-curricular initiatives, or workshops. I decided to self-publish this book to keep costs low and speed-up the time to market. More importantly, lean direct-to-consumer business models are perfectly aligned with my philosophy of knowledge democratization and social innovation. Platforms and technologies like Amazon, Createspace, E-readers, and Elance, made it easier to navigate the book publication process while adding a sense of adventure to it.

I sincerely hope that you enjoy reading the chronicles as much as I enjoyed writing them.

Erokamano Ahinya!

Khanjan Mehta
State College, PA
August 2013

Acknowledgments

A HUGE Thank You to Jabez Issa Mohammed for his phenomenal job on the illustrations for this book. Issa is a fulltime wildlife painter based in Nyeri, Kenya. The sketches were completed as a commissioned project over a six-week period during May and June of 2012. The sketches went through multiple iterations and revisions. Issa taught me how to accept constructive criticism and go back, quite literally, to the drawing board again and again and again – with a smile.

Gori Gaitano connected me to a host of very interesting people including chemists, teachers, used shoe vendors, coffin manufacturers, HIV patients, boat owners, pineapple sellers, piki piki drivers, fishermen, fishmongers, and local investors in Kochia, Homa Bay, and surrounding areas. Gori went out of his way to identify the right people to talk to, organized meetings with them at short notice, and served as a translator. He taught me how to ask sensitive questions without creating awkward situations.

Special thanks to Paul Maina, Director of the Children and Youth Empowerment Center (CYEC) in Nyeri, Kenya, and a part of the extended Mehta family. Paul was the first person I talked to about this project and he has been a steadfast believer ever since. Having lived in various parts of Kenya and traveled extensively across the world, Paul provided excellent critiques from diverse perspectives.

Several individuals reviewed the stories and/or provided feedback: Carl Hammerdorfer, Jeff Brown, Audrey Maretzki, Toby Cumberbatch, Mark Henderson, Iana Aranda, Cathy Nguru, Nelson Onyango, Auma Obama, Steve Suffian, Rachel Dzombak, Jeff Lackey and Ayushman Khazanchi. Everleigh Stokes copyedited the manuscript meticulously and I am grateful to her for that.

I did not develop most of the specific solutions presented in this book and I deserve no credit for them. Credit should be given to the innumerable researchers, innovators, and entrepreneurs across the world that shared their ideas through formal channels like conferences, books, and journal articles, or informal conversations over tea, coffee, or warm Tuskers. I am particularly indebted to the people of Kenya, and specifically Kochia, Nyeri and Nairobi, who have taught me so much about life, liberty and the pursuit of happiness.

I would like to particularly acknowledge my tribe – the wonderful community of innovators and educators at the National Collegiate Inventors and Innovators Alliance (NCIIA). There is so much they have taught me over the last decade. I have also learned a lot from the work of Paul Polak, Guy Kawasaki, Jan Chipchase, William Easterly, Hans Rosling, and the folks at the Abdul Latif Jameel Poverty Action Lab (J-PAL). Joel Friedlander's excellent blog, The Book Designer, provided a wealth of very practical information about the book publication process.

My students – too many to list here – encouraged me to keep working on the stories. Several issues covered in this book can be traced back to original engaged scholarship projects they conducted. It is exhilarating and gratifying to work shoulder-to-shoulder with some of the most amazing young minds, hyper-driven to change the world. I just love my students and cannot thank them enough for making this journey fun and exciting.

The research behind the stories in this book was done over a three-year period and writing the first draft took a year more. The research was supported, in part, by a grant from the Africana Research Center at Penn State. An impact investment from my daughter's college fund allowed for thorough data collection, the commissioned illustrations, and the publication of this book.

My parents, Rashmi and Shaila Mehta, brother, Chanakya, and sister-in-law, Priyanka, firmly believe that everything I do is related to saving the world. They express their love for me, and confidence in my work, by taking over all household chores and mundane tasks, and cooking up awesome meals that meet my exacting standards. My wife, Toral, patiently read and critiqued the stories several times. The assurance that at least one person would read my stories kept me going through the countless nights it took to write every single one of them. We welcomed our daughter, Tashvi, into this world in June 2013. I am excited to have another assured reader, maybe even an editor!

None of the shortcomings of this book should be attributed to any of the individuals mentioned. After all, I made everything up. For whatever is good in these stories, I thank them all very deeply.

About the Author

Khanjan Mehta is the Founding Director of the Humanitarian Engineering and Social Entrepreneurship (HESE) Program at Penn State. HESE is an integrated learning, research, and entrepreneurial engagement program that brings together students and faculty across campus for the rigorous research, design, field-testing, and launch of technology-based social enterprises in resource-constrained settings. HESE espouses the philosophies of Empathy, Equity and Ecosystems to create a vibrant and emergent framework for radical collaboration that leads to the development of sustainable and scalable solutions. Sustainability, in this context, refers to the notion that solutions must be technologically appropriate, socially acceptable, environmentally benign, and economically sustainable. Mehta has led HESE ventures in Kenya, Tanzania, India, China and other countries. These ventures range from telemedicine systems and ruggedized biomedical devices to low-cost greenhouses, solar food dryers, cell phone-based social networking systems, and knowledge sharing platforms for self-employed women.

Mehta's research interests encompass affordable design; systems thinking; social entrepreneurship pedagogy; agricultural technologies and food value chains (FVCs); global health and telemedicine systems; cellphones, social networks and trust; indigenous knowledge systems; development ethics and grassroots diplomacy; women in engineering and entrepreneurship; and informal lending systems for microenterprises. The objective of these research endeavors is to democratize knowledge and mainstream HESE as a valid and rigorous area of learning, research, and engagement. Mehta has served on several university-wide and international committees and taskforces. He has delivered invited talks and keynote speeches on technology innovation, social entrepreneurship, and global sustainability at several universities and international conferences. He lives in State College, PA with his parents; wife, Toral; and daughter, Tashvi.

#1

Obongo's Scramble for the Signboard

Like the rest of the inhabitants of Kochia, Obongo was excited about the new solar power project. Obongo and his wife Janet were leaders of the Empower Kochia Group, a Community-Based Organization (CBO) working on various development projects to improve the lives and livelihoods of the inhabitants of Kochia and surrounding areas. Government officials and Chief Peter Achieng from the Sustainable Utopian Village (SUV) Foundation had come to Kochia about three months back to congratulate the people on their good fortune. After a year-long screening process that involved studying thirty sites and interviewing over 300 people, Kochia had been selected for this project. An array of five large solar panels were to be installed for people to recharge their LED lanterns. Kenya's electrical power system was unreliable and very expensive. Remote areas like Kochia had never had electricity and the people generally used kerosene lamps at night. Since the last two years, a select few inhabitants of Kochia had purchased car batteries for powering LED lamps. It was common for them to travel upwards of 10 kms and spend half their daily income every two weeks to get their batteries charged.

Chief Achieng had explained to Obongo that the solar panels would convert sunlight into electricity. The people of Kochia would have to purchase LED lanterns that would operate on this electricity. Every week, they would have to take their lantern to the project site and get it recharged. It would be like going to the water tap and waiting in line to get your jerry can filled up. Obongo was not quite sure how it would all work but Peter was a trusted friend and if he said so, it must work. Everyone would finally have light at home in the evening; no more eating in the darkness. Obongo was happy that he would finally be able to see his dear wife Janet's face when they would sit down for dinner and chat for an hour or two afterwards. Obongo had a set routine every evening. He would listen to his radio for an hour before dinner. After dinner, he would check on his seven children, two cows, five goats and then come back to his hut and talk to Janet. The topics of conversation were the same every day. They would talk about the children, how much milk the cows and goats were giving, the cellphone calls they made on that day, and general gossip about the members of the Empower Kochia group. The solar power project had also made it to their daily conversation - taking up the spot between the goats and the cell phone calls.

Okello had explained to Obongo that he would save over three hundred Shillings[1] a month by switching from kerosene lamps to the LED lanterns. The lanterns would provide more light than the kerosene lamps and not produce those nasty fumes. He had mentioned something about saving the earth. Obongo was a frugal man and understood the importance of saving water. He was confused about this business of saving the earth but if Okello thought it was important, it must be. Okello knew everything about everything. They had studied together in secondary school and while Obongo quit after Form 4, Okello had gone to Homa Bay and completed Form 6. Okello did not have money to go to university. He worked various jobs in Nairobi, Kisumu, Eldoret and Mombasa before coming back to his homeland to settle down. He started a small medicine shop and looked after his half-acre farm.

Everyone in Kochia had great expectations from Okello. They were convinced that if Okello really put his heart into it, he could rise to great heights. Maybe even become the President of Kenya some day, or at least a senator in the Kenyan government. Okello, on the other hand, had no political ambitions or interest in bureaucratic processes. Ever since he was a child, he was very inquisitive and loved to solve problems. He liked to build things – toys, furniture, mud sculptures, farming implements, matatu[2] decorations and radios. Upon returning from Mombasa, he invested his savings in various tools for his little workshop. He could be found working on some new project in his workshop at odd times of the day and night. He loved children and would make them toys with lights and sound. He would help people build their homes and toilets, fix their cellphones and radios, and rent out batteries. He didn't particularly seem to care about making money either. Sometimes he would just give away

---

[1] 1 US Dollar = ~84 Kenyan Shillings (KES. or KSh.)
[2] Matatus are 11-seater or 14-seater vans widely used for public transportation across East Africa. The motto of a matatu is "There is always room for one more!"

his creations or fix people's appliances and refuse to accept money in return.

"Solving a problem and seeing you happy is my biggest reward. If I have money in my pocket, I will spend it on something frivolous. Rather, I will save it as a favor in your pocket and someday when I need something, you can return the favor," he would tell everyone.

After a year and a half of putting aside a thousand Shillings every month, he finally purchased a second-hand laptop for KSh. 20,000 and a USB internet modem for KSh. 2,000. Access to the internet opened up a whole new world. Okello would spend days and nights learning and building all kinds of things. Gradually, he came to be known as the engineer and problem-solver of Kochia. Everyone sought his advice before buying a new technology product, engaging in a new business venture, trying a new fertilizer, or essentially doing anything new or different. Okello would admit the boundaries of his knowledge but strive to find answers to people's questions. It took away a lot of his time but he enjoyed it. He just couldn't turn anyone down. When people started seeking his advice on buying cows, impotence problems, and negotiating dowries, he drew the line. He put a sign on his door declaring that he would only answer questions related to technology and new businesses. People just ignored it. Finally, when he intentionally advised a rich man to buy a sick ox, the problem was solved. The ox died a week later and word got around that Okello did not know much about cattle. Okello was now able to devote more time to his own projects, and those coordinated by his dear friend Obongo for the Empower Kochia group.

Obongo woke up at his regular time of 6 AM on Monday morning and started thinking about the week ahead. There were only six days left before the launch of the solar power project. There was so much work to be done. He had to travel to Homa Bay to invite the District Officer (DO) and District Commissioner (DC) to the ground breaking. The DC and DO would be invited by Chief Achieng but it was still essential for him to personally invite them. He had to contact all the members of the Empower Kochia group and confirm that they were prepared to be present on Sunday morning. He had to arrange for name badges and safety pins for all the office-holders. There were so many more things to do but first and foremost, he had to get the project signboard made! Chief Achieng had suggested that a big professionally-painted signboard would be received very positively by the chiefs of the SUV Foundation. After all, this was a very big and important project that would mark a new chapter in the history of Kochia. Obongo presented this idea to the CBO members who were very supportive and resolved that no expense should be spared to prepare a signboard that fits the stature of the project.

Obongo decided to start his day by talking to Godgift about the signboard. It was a 45-minute walk across his friends' farms to reach Godgift's little shop in Imboyo market. Obongo started out for Imboyo market at once - there was no time to lose.

"The ground breaking of the solar power project is on Sunday at 10 AM. Come to the site directly after church. Don't forget!" he would shout as he passed people's homes. It was barely 8 AM when he reached Imboyo market. Barring the M-Pesa[1] kiosk, the rest of the shops were closed and the huts where the people lived were just beginning to stir.

"A little too early," Obongo thought to himself, "Godgift is not going to open his shop for at least two more hours!"

He settled down on a chair offered by a lady in one of the huts. He had seen her many times but was not sure whose wife she was. A number of thoughts ran through his head: things to do for the groundbreaking; how he would greet all the important people; the menu for the feast sponsored by the SUV Foundation; from whom he would buy the goats; how the goats would be cooked; how he would bargain down the price of the goats. After dwelling on the goats for a few more minutes, his mind settled on the finances of the Empower Kochia group.

Obongo always knew which members had their dues paid in full and whose contributions were pending. "...my good friend, I know that business is not very good right now and your child was recently sick. But if you don't pay your dues on time, how will our group complete all these projects? How will we improve the life of our people?" Obongo would urge the defaulters. "It is just 100 Shillings a month – the cost of two sodas."

He always knew how much money was in the group's bank account. Last month, the balance was over KSh. 8,000. When the rent for the group's tiny office space, which had accrued for six months, was settled, the balance dropped to KSh. 2,550. Fifteen members were yet to contribute their monthly dues. That would put their total balance at KSh. 4,050. He remembered the day the bank manager at United Kenya Cooperative Bank had called him into his office and they had a soda together. The account balance stood at a majestic KSh. 22,600 on that day and they had discussed various ways the funds could be invested so that they would grow into a larger amount.

"Those were the days. If only I had not listened to the manager's

---

[1] M-Pesa is a mobile-to-mobile money transfer system operated by Safaricom.

Obongo Waiting Outside Godgift's Shop

fanciful ideas, right now there would be so much more money in the account," Obongo reminisced. He wrote up the names of the fifteen group members whose dues were pending. He decided that after he had talked to Godgift about the signboard, he would go around and collect money from all the members. He might even goad them to pay for the next month!

It was past 10:30 AM when Godgift finally appeared at the shop. Obongo could not stop staring at the gigantic rusted lock that held the rotting doors together. "One could easily pull the doors out from the hinges," he muttered under his breath.

"You are very lucky that I decided to open the shop today," Godgift insisted. "Business has been so slow in the last few days that I don't see the point of opening the shop and sitting here all day. I might as well stay at home with the children. How can I help you?"

That's the moment Obongo was waiting for! He took a deep breath and burst into an ear-to-ear smile. For the next thirty minutes, he narrated to Godgift everything he knew about the solar power project - from the sun's energy to Okello's smart ideas to the menu for the gala feast to be held on Sunday. A small crowd had gathered by the time Obongo was done explaining the project. "Don't forget gentlemen," Obongo said to the crowd, "Sunday morning, directly after church...and I have been told that the MP himself will stop by to grace this occasion."

"This is a very good project. It will benefit all of us," Godgift agreed. "Thank you specially for coming all the way here, early in the morning, to tell me about this project."

"Karibu Tena[1]. I came here with a purpose." Obongo smiled. "I want you to play a larger role in this project and leave your mark on the history of Kochia."

"I am honored," Godgift replied. "But let me be clear. This time I cannot provide my services for free. Business is not good. I will leave as many marks on our history as you insist but I need my fair wages."

"Surely," Obongo assured, "the group has already sanctioned the funds for this effort. We need a large signboard on a metal sheet with a wooden frame around it. The metal should be thick gauge and the wood must be termite-resistant. The name of the project is 'Solar Power Project' and the partners are the President's Office (Government of Kenya), the Sustainable Utopian Village (SUV) Foundation and the Empower Kochia CBO. The words should be painted with oil paint that will stay for at least ten years. Every two years, we will get it repainted so

---

[1] Karibu Tena = You are welcome (Kiswahili)

6

that it looks brand new...and of course you will be asked to repaint the sign."

"Did you say it is a ten-year project?" Godgift gave a shy smile. "I am so proud to play a pivotal role in such an important long-term project."

"Indeed," Obongo confirmed. "Depending on when the project itself starts, it might even be longer than that."

"When will the project commence?" Godgift inquired. "At that time we will have to place several signboards to direct everyone to the project site. Why don't we start working on those signboards now? Then all our people and the visitors will know exactly where the project is going to be located!"

"No, No, No, my friend," Obongo said. "For now, the group has only sanctioned funds for the main signboard. But, you have to give us a very good rate. As you know money is very tight and this is all for the improvement of Kochia!"

After an hour's negotiation with six bystanders expressing their opinions on the correct price, the kind of wooden frame, and the precise shade of the blue paint, the price was set at KSh. 4,000. This price included the installation of the signboard at the project site as well as repainting the text every two years for the next six years. The signboard was to be installed on Saturday morning and that's when the KSh. 4,000 would have to be paid.

"There is nothing to worry about. The money for your wages has already been set aside." Obongo swiftly turned down Godgift's request for an advance.

"Godgift does a good job but always charges so much money. KSh. 8,000 is certainly outrageous! The signboard should not cost more than 2,000 bob[1]. Thank heavens for supporting this project. We got the signboard done for 4,000 bob. Now, there is nothing to worry about for the next ten years," Obongo mumbled to himself as he set off on his journey, determined to collect the KSh. 1,500 in missing dues. He went to five houses that evening and spent between ten minutes to two hours explaining the solar power project and coaxing the members to pay their monthly dues. He was able to recover dues from three of the members while the other two asked him to come back the next day. He had to collect money from 12 more members and he had four more days to do so. After those four days, he would have KSh. 4,050 - enough to have the signboard completely paid for. The sun had set when he reached home - another long day with so much accomplished.

---

[1] Bob = Slang for Shillings.

That night Obongo truly enjoyed his modest sukumawiki[1] and chapatti[2] dinner with his family. His nightly discussion with his wife focused on his adventures of the day and his plans for Tuesday. He decided to set off early on Tuesday morning to collect dues from the other twelve members. The reputation of the Empower Kochia group was at stake, and so was his.

"Maybe there will be some faults with the signboard and then I will pay Godgift only KSh. 3,900. That will leave me with 150 bob that I can use to buy a soda for the District Commissioner, the District Officer, the MP, Chief Achieng and me. I will just pay for the ice myself so that we can enjoy a cold soda together. Once the project starts and everyone can see the potential in Kochia, more donors will come and there will be many more projects. In addition to more donors, once we demonstrate some success, we will increase the monthly dues to 200 Shillings. Then I will have some funds to move around and meet more partners. I can even ask the group for a small stipend," Obongo thought to himself. He was smiling when he finally fell asleep.

Tuesday and Wednesday were long days. Obongo went door to door all over Kochia from seven in the morning to eight at night. He was able to collect dues from six more members. Now, he had KSh. 900 in his pocket and KSh. 2,550 in the group's bank account, bringing the total to KSh. 3,450. Six more members to go! He tried to hide his worries from Janet but failed miserably. As he tried to fall asleep, he was thinking about the people from whom he had to collect money.

Philip was one of the group's most active and popular members. His home was closed. "Maybe, he found a contract job in Homa Bay and is staying with his brother. I should go to Homa Bay to withdraw money from the bank tomorrow rather than Friday...and also check on Philip at the same time," Obongo made plans for the next day. Four of the Empower Kochia members lived in Ngegu, a small fishing village on the way to Homa Bay. He decided to visit them first and then go to Homa Bay. If everything went as planned, the only person left would be Reverend Ndiege.

"Yai yai yaaiii!" Obongo sighed. Last time when he had gone to Rev Ndiege to collect dues, the Reverend had asked him to wait for almost five hours while he took care of church duties. Finally, he had come out and explained how his finances were not very good and asked Obongo to come back after two days. It took three more visits and a cumulative wait

---

[1] Sukumawiki = Kale. Sukumawiki literally translates to "push the week" and is a staple food across East Africa.

[2] Chapatti = Indian flat bread made from wheat flour; another staple across Kenya.

8

of eleven hours before Obongo walked home a winner - with 100 Shillings in his pocket.

Thursday did not go as planned. As Obongo was about to step out in the morning, the sub-chief of Central Kochia walked into his house to discuss the plans for Sunday. The discussion lasted over four hours and the sub-chief finally left at 2:30 PM only after he was convinced that everything would go smoothly. Now, there wasn't enough time left to make the trip to Ngegu, the bank in Homa Bay town, and the municipal offices to invite the DC and DO. Obongo decided to visit the Reverend instead. The Reverend greeted him very warmly and inquired about the plan for Sunday and the status of the signboard.

"Don't forget to check on Godgift again!" the Reverend warned Obongo. "All of Kochia knows how bad his spellings are. Last time..."

Obongo was not in the mood for any more discussions but he patiently heard the Reverend's stories about Godgift's spelling errors. He had to wait just 30 minutes to witness a miracle. The Reverend pulled out a crisp 100 Shilling note and gave it to Obongo, "I will be at the site at 11 AM sharp and I will bring all my congregants with me."

The reverend understood the reason for the surprised look on Obongo's face. He looked at the heavens and smiled. Obongo was back home in less than an hour and had successfully collected the dues from the Reverend! On the way home, he decided to stop by Godgift's shop. Godgift had the correct design and spellings on paper and was just getting ready to start painting them on the board. Obongo waited for a while but then decided to head back home and listen to his radio. He was curious if the local evening news broadcast would mention the ground breaking ceremony and the solar power project.

Obongo boarded the first matatu to Ngegu on Friday morning. He went straight to the group members' homes but all four of them were out fishing on the lake. He was assured by the member's kin that the 100 Shillings were ready, but he should return in the afternoon and speak to the men before collecting the money. It was almost noon when Obongo reached the bank in Homa Bay. He was hoping that the bank officer would ask him why he was withdrawing so much money from the group's account. The bank officer simply verified Obongo's and the treasurer's signature and handed him the KSh. 2,550. He advised Obongo to maintain a small balance in his account before moving on to the next customer.

"The bank officer did not even care to ask me why I am withdrawing so much money! These young people don't know how to engage with customers," Obongo walked out of the bank disheartened. The DC and

DO were not in their respective offices and he left a warm invitation for them with their secretaries.

The next stop was Philip's brother's shop. Peter knew nothing of Philip's whereabouts and refused to pay his brother's dues. Without pressing the matter further, Obongo rushed to the matatu stage. Thankfully, the bus to Kisumu left soon and dropped Obongo at Ngegu thirty minutes later. He was able to quickly collect dues from all four members. They insisted that the next project be situated in Ngegu so that they didn't have to travel such a long distance. Obongo promised them another solar project that would be the pride of Ngegu. He was glad that everything in Ngegu worked out well. He put the KSh. 3,950 in a plastic bag, neatly folded it up and put it in the inside pocket of his old grey jacket. Obongo was disappointed. He was 50 Shillings short. He would surely lose face if people would find out that he had not managed to put together the KSh. 4,000 for the signboard.

Obongo would have just added the 100 Shillings from his pocket. Over the years, he had contributed thousands of Shillings to various group projects. Then, three months back, he refused to buy his daughter a cellphone but contributed 500 Shillings to a cooperative farming project. That was the straw that broke the camel's back. Janet did not take very kindly to Obongo's judgment. The farming project's failure added fuel to the fire. After a lengthy argument and a week-long cold war, Obongo promised to never contribute any funds besides the regular monthly dues. Given the importance of this event, Obongo considered seeking a waiver from Janet. After considerable thought, he decided to save the favor as a last resort. He started praying that Godgift would make a spelling mistake. The budget for the sodas and ice was bothering him too. That night he lay awake for two hours tossing and turning - acting and re-enacting how he would tell Godgift that his work was only worth KSh. 3,900 Shillings...or even worth KSh. 3,800!

Saturday morning was full of excitement. Over 35 people had gathered at the site to commemorate the installation of the signboard. When the signboard finally arrived on a bicycle, it was covered in newspapers so that it would not get dirty. Godgift insisted that the newspapers be kept on the signboard until the actual ground breaking ceremony. "At that auspicious moment, the MP will tear off the newspapers and inaugurate the signboard." Godgift even brought along a few of his friends to support his idea. Everyone seemed to agree with Godgift's plan. After a heated two-hour debate, Obongo had to concede defeat. He also ignored his promise to Janet and added personal funds to hand out the KSh. 4,000 to a delighted Godgift, who quickly counted the crumpled notes, put them in his pocket, and walked away. Obongo was an honest man and resolved to make a candid confession to Janet about the extenuating circumstances that led him to add the paltry sum of 50 Shillings for the signboard. Four volunteers had come forward to guard the signboard overnight until the formal inauguration. Obongo had lost interest in the signboard now. His thoughts revolved around having a soda with all the important people on Sunday.

Sunday morning was very hectic. Chief Achieng had called a number of times to check on the preparations. He informed Obongo that the SUVs were on their way to Kochia, picking up dignitaries - local chiefs (and their relatives), civil servants, businessmen, NGO workers and others along the way. The ground breaking ceremony was to commence at 10 AM. The school headmaster, Mr. Masinde, had promised to bring his children to perform a folk dance for the esteemed guests. The SUV Foundation had arranged for a megaphone system so that the speeches could be clearly heard by the 200-strong audience anticipated at the inauguration. The foundation also provided the groceries for a meal of ugali[1], sukumawiki, beans and goat stew for all the guests. Under Janet's leadership, a team of twenty women had been toiling since early morning to prepare the meal. All the Empower Kochia group members and a few other guests brought in fresh pineapples from their farms to share with everyone.

Finally, crowds started gathering around 11:30 AM. As promised, the Reverend arrived with his entire congregation and Mr. Masinde arrived with his 60-member school dance troupe. The Reverend was not the kind who would waste a minute. The school children were a captive audience and a long sermon followed. Screams of "Yesu nakupenda[2]" and peals of laughter from the children as well as adults reverberated in the air. Rev. Ndiege was adept at preaching to young people in an intelligent and entertaining manner. There was a sense of euphoria that comes with great hope and engagement in a community that one can truly identify with. Obongo was happy. He had five big bottles of soda in a plastic bucket full of ice hidden away in a safe place.

There was great jubilation in the crowd when a dust storm kicked off on the horizon. People scurried around and informed everyone that the officials had arrived. Obongo looked at his watch - it was 12:45 PM. "Thank God, everything is going as planned," Obongo cheered the women who were now busy slicing juicy pineapples. "Please make sure that the meals are ready at 3 PM sharp." He rushed back to gather

---

[1] Ugali is a staple food made by boiling cornmeal until it has dough-like consistency

[2] Yesu Nakupenda = I love Jesus (Kiswahili)

everyone and welcome the dignitaries.

The fleet of six SUVs, specially decorated for the occasion, arrived at the project site in style. Obongo and the chair holders of the Empower Kochia CBO were standing in formation to greet the visitors. Chief Achieng and the District Commissioner were the first to alight and greet everyone. The dignitaries and guests from the neighboring towns poured out from the SUVs and engaged in an elaborate round of greetings and handshakes with the crowd.

Chief Achieng held Obongo's hand and pulled him aside, "I have a message for you. The MP himself called me this morning and pledged his support to the project. He had some work come up today and could not join in the festivities but he has promised to pay a visit to Kochia very soon."

"I understand," Obongo drawled. He took a deep breath. "And what about the District Officer? He called me just yesterday evening and promised that he would grace the occasion."

"Unfortunately, he is also very busy. You know these fishermen keep breaking the law by using very fine nets. He had to resolve some problem regarding that issue. Let me assure you that he is also very supportive and will be here once the project has started!"

"Many people have been asking me when the project will actually start," Obongo remarked. "Please address that question in your speech."

"I have been trying to find that out myself," Chief Achieng confided. "It is beyond my control. Let me assure you that I was instrumental in making sure that this project comes to Kochia. I am committed to you people. Now that we have started the project, with God's support, I am sure we will also complete it someday."

Obongo commenced the celebrations with a welcome speech. He invited the Reverend to say a short fifteen-minute prayer. This was followed by the school children's folk dance performance and speeches by the District Commissioner, Chief Achieng, and the project engineer. Okello was called on by the crowd to translate the engineer's speech into simple words. Okello stepped up to the occasion and explained in details how the solar power project will eventually change the lives of the people of Kochia by providing them light while saving time and money. Okello responded to a barrage of questions posed by the audience. A few guests made formal speeches to express their gratitude to the SUV Foundation and other sponsors and expressed their excitement in seeing the project begin. Chief Achieng was requested to explain the timeline for the project. In a circuitous manner, he indicated that the solar panel installation would be initiated within three months. Much to Okello and

Innauguration of the Solar Power Project

Obongo's dismay, he refused to provide a specific date when the project itself would be inaugurated and people would be able to get their LED lanterns and cellphones charged. Obongo pleaded with Okello to hold back and not challenge Chief Achieng in front of the entire crowd. Okello relented and walked away from the project site without looking back.

At 3:30 PM, it was finally time for the groundbreaking and the inauguration of the signboard. Godgift ran ahead and moved everyone away to make space for the dignitaries. He occupied a prime spot right next to the signboard.

"The correct person to inaugurate the signboard is our MP," the DC declared over the megaphone. "But as you all know very well, our MP is a busy man and could not make it to Kochia today. He has pledged support to this project and on his behalf, Chief Achieng and I will officiate the inauguration." There was a loud applause from the crowd as the DC followed by Chief Achieng shoveled some mud and collaboratively tore off the newspaper wrapped around the signboard.

"Yai Yai Yaiii! Didn't I warn you…?" Reverend Ndiege exclaimed as Obongo stared at the ground and scratched his head. The crowd cheered and danced as a beaming Godgift gave a theatrical bow and joined in the revelry. The "Salor Power Project" was thus inaugurated.

"Today is a historic day for Kochia," Obongo proclaimed over the loudspeaker system, "The Government of Kenya, SUV Foundation and Empower Kochia CBO are working together shoulder to shoulder. This has been possible only because of the hard work of the DC, Chief Achieng, and, of course, our MP…who, as you all know could not make it here today. He has promised us a visit very soon when I am sure we will have a feast that rivals today's celebrations. As this sign proclaims, we have started a very important project and very soon we will have light in Kochia." The crowd jubilated and continued their celebrations while the women started serving the meals. Obongo switched off the megaphone and turned to the DC and Chief Achieng, "Today has been a very tiring day for you and now it is time to have something. So, please…" He led the way to his humble home where Janet and the Reverend were waiting with five ice-cold large bottles of soda.

#2

Janet's Momentous HIV/AIDS Workshop

"Why don't you go to Kisumu and visit your sister?" Obongo suggested to Janet. "Her health is getting worse every day. Charity told me this morning that the doctor has given her just a few more days to live."

"I know," Janet sighed. "When I spoke to Charity two weeks back, she told me exactly the same thing. I want to see my sister before she passes away. I will surely go next week."

"That might be too late. Do you remember how I kept postponing my visit to Philip's ailing father and then it was too late."

"I just cannot go this week. I have to attend the HIV/ AIDS workshop. It is very important that I learn to do home-based care of HIV patients perfectly."

"But Janet, your sister is dying from AIDS. She only has a few days to live. And you have received HIV training in the past. If you leave this afternoon, you could be back in time for the workshop."

"That is not possible because I have to prepare for the workshop. I will leave for Kisumu right after the workshop is over."

"OK, do what you wish," Obongo snapped. "I have told you what I think."

"And I have heard you." Janet walked off to the kitchen. "I will talk to Sister Phoebe when I see her this afternoon." Janet cooked a light meal of boiled eggs, sukumawiki and chapattis and asked her daughter to serve it at lunchtime. She started her hour-long walk to Sister Phoebe's home for HIV/AIDS patients.

Sister Phoebe, a catholic nun, was one of the most respected citizens of Kochia. She was born there and had devoted her entire life caring for the people. After completing her religious education, she chose to serve at a clinic operated by the Catholic church because she wanted to improve community health. She spent a decade at the clinic counseling patients and providing basic care. Though she had no formal medical training, she became a nurse by practice. When the HIV epidemic worsened, clinics and hospitals were grossly overburdened with HIV patients. Sister Phoebe started providing home-based care to patients whose families could not care for them due to stigma, poverty, or personal health problems. She pioneered this practical approach of visiting patients at their home to provide medicines, nutritious food, spiritual strength, and assistance in daily chores. While this approach worked for patients in early stages, patients who had developed advanced AIDS required intensive care. With the help of local Samaritans, Sister Phoebe refurbished an abandoned community school and converted it into a home for terminally-ill HIV patients. She lived with the patients and took responsibility for every aspect of the home's operations, from fundraising to cooking, healthcare, ministry, and managing volunteers. Over the years, she was able to build-up and sustain a three-member staff consisting of a cook and two full-time caregivers. Sister Phoebe mentored Janet and several others to initiate and operate their home-based patient care activities.

"Good afternoon, Sister Phoebe." Janet knocked on the door and walked in.

"Janet! What a pleasant surprise. Please come in. What brings you here?"

"I was just going on my home-care rounds when I decided to pay you a courtesy call and seek your advice about something that is troubling me."

"I am happy you came. I was going to call you today. There is someone who has come to me several times to ask me how he can help our people. I suggested that he could get involved with home-based care. He wants to learn more."

"Did you say this person is a man? Right now, all our group members are women. Having a man would be very helpful, especially to work with the older male patients. Who is this person?"

"First, let me assure you that he is very genuine and committed this time. So you must really talk to him before deciding whether you want to involve him or not."

"Sister Phoebe, who is it?"

"Odhiambo!"

"Yaai yai yaai! Odhiambo!"

"Janet – just talk to him first. He is very serious about helping."

"Tch tch sister, his track record is very poor. He is always joking around about everything. He will make fun of the HIV patients and cause them more suffering."

"...or he might provide them some much-needed comic relief! If he sets his mind on something, he can do a very good job. If you remember, he worked shoulder to shoulder with Okello and Obongo to refurbish our home. He worked day and night all alone over five days and painted this entire place. Every few weeks, he comes here and works on the shambaa and tells stories to the patients. They eagerly look forward to his visits."

"Yes, he is a good person but he needs to get serious. Since you insist, I will talk to him."

"The only problem," Sister Phoebe continued, "is that while he is happy to volunteer once in a while, what he really wants to do is to help people and earn money at the same time."

"See, this is the problem with Odhiambo! How is that possible? How can he expect money from the HIV patients who have nothing, absolutely nothing, and are at the end of their lives?"

"Don't you earn a little money when you provide home-based care?"

"Sister, you initiated me into this work. As you know, just like you, I volunteered my time in the early days. It was physically strenuous work and I had frequent headaches. Then two years back, this NGO came to Homa Bay to help with the HIV burden. Now they provide us some funding. But, they don't pay us a salary. When I go to the office to report my monthly activities, I get a conveyance stipend of 2,000 Shillings. Since my actual travel cost is only 100 Shillings, the rest of the money can be considered a salary."

"Is that it? I remember you told me that you are always on the lookout for patients who might qualify to receive a chicken or a goat..."

"Oh that!" Janet smiled. "Depending on their condition, some individuals qualify for a chicken and groups can qualify for a goat. After the patients get their HIV tests done and other paperwork is complete, I give them the chicken or goat. If we give them money, they spend it on unnecessary things. So that is not allowed. I get the cash from the office and I buy the chicken or goat and give it to the people. Then I return the receipt and the remaining money to the office. I have many friends in the market and they help me make a little bit of money. You know how it works sister!"

"Janet! That is not fair!"

"Sister Phoebe," Janet explained, "I know it is not completely right but all the health workers do that. Even the NGO people know it. Because of their rules, they cannot pay us for our work. At the same time they know that we are also poor people and need to feed our families. This is actually a very inexpensive and practical way to incentivize us and keep us working for the HIV patients. When we are helping the HIV patients, we are getting the NGO's work done."

"We can talk about right and wrong for hours," Sister Phoebe said, "but I can see how this is a practical solution."

"Anyways, to answer your first question, every month we earn between 2,000 and 3,000 Shillings. Many of us also engage in other income-generating activities to supplement this money."

"You should explain this to Odhiambo when we meet him at the HIV/AIDS workshop. I had nominated him and he was invited. I spoke to him this morning and he is very excited about it."

"We have had a few other men work with us but it is very difficult for them. Providing care involves washing, cooking, feeding, cleaning, purchasing household things, taking the patients to the toilet, helping them take a bath, and making sure they have taken their medicines. Men are not used to doing such jobs. They are excited about helping people and do it for a few days, even a week, and then they give up. Also, the money is not adequate for them to support their families."

"Odhiambo can try and see what it is like. He might like the work or he might decide it's not for him. Either way, he will learn many new things. Maybe he will find something else that suits him better. Anyways, you said you wanted my advice?"

"Yes, my sister who lives in Kisumu has AIDS. I was informed that she is now in her final days. Obongo wants me to visit her this week and I really want to see her too. But, the HIV/AIDS workshop is this week and I don't want to miss it."

"I am very sorry to hear that," Sister Phoebe commiserated. "That is a difficult situation. I think that since you have been to other HIV workshops in the past, you should visit your sister. If you don't meet her, you will regret it for your entire life."

"That is exactly what Obongo said as well," Janet acknowledged, "I will think about it some more."

"It is your decision and no one else should decide for you," Sister Phoebe reassured Janet.

"Thank you Sister." Janet clutched Sister Phoebe's arm. "I will leave now but we are together."

"Yes, we are! And don't forget to talk to Odhiambo," Sister Phoebe reminded Janet as she hastily dashed out of the door to start her rounds with the patients.

"AIDS is not American idea of discouraging sex," affirmed the training coordinator struggling to suppress laughter. "Everybody here knows what AIDS stands for? Does everybody know?"

"YES," was the unanimous response from the 15 or so people sitting in the tiny dimly-lit room.

"Can you tell me what AIDS stands for?" the coordinator asked as she surveyed the room. About half the people in the room raised their hand. Janet was one of them. After mulling over her dilemma all night, she had decided to stay her course and attend the workshop. Attendance at the two-day workshop was by invitation only. Janet had been invited because she was the leader of the Empower Kochia CBO. The coordinator looked at Janet and smiled.

"AIDS is Acquired Immune Deficiency Syndrome. HIV is Human Immunodeficiency Virus. HIV/ AIDS is a killer disease that is claiming the lives of millions of Kenyans every year," Janet said in one breath.

"Ayyyy," the coordinator agreed and pushed her chin up. "AIDS is killing Kenyans like goats and sheep in an abattoir."

"Since the first case of HIV and AIDS was diagnosed in 1984, Kenya has witnessed enormous devastation and erosion of socio-economic gains that have taken so many years to put together." The coordinator carefully read from the HIV/AIDS Training Manual provided by the government. She had memorized most of the sentences she was supposed to read while conducting the two-day HIV/AIDS training workshop for local chiefs and community workers. She had conducted these programs all around Nyanza province and came back to Kochia to teach the course every two months. Kochia was her favorite location because she knew everyone so well.

"We must commence our workshop with a prayer," the coordinator suggested and motioned the participants to rise. Everyone in the room stood up, formed a circle and said a short prayer. They thanked God that they were free from HIV and asked for strength and support to care for their friends and relatives who were suffering from AIDS. The participants were an equal mix of men and women and ranged in age from 25 to 55. Most of them had more than one trade – they were fishermen or fish mongers, they sold vegetables or fixed bicycles, some were jua kalis[1] and some worked in small shops. Most of them farmed sukumawiki around their homes and kept poultry. All the attendees had one thing in common - they cared for, or were interested in caring for,

---

[1] Jua kalis literally means "hot sun" in Kiswahili. It refers to workers in the informal sector, especially metal workers and carpenters.

people who were living with HIV/AIDS. Everyone settled down quickly after the prayer and a round of introductions commenced.

"We all know each other but it is still important to introduce ourselves and tell our friends about our work with HIV patients," the coordinator said. She introduced herself and then looked at Sister Phoebe.

"I am Sister Phoebe" was the briefest introduction of the morning. Everyone knew Sister Phoebe. They loved and respected her for her selfless contributions to Kochia over nearly two decades.

Mary held her fifteen-month old infant close to her and tearfully narrated how her husband succumbed to AIDS and left her with six children. Her second-to-last child was HIV positive and hence she was afraid to get her youngest one tested. Everyone felt sorry for Mary and another quick round of prayers ensued.

"I am Peter Odhiambo. Just call me Odhiambo. I am here to learn how I can help our people. But let me tell you, I am not convinced about this AIDS business. There are so many diseases...TB, cancer, malaria, pneumonia...AIDS is another disease just like the others. All diseases kill Kenyans. I am going to die someday – today or tomorrow. I have read in the newspapers that AIDS is an American disease. I don't think we Kenyans need to worry about it because..." Odhiambo rambled on for ten more minutes before heeding the coordinator's pleas for him to stop so that they can complete the introductions. Janet looked at Sister Phoebe and nodded her head in disapproval.

It was a good 25 minutes before it was Janet's turn. Janet knew almost everyone in the room. She stood up and explained the various activities conducted by the Empower Kochia CBO members including AIDS awareness, HIV support groups, home visits and income generation projects for HIV patients. She explained how they got funding from the new NGO in Homa Bay, SUV Foundation and community members, and used it to care for AIDS patients. "If you know any advanced HIV patients who have financial problems, let me know. I can connect them with our NGO, which has money available for buying a hen for eggs, or patients can come together and buy a goat. But they have to identify themselves, come to a Volunteering Counseling and Testing (VCT) Center with me, and sign all the papers. It is very easy and I can help you every step of the way."

Odhiambo was very skeptical. "So many people die from malaria every year and the government does not do anything. Americans come and tell us about their diseases and the government is giving away billions of Shillings. I think that it is better for me if I have HIV so that I can get

The HIV/AIDS Workshop

all these free things. Surely, this is a conspiracy by the Kikuyus to get more Luos to acquire HIV and die from AIDS. Then they can rule the country without any obstacles."

The coordinator grimaced. "You cannot separate a Kenyan man from his beliefs."

"None of our funding for home-based care comes from the Government. The funds are provided by some NGOs and churches," Janet clarified. She looked at her watch. It was ten more minutes before the tea break. After three more introductions, everyone got up to get some tea and mandazis[1].

"Did you hear that Philip is not in Kochia. No one knows where he is," Janet mentioned to a group of participants who were trying to identify the fishing boats on the lake.

"I saw him a few days back having a soda with the tall Kikuyu woman. I smell a fish – a nice big tilapia," Elizabeth Atieno suggested with a mischievous grin.

"They were also seen in Kendu Bay together," another participant added.

"Obongo might be going to Kendu Bay on Friday. I will ask him to inquire about Philip's whereabouts." Janet's offer was met with approval from everyone.

"Please ask Obongo to inquire," Odhiambo urged. "Philip is our brother and he is from Kochia. We should know where he is and whether everything is fine with him or not. I have heard that a Kikuyu has bought a lot of land near Kendu Bay. Not good. I am telling you. You cannot trust these people. Why should a Kikuyu buy land in Kendu Bay? We have so many beautiful Luo women in Kochia. Why should Philip run away with a Kikuyu woman?" Everyone slowly excused themselves or moved away until Odhiambo was left chatting with Jokongo, the village drunkard who was attentively listening and nodding to Odhiambo's harangue.

The break ended and the training session got underway a little after 11 AM. The coordinator finally started the first session on facts about HIV/AIDS, and prevention and control mechanisms. "The government has finally released the new report on HIV in Kenya," the coordinator remarked. "7.1% of Kenyans between 15 and 49 are HIV positive. Women are more likely to be infected than men. 8.4% of the women are infected whereas only 5.4% of the men are infected. In particular, young women between 15 and 24 years are four times more likely to be infected

---

[1] Mandazis are East African donuts. They are not as sweet at American donuts and don't have any frosting or glazing.

than young men of the same age group." There was absolute silence in the room as the coordinator stopped reading and gave everyone a chance to reflect on these numbers. "We have a very big problem in Nyanza," she continued. "14.9% of the people in Nyanza are HIV positive."

"And needless to say, they are all Luos," Odhiambo added in a matter-of-fact manner.

"I noticed that there are many more HIV positive women than men. I thought that most women get the virus from men. Can you please explain?" Elizabeth asked the coordinator.

"Women are more susceptible to HIV infection than men due to many reasons. First of all, biological factors are a major contributor to infections amongst younger women whose vaginal tracts are still immature. Older men are more likely to be HIV positive than younger ones. The older men have money and are able to form short-term alliances with younger women and thus spread the infection. Then there are gender norms, lack of education, gender inequities and unhelpful cultural practices like wife inheritance," the coordinator explained.

"If there is just one thing we can do," Sister Phoebe said, "it is to educate young girls about the dangers of sleeping with older men. We must educate older men at the same time but that is much more difficult."

"Kenya's HIV prevention strategy focuses on 'ABC' - Abstain, Be faithful, and use a Condom. The ABC approach has helped many people avoid infection," Janet raised her voice and demanded. "But tell me, how many women are in a position to abstain from sex, rely on their partners for fidelity, or negotiate condom use? HOW MANY?" There was authority and passion in her voice. There was pain and concern in her voice. She worked primarily with HIV positive women and understood their circumstances and challenges very well. The entire room nodded solemnly.

"My pastor told me that as a Christian, I should not use condoms and also discourage other people from using them. What should I do?" a middle-aged man asked the coordinator. The entire room broke into loud debates. This was a particularly complicated issue. The church did significant amount of work on AIDS prevention and home-based care of HIV patients but prohibited the use of condoms, going as far as spreading rumors that they have tiny holes in them, or that condoms are pre-infected with HIV. The common people were confused about the conflicting information coming from the government, NGOs, and the churches. They often trusted their church more than the government or NGOs. Different churches had varied opinions on the use of condoms and that further added to the confusion.

"Shhhhhh," Sister Phoebe quieted the room. "This is a very difficult question and I think that the decision should be made by the person individually. God does not want you to use condoms but God also wants you to have a long and honest life. You should be faithful to your wife and encourage your friends to also be faithful." Everyone was surprised by Sister Phoebe's response as it was against the teachings of her church, which strictly forbade the use of artificial contraception.

"As a Catholic who has devoted her life to Christ," Sister Phoebe continued, "I agreed with the Vatican that condoms should not be used. Then, I went to a training seminar in Nairobi and learned that 5.9% of couples are HIV discordant meaning that one partner is positive and one is negative. I thought that if I tell a discordant couple not to use a condom, the other partner will also get infected. If I tell them to abstain from sex, they are going to break the marriage and that puts more people at risk. I got an opportunity to discuss my dilemma with the Archbishop. He is a kind man. He explained that the use of condoms to prolong the lives of infected couples was consistent with Church teachings, despite the Vatican's opposition to the use of contraceptives for family planning and to prevent HIV infections. After that incident, I have thought about this issue many times and concluded that condoms are helping us more than hurting us. I am not here to judge people, I am here to help people and if using condoms helps them lead a happy and honest life, then it is no problem."

"But, if you live an honest life, you will never need condoms," a man argued.

"You can live an honest life, but how do you know your spouse is also always honest?" Janet retorted. "And no one is forcing you to use them. As Sister Phoebe said, we must not judge people. Our job is to educate people and then they can make their own informed decisions."

Most of the people in the room agreed with Sister Phoebe. Some disagreed. Odhiambo was convinced that the Vatican must be full of Kikuyus.

After discussing more facts related to HIV/AIDS in Kenya, the group finally broke for lunch at 1 PM. The lunch consisted of sukumawiki, potatoes, boiled eggs, rice and beef stew. The gentle breeze from the lake was too tempting for some of the attendees. The men took a short nap under the trees while the women chatted away. Training resumed at about 2:30 PM with a seminar on home-based care. Home-based care refers to fulfilling basic nursing care needs by formal or informal caregivers to HIV/AIDS patients in their own homes. Most trainees were already providing home-based care to people in communities with financial support from NGOs and logistical support from the health ministry. Caregiving involved the patient's general hygiene, physical therapy and behavioral change. Another aspect was caring for young children who were orphaned by the disease. They were hungry, suffered poor health, missed school, and ended up in conditions where they were subjected to economic and sexual exploitation. Often times, patients in advanced stages would contract tuberculosis and the caregivers had to isolate them in their homes to avoid infection. Working with such patients often put the caregiver's own health at risk. A relatively risk-free and high-impact task was educating patients about how they can make their food more nutritious. It was certainly not easy!

Farming had never been a vital component of the Luo people's identity. They identified themselves as fishermen and not farmers. HIV/AIDS destroyed the agricultural system completely. Unlike other diseases, HIV took away the fittest rather than the frailest members of society. As workers died, food production fell and hurt the nutritional status of the population. In the severely impacted regions, fresh food had to be brought in from outside, and hence, was very expensive. There were very few food products in the market that met the special nutritional requirements for HIV patients, and the ones that existed were mostly unaffordable. Food companies were afraid to explicitly mark products as beneficial for HIV patients in fear that the general population would stop buying them due to the attached stigma. Hence it was essential to train the home-based care providers in helping patients eat a balanced diet from the few natural foods that were easily accessible to them. The workshop participants particularly enjoyed this session and were excited about sharing their knowledge of nutrition with their own families and patients. Analysis of the nutritional contents of various food preparations continued over the tea break.

The next session was about socio-cultural aspects of HIV/AIDS. Occasionally, curious people would stop by, peer in through the door, listen to some of the conversations and leave. The participants discussed various socio-economic factors and cultural practices that promoted the spread of HIV. There was general agreement on most issues until the coordinator mentioned how modern technology including the internet, cell phones, television, and the transportation system were accelerating the spread of HIV.

"Okello was telling me about the internet," Elizabeth interjected. "He said that it works on a computer and it is very useful. It can help you find donors and get information about fish prices or nutritional food products and anything else that you might want to know. But he did not say that it leads to HIV!"

"I have a cellphone," another attendee added with fear in his voice, "but I did not realize that it also causes HIV infection."

"How do cellphones cause HIV infection?" everyone asked the coordinator.

"OK - I don't know but I will call the chief in Kisumu this evening and ask him," the coordinator promised.

"Don't use your cellphone to call him!" Elizabeth suggested.

"With a cellphone, men can talk to more women and then they become more promiscuous," Janet theorized.

"I think you are right – that is the reason," the coordinator nodded in agreement.

"That's why I do not let any women in my home use a cell phone," an elderly gentleman boasted.

"I propose that as pointed out by the respected coordinator earlier today, we should all wear condoms when making cell phone calls," Odhiambo suggested. The entire room burst out laughing. Odhiambo considered this as validation for his smart idea and settled down with a proud grin on his face.

"How does the transportation system increase the spread of HIV infection?" the elderly gentleman wondered. "Should I forbid my family from traveling by matatus and busses?"

"I can answer that," Janet jumped in. "The transportation systems contribute in many ways. When truck drivers go on long journeys, they are likely to engage in risky sex and spread the disease from one region to another. As more roads open up, the trucks go there with their goods and also take the HIV virus with them. Then you also have the migrant workers that travel place to place for work. A lot of these workers are men and, when they are away from their wives for so long, they engage in risky sex with sex workers who are more likely to be HIV positive."

"Thank you Janet," the coordinator beamed. "You have really become an expert on HIV now!"

The video scheduled for that evening had to be cancelled because there was no power. The group dispersed at 6 PM. Half the attendees started walking home while the other half waited for matatus. Janet and Elizabeth were neighbors and decided to walk home together. The one and a half hour journey would provide them ample time to catch up with each other's lives. They talked about their children, their goats, and the attendees at the training session. They speculated on which of the attendees were HIV positive and who attended the seminar just for the free food.

"If they didn't make the attendees stay the entire time to get tea and lunch, all of Kochia would apply for the workshop," Elizabeth remarked.

"So, how did you get invited to the workshop? If I remember correctly, you are not providing home-based care anymore," Janet sheepishly inquired.

Elizabeth grinned. "Ah…you see, my sister-in-law is now old enough to provide home-based care. Since she had to go to school, I am attending the training on her behalf."

"Yes, I remember little Apondi – so she has grown up. Now you will have to go home and teach everything to her again," Janet sympathized.

Elizabeth looked away from Janet's gaze. "I am very tired and tomorrow I have to wake up early again. But I will certainly train her next week," Elizabeth mumbled under her breath as she parted ways to reach home. Janet knew all too well that it would never happen. She walked home contemplating whether home-based training of providers was essential to providing better home-based care. She called her sister on the way. Although she could not speak to her sister, she spoke to her niece Charity and learned that her sister's health was the same as earlier.

The second day started promptly at 9:15 AM with a prayer led by Sister Phoebe. Four of the attendees were missing. The first session of the day focused on the national response to HIV/AIDS.

"The Kenyan Government has specified three priority areas," the coordinator said. "The first priority is to prevent new infections, the second priority is to improve the quality of life of people infected and affected by HIV/AIDS, and the third priority is to lessen the socio-economic effects of HIV/AIDS. It is very important that all of you memorize these priorities. If you ever go to another workshop, or there is a government inspection, you will be asked these priorities." She made all the attendees memorize and recall the three priority areas. Attendees who successfully memorized the priority areas were allowed to go out for a breakfast of tea and chapattis. Most attendees thus enjoyed a long tea break, a large portion of which was spent recalling Odhiambo's antics.

After the tea break, the group discussed Voluntary Counseling and Testing Centers (VCTs) and patient counseling techniques. The chief counselor from the VCT in Homa Bay town had come down to give a guest lecture to the participants. "I am very happy that all of you are joining us in the fight against HIV / AIDS," the counselor said. "The future of our country and all our people is in your hands. Almost half of all new HIV infections occur among young people under the age of 25 and they are mostly caused due to unprotected sex. Voluntary Counseling and Testing centers, or VCTs for short, are where people come to get tested for HIV. It is free of cost. All of you are on the frontlines of community health. We want you to send every single person to us. We want every Kenyan to know their status. We also provide confidential and personalized counseling to our customers. We educate them about high-risk behaviors and encourage them to always be on the safe side. Even if the people, especially young ones, insist that they know their status and there is no need, please send them to us. Every time they come to us, we explain the basic rules for avoiding HIV and living healthy and productive lives. This boosts their confidence."

"Do you also provide free condoms?" a participant asked.

"Yes, we provide free male condoms and also teach people how to use them," the counselor said. "Everyone has heard about condoms but many people don't know how to use them correctly."

"You are encouraging the young people to be promiscuous and get infected," the elderly gentleman alleged.

"Our goal is to decrease HIV and other infections," the counselor explained, "and education about abstinence, being faithful, and using condoms, the ABC approach, has proven to be effective. However, neither of these three approaches by themselves are adequate."

"It used to work in our time," the man argued. "Our society has become morally bankrupt."

"Let God be our witness," the counselor challenged the group. "How many of you never engaged in sexual acts before you got married? How old were you when you got married? 20 years? People are getting married later in life – both men and women. What makes you think that all of them will remain abstinent until they get married? Maybe some of them are very religious or have self-control. But will all the young people, millions of them, stay abstinent? How is that possible?"

"It is not possible," Odhiambo declared. "It will never happen in Kochia, much less in all of Kenya."

"The reality is," the counselor continued, "no matter how much we preach about abstinence or how much we scare people, they are going to have sex. We have done research across Kenya and found that providing free and easy access to condoms helps reduce the number of new HIV infections while also helping HIV positive people avoid opportunistic infections. Let me be clear: our goal is to reduce HIV infections."

"So, counselor," Odhiambo asked, "I want to help our people. I am very confident that I will be able to tell them engaging stories and discourage them from doing risky things. What are the qualifications to work at a VCT?"

Lunch Overlooking Lake Victoria

"You need to have a secondary education and then we will provide you with three-weeks of training on how to administer the tests and counsel customers," the counselor informed. "But we don't have any jobs right now. You should keep checking with our office every month."

"I read in the newspapers that there was some problem with faulty HIV tests," Sister Phoebe asked. "Is the problem resolved?"

"We had a problem with some of the rapid test machines," the counselor concurred. "They were returning wrong results. All those machines have since been returned and new machines have been obtained. We had to turn people away for a few weeks as we switched over to new machines but everything is fine now."

"So, should we encourage people to get tested once again," Janet wondered.

"Surely, please encourage them to come back for testing," the counselor earnestly requested. After a few more words of encouragement for their noble work on the frontlines of the national battle against HIV, the session was adjourned.

"Since no local chiefs are attending the course, the afternoon session on the role of chiefs in prevention, control, and epidemic management has been cancelled," the coordinator announced to the delighted group. "So now we will take lunch and reconvene in four hours."

Lunch was an elaborate affair under a cluster of palms overlooking the grand lake. The four attendees who were missing since morning miraculously appeared in response to the aroma of chicken stew and fried tilapia wafting around the tables. All the participants had a hearty meal. The men enjoyed a siesta in the pleasant breeze and then engaged in intense political debates. Screams, swear words, and guffaws of laughter filled the air. Odhiambo was the star of the afternoon. The women settled on the ground and stretched out their legs. They exchanged stories of their own experiences with home-based care. They talked about their fears and aspirations, their children and husbands, their livelihoods and struggles.

One of the participants divulged that she was HIV positive. She narrated how she might have contracted it from her husband and how she was fighting it by growing her own vegetables and eating a balanced diet. She shared several lessons on growing fruits and vegetables for domestic consumption and the marketplace. The rest of the women were taken by surprise when she informed them about her plans of making her HIV status known to everyone. The workshop coordinator applauded her courage and explained how important it was for HIV positive people to come out and serve as role models. This discussion continued into teatime and provided the perfect backdrop to learn about the challenges of stigmas and discrimination. When the workshop reconvened at 4:30 PM, the coordinator requested the woman to share her journey with HIV with the entire group. Some participants moaned and others wept, but everyone listened intently and clapped with respect and admiration as she completed her story with a smile. The group discussed prejudice, negative attitudes, abuse and maltreatment directed at people living with HIV/AIDS.

"I was excommunicated by my family, all my neighbors, and everyone in the community when my husband was diagnosed with HIV," Mary recounted. "My husband's family took away our small boat and fishing nets. They said we were immoral people and God was punishing us. Our livelihood was snatched away and my husband was too weak to fight back. There was no food to eat until Sister Phoebe and Janet came and helped us."

"I am still trying to get the boat and nets back," Janet fumed. "Those scoundrels have to return them. I am meeting with the DC again next week to get his support."

Sister Phoebe had brought with her a news article that she had received from the Nairobi office. She read aloud a quote by the United Nations secretary-general Ban Ki Moon, "Stigma remains the single most important barrier to public action. It is the main reason why too many people are afraid to see a doctor to determine whether they have the disease, or to seek treatment if so. It helps make AIDS the silent killer, because people fear the social disgrace of speaking about it, or taking easily available precautions. Stigma is the chief reason why the AIDS epidemic continues to devastate societies around the world."

The discussions and stories related to stigma continued. Janet looked at her watch. It was almost 5:30 PM. She kept staring at the coordinator but could not meet her eyes.

Finally at 6 PM, the coordinator announced that it was time for the workshop to conclude and certificates to be awarded to the participants. "Now, all of you are trained and certified HIV/AIDS care providers," the counselor said. "Congratulations and good luck in your work. Let us pray that God will clear all the hurdles from our path and make Kenya free of the HIV/AIDS disease."

The attendees were individually awarded their certificates amidst loud clapping, hooting, and whistling. Each and every participant expressed their gratitude to their parents, families, miscellaneous people, and the course coordinator. Odhiambo's mother, wife, children, and three brothers had been waiting outside for the past two hours. They cheered

Odhiambo when he received his certificate. One of his brothers indicated that a celebration was in order.

"I was told that if we are actively involved in providing care, we can attend more workshops like this one. Is that true?" Odhiambo inquired.

"Surely," the coordinator said. "The next workshop will be after two months. We will inform you about the date through Janet one week in advance. As long as you are providing home-based care, you are welcome to attend."

"Sister Janet," Odhiambo said, "I liked this workshop very much. Please let me know when the next workshop is. I wouldn't miss it for anything in the world."

"Indeed," three of the men chorused. "When you find out, let us know. If you will attend, all of us will join you too. We make a very good team."

On behalf of all the attendees and the people of Kochia, Janet gave the vote of thanks to the coordinator, the guest speakers, and all the workshop sponsors. Finally, Sister Phoebe asked everyone to rise as she led the prayers. After exchanging phone numbers and making promises to stay in touch, the workshop participants went their separate ways.

"Sister Phoebe," Odhiambo said. "Thank you so much for nominating me to attend this workshop. I learned so much over the past two days and I have decided that I want to devote myself to serve the people of Kochia. As per your advice, I have already discussed with Janet the financial aspects. I think it will work for me. I also have other ideas on how to earn money while helping people. I will follow up with her shortly about getting started with home-based care."

"Here she comes," Sister Phoebe said. "Talk to her right now. There is no need to wait."

"The problem is this." Odhiambo held up his certificate and grinned. "My entire family has gathered to celebrate my graduation. I need to rush home right now. As soon as Janet is back from Kisumu, the first thing I am going to do is talk to her and start working immediately." Before Sister Phoebe or Janet could say a word more, Odhiambo had disappeared. His voice and laughter could be heard for several minutes more.

"So, Janet," Sister Phoebe asked, "Are you going to Kisumu tomorrow?"

"Yes," Janet replied, "My sister's health is stable right now. I will leave early tomorrow morning and stay with her for three or four days. I want to be there with her in her final days."

"I was surprised to see you yesterday morning," Sister Phoebe

Odhiambo's Graduation

admitted. "I was convinced that you would go and visit your sister."

"I thought about it a lot. I really did. I concluded that my sister is dying but she has lived a good life. She is 49 years old and has already received nine bonus years. Now, her fate is sealed. There is nothing anyone can do to change it. She has many complications and is in pain. She is always sleeping and does not even recognize me. If I visit her, it is really for my sake, not hers. At the same time, I can come here to the workshop and learn something new and improve my work. I can share my experiences and make some new friends. If my presence here helps one person, whether immediately or in the long-term, isn't that reason enough to be at the workshop? So, I chose to attend the workshop in hopes of helping someone, someday, somehow."

"Bravo Janet!" Sister Phoebe cheered. "We all have to stand before the judgment seat of God and answer for our actions. God will certainly commend you for this selfless decision."

"Thank you Sister," Janet drawled. "But since you brought up God and judgment, I must admit that I also had a small selfish motivation for attending the workshop. I will tell you about it some other time. Right now, I really want to return home to cook supper and prepare for my journey tomorrow."

"That is OK." Sister Phoebe smiled. "You don't have to tell me. Just be true to yourself and God. But I wanted to ask you one question. You have attended many such workshops in the past and you have all the knowledge. On some topics, you actually know more than the coordinator. Then why did you insist on attending the workshop?"

"Ummmm...Sister Phoebe," Janet stammered. "I have the basic knowledge but things are always changing. This is an opportunity for me to revise my knowledge and stay up-to-date with new advances. Through the workshop, I find more patients and discover new resources. When I come here, I meet other caregivers and we learn from each other. As you know, it is difficult for us to share our problems and experiences openly. There are so many social norms, taboos, stigmas, and discrimination. Here we can trust each other and communicate openly. Every time I come here, I return home refreshed and energized to go and help my patients."

"But you can meet with the other caregivers anytime you want. Isn't everyone from this area? I am wondering whether such workshops should be offered only to new caregivers?"

"All of us know each other," Janet explained, "but we never meet by ourselves because we have to pay for the expenses. Here we have two days with very good food and a nice relaxed environment. It is much more conducive to an open conversation."

"You are confirming something I always believed," Sister Phoebe remarked. "Such workshops are very valuable but the value is not always what people think it is. The seminars and lectures are helpful for the new participants. But the formation of a trusted community with honest discussions and lateral knowledge sharing is much more important."

"Indeed. The most useful parts of the workshop are the breaks," Janet affirmed, "Also, you cannot forget that the caregivers are not paid to do this work. We consider attending such workshops a major benefit of being a caregiver. Let me tell you – the number of health workers will drop if such incentives and opportunities are taken away. All the health workers are excited when they get started. The difficulty is in sustaining that motivation after the first 3-6 months. Attending one of these workshops every two months is a very effective motivator." After wishing each other well, Janet and Sister Phoebe parted ways.

Obongo was pacing outside his homestead when Janet walked in at 8 PM. "I am so sorry," she said to her husband. "The workshop went on till 6:30 and then it took me a long time to get a piki-piki[1]. It is becoming very difficult to get a ride in the evenings."

"Pole sana[2]. You must be tired," Obongo said. "We have a surprise for you. Our children have grown up now. They have prepared supper for us. Let us eat and then you can start packing for your trip tomorrow."

The children ran out and warmly congratulated Janet, who greeted and hugged each one of them in return. Obongo and the children followed Janet into the inner bedroom. In the flickering light of the kerosene lamp, she carefully removed the file marked "HIV/AIDS HOME-BASED CARE". She proudly looked at her graduation certificate and ran her fingers over it. She smiled and placed it on top of the stack of twenty-four certificates she had received so far for attending HIV/AIDS training workshops.

"I have finally reached my silver jubilee." She turned to her family and declared with pride. "I am so grateful to God for giving me such a supportive family and helping me become one of the most experienced HIV/AIDS workers in all of Kochia."

---

[1] Piki Piki = A motorcycle. Increasingly being used as a commercial taxi to transport 1-3 people over relatively short distances. Piki Piki is an onomatopoeia based on the sound of the motorcycle's horn.

[2] Pole Sana = Very sorry (Kiswahili)

#3

Okello's Foray into Social Business

"I fail to understand how someone as educated and accomplished as Obongo can act in such an irresponsible manner. I was sure he would set an example for our people by organizing a modest funeral," Sister Phoebe said. "This has to stop. When people die, we have a funeral. Then because of the funeral, many more people die. This continuous cycle is destroying our communities."

"The funerals are certainly killing our people," Okello concurred. "But right now we need to support Obongo in every way we can. He really needs us."

"This is the time for Obongo to prove himself as a leader. His father was one of the first teachers in this area. All his life he worked for the betterment of the people. This is the perfect opportunity for Obongo to honor his father's legacy!"

"We have spoken to him twice and he has refused to scale down the funeral arrangements," Okello said. "We must look at the situation from his perspective. He told me that he wants his own funeral to be simple but he is scared of organizing a frugal funeral for his father. All of Kochia is going to judge him and his love for his father."

"Yes, I know our people. They will talk about it for a long time. But someone needs to stand up. If not Obongo, who will oppose such destructive traditions and unfair expectations of the people?"

"I have never understood why we are so preoccupied about funerals - the burial place, the rituals, the feasts, the number of cows slaughtered. People even go to courts to fight over how a funeral must be conducted and where a person must be buried. There are so many more important problems we need to address."

"The problem is that funerals have become venues to assert the family's stature and social class," Sister Phoebe remarked. "Honoring the dead leaves the living relatives bankrupt and pushes them further into the vicious cycle of poverty. Hundreds of mourners travel long distances to burials in the rural homesteads where the person was born. The mourners expect to be fed cows and goats and chicken and fish and will remember the funeral for everything that was missing or not done right. If families don't meet the mourner's expectations, they are ridiculed or ostracized."

"I have seen very many funerals," Okello added, "and it is not unusual for families to sell their cattle, boats, or ancestral land to afford an extravagant funeral. It is frustrating to see our friend go down the same path. It is easy for us to sit here and argue but when you are in that situation, it is very difficult to go against traditions. For something as sentimental as your father's funeral, how can you go against your culture?"

"Let me tell you something." Sister Phoebe clenched her fists. "I am getting very tired of our culture. Whether I am working with HIV patients, attending health workshops, establishing women's cooperatives, or counseling young girls who have been defiled by their teachers, everywhere I go, all the problems are because of our culture."

"Sister Phoebe, I have never seen you angry and frustrated like this," Okello empathized. "Please don't be so harsh on yourself. These are all very complicated and systemic problems. They emerge from our traditions and culture as well as from other factors such as poverty, colonialism, politics, economics, corruption and human nature."

"Sorry, I got carried away. Navigating our culture to solve community problems is one mountain after another. I am losing hope that we will ever free ourselves from these shackles of tradition and culture that are colonizing and controlling every facet of our lives and keeping us poor."

"Sister, we must make a distinction between traditions and culture," Okello suggested. "Our traditions have been handed down to us over time. Some are rational and others are not. Our traditions might be stuck in time but our culture is not. Our culture is dynamic and evolves with time. Our dress, clothes, food, language, taboos, social norms, community courts are all elements of our culture. Just think how much they have changed, just in the last five years. As our culture evolves, for better or for worse, we collectively decide which traditions we want to keep and which ones we want to bury in the graveyard of time. While our communication habits can evolve overnight with the integration of cellphones, our funeral processes will need a few generations to change."

"I have been told that nowadays, without a cellphone, you cannot have a funeral," Sister Phoebe said. "I am not sure if our dependence on technology is healthy but I wish there was a way to expedite this process of throwing out traditions that hurt our people."

"Maybe, there is! People like their traditions because they provide comfort, a connection to the past, and most-importantly, a sense of identity. If you talk about throwing away traditions, people will consider that an attack on their identity. Instead, we must think about practical ways to make traditions obsolete by envisioning a new social reality and championing a new identity."

"Ever since you got that laptop computer, you sound more like a professor. Can you explain to me what you mean by a new identity?"

"I need to think some more," Okello scratched his head and mulled it over for a few moments. "You said that our biggest problems are our traditions and culture. While that may be true, I also think that, it is inside our traditions and culture that we must look to find the biggest opportunities for social change. As for identity, have you noticed how Janet and the other health workers have integrated their work into their lives? Janet and Obongo were at my home yesterday. Janet scolded me for the shabby state of the kitchen, the unhealthy food I was eating, and for the puddle of water outside my window. She lectured me for fifteen minutes until Obongo stepped in. Thank God these health workers don't walk around with canes for I would have been on the receiving end of one yesterday! Being a health worker is now part of Janet's identity; that is how she sees herself, not only when she is working, but all the time. From Janet, the mindset of being health savvy has spread to her family, other health workers, and to her friends."

"I get your point," Sister Phoebe's eyes lit up. "If people are empowered and start thinking about themselves differently, they will take that mindset wherever they go and incorporate it into whatever they do. We want our people to build their confidence and start thinking of themselves as health workers, problem solvers, innovators, educators..."

"...and mavericks," Okello grinned. "Instead of taking traditions for granted, we want our people to engage in a respectful and meaningful discussion. We don't gain much by constantly questioning every tradition. But as we discuss our traditions and culture, recognizing opportunities and acting on them to reap economic and social rewards will be a stronger and more positive approach to advancing our culture and making unhelpful traditions obsolete. Slowly, the ideas, stories, opportunities, and successes will spread and we will have this new social reality."

"So, where does this process begin?" Sister Phoebe asked with skepticism, "and how do we know it will not lead to failure?"

"Failure is guaranteed! We will fail more times than we will succeed," Okello warned. "But recognizing failure as a way of learning also has to become a part of our mindset and our identity."

"I have been working with HIV patients, or those at risk, for ten years now," Sister Phoebe said, "and now I can slowly start to see some behavioral change amongst the people. Isn't that a new social reality?"

"Indeed," Okello agreed. "Your work with the health workers is the best example of this change in mindset. The only thing missing is the integration of incentives to keep the health workers engaged and to attract more workers over time."

"How do we, as a community, start on this long journey?" Sister Phoebe asked.

"By taking the first step! Our people consider us community leaders. Hence, we have to champion this social innovation process. We must begin by standing with Obongo in this difficult time. As we help him with the organization of the funeral and the various events, let us strive to understand the problems, understand the motivations, and identify opportunities for change. We must meet and talk on a regular basis. Once the funeral is behind us, we must include Obongo and Janet in our conversations because they might have a different perspective than us. As long as we keep observing and talking, I am sure that many opportunities will present themselves."

"Wait a minute," Sister Phoebe clarified. "You have convinced me that I should participate in the funeral in solidarity with Obongo and Janet. But I really don't feel comfortable organizing the events."

"That is fine," Okello replied. "You can spend more time with Janet and I will be with Obongo. We must also talk to other people and get their views."

"Ayyy," Sister Phoebe agreed. "But now, I must hurry home to complete my duties. I need to reach Obongo's home in three hours."

Sister Phoebe marched off to her home for HIV/AIDS patients while Okello returned to his workshop to research funeral coordination companies. After spending two hours on his clunky laptop, he decided to head over to Obongo's place and start planning the funeral for Obongo's father.

Obongo Sr., a retired primary teacher, had traveled to Nairobi to join over 30,000 retired teachers from around the country that had gathered to protest the non-payment of pension for over fifteen years. Teachers from every corner of Kenya had converged in Nairobi for the third time to plead for their rightful pensions. Two earlier protests, four and nine years ago, were unsuccessful and hence Obongo was not thrilled about investing his meager savings in his father's travels. However, Obongo Sr. had made up his mind and there was no point arguing. The four-day trip turned into a three-week sojourn that included participation in two rallies and over thirty visits with long-lost family and friends. The old man lived a simple sedentary life at home. However, traveling to the big city with friends always brought about a radical transformation in his personality and habits. He was too polite to turn down drinks, and too proud to refrain from showering lavish gifts on the friends and family he visited every day. Obongo exhausted all his cash savings and was forced to sell three of his goats in order to M-Pesa money to Nairobi twice over this three-week period.

The old man's charity and his son's sacrifices must have pleased the Gods. The parliament passed a resolution to release KSh. 3.34 Billion (about USD 40 Million) to the teachers in pension and back payments. Obongo Sr. stood to receive over KSh. 3.5 Million for the fifteen years of unpaid pension. Obongo started trembling when he heard the news on the radio. He decided to rush to Nairobi and bring his father back home. He was scared that his inebriated and euphoric father would spend all the money he was hoping to receive. It did not matter to Obongo whether the pension funds came through or not. He just wanted his father back at home where he could no longer promise people TVs or goats or cows or cars. After all, there was no guarantee that the government would actually release the funds. One spokesman for the teachers was worried that the money would never be given to them and would simply return to the treasury at the end of the year. Another spokesman was convinced that a new tax would be instituted on pension back payments which would leave the impoverished retired teachers with a worthless sum of money while taking away their power to protest again in the future.

The night bus to Nairobi had already departed. Instead of waiting for almost 24 hours to board the bus next evening, Obongo decided to start for Nairobi early in the morning by matatu. This would be a longer, costlier, and more painful journey with numerous stops on the way.

"Every hour, baba is promising away tens of thousands of Shillings," Janet lamented.

Obongo gasped at the humor and horror of the situation. "Imagine the stampede in Kochia if we receive the funds…or if we don't. Everybody will come to celebrate and request their promised gifts, or they will come to console us and curse the government. Either way, we will have to feed a few hundred people."

"Yes, all our savings will be gone," Janet burst out laughing. "You better hurry to Nairobi and bring father home."

If everything went as planned, Obongo calculated that he would reach Nairobi in the evening, immediately round up his father, and then take the night bus back to Kochia.

The first rays of the sun were just piercing the sky when the phone's loud ringtone woke the entire house. Janet and four of the older children gathered around Obongo as he rubbed his eyes, waited for a few rings, and pressed the talk button.

"Hello. This is Inspector Kariuki from Thika police station. Can I speak to Mr. Obongo?" It was the calm and seasoned voice of a professional who made umpteen such calls every day.

"This is Obongo speaking."

"Mr. Obongo, I am sorry to disturb you at this hour but I am very sorry to inform you that someone you know passed away in a matatu accident on Thika road a few hours ago. Your phone was called several times by the deceased person and hence I am calling you to determine his identity. The deceased person is an elderly male, about 70 years of age."

There was a long silence. The inspector was expecting it. Eventually, Obongo queried the inspector about the deceased's phone number as well as facial features. The physical description accurately matched with his father and so did the phone number.

"A lorry crashed into a matatu on Thika road. The driver and all fourteen passengers were killed," the inspector said. He provided details about the accident and the morgue where the body would be stored. Obongo was informed that the police formalities would be complete only after a formal identification was conducted. The inspector offered his condolences and hung up.

Obongo could feel the energy escape from his body. He felt a boulder on his chest. He slouched into his old wooden chair and stared at the ceiling. Janet and the children started crying. It took a couple of hours for Obongo to regain his composure. He started thinking about what he should do next. He was going to wake up and get ready to leave for Nairobi and bring his father back home. Now he would have to bring his lifeless body back. How could a man who had survived wars and famine and deadly diseases succumb to an accident?

"It is God's will and who are we to intervene?" Obongo conceded. "And now we have to rise to the situation and fulfill our duties. My father lived a respectable life and his funeral will be remembered by the people of Kochia for a long time."

This was no easy feat. Fourteen burial rituals were to be organized and executed over the next two months. Hundreds of mourners were to be entertained at the cost of a few hundred thousand Shillings.

Obongo's two-hour strategy session with Janet culminated in a list of twelve members for the funeral committee. Invitation to the committee was an honor as well as a responsibility. Any friction between members could compromise the sanctity of this project and impact its smooth operation. Obongo immediately called his best friend Okello and requested him to transfer some phone credit over to him. Several phone calls would have to be made over the next few days. Okello graciously accepted the invitation to serve on the funeral committee and promised to come over in the afternoon. Obongo heaved a sigh of relief when Okello also promised to set up and manage the audio and video systems for the various burial ceremonies. Sister Phoebe, on the other hand, agreed to come over and help but turned down the invitation to the funeral committee by explaining that she was very busy with her responsibilities at her home for HIV/AIDS patients.

Professor Onyango from Nairobi University, a distant relative and good friend, was invited to be the Nairobi liaison for the funeral committee. This was a particularly important job since a Harambee would have to be conducted in Nairobi to raise the funds to bring the body back home. Professor Onyango expressed some apprehension since he was extremely busy with his teaching, research, and entrepreneurial ventures in East Africa. "I am already serving on three university committees, two conference committees and two other funeral committees. You see…very many Luos die in Nairobi and I am requested to conduct the harambees. It is becoming more and more difficult. But Mzee[1] Obongo was my primary school teacher and I owe my professional success to him," the professor told Obongo on the phone. After some deliberation and consultation with his wife, the Professor finally called back after an hour and agreed to conduct the Harambee in Nairobi and coordinate with the morgue. The professor suggested that it would be wise to formally identify the body first and confirm the identity of the deceased before the formal death announcement was made. He took it upon himself to rush to the morgue and complete the formalities.

Obongo, Janet, Sister Phoebe and Okello spent the next few hours laying down the charter for the funeral committee and eagerly waiting for the Professor's report from the morgue visit.

"Hello. Onyango here. Sorry it took so long but you know the traffic

---

[1] Mzee = Honorific title for an elderly gentleman (Kiswahili)

Dero – Traditional Luo Granary

on Thika Road and there are always a few accidents. I have completed the police formalities and now there is no doubt in my mind that the body is Mwaalimu's[1]. He is now resting at peace in the morgue. I have made a 3,000 bob payment for two weeks. Let us discuss the harambee dates in the evening. I have already reserved next Sunday on my schedule." The professor gave his matter-of-fact report, offered his condolences and hung up. Obongo was glad to have the Professor by his side. He did not have to worry about the harambee in Nairobi or even travel there until the funeral. All the action was centered in Kochia. The four-member team decided that two harambees were in order – one in Nairobi to cover the expenses of bringing the body and the mourners to Kochia and another one at home to cover the local expenses.

Harambee literally means "let's all pull together" and captures the Kenyan spirit of working together to overcome problems. In popular usage, people associate harambees with fundraising. Harambees could be organized for weddings, funerals, hospital bills, university fees or almost any other cause where an individual cannot meet the expenses. Professor Onyango once successfully conducted a harambee to raise funds for traveling to an academic conference in the United States! However, harambee is much more than fundraising. Harambees foster community self-reliance through collaborative effort in a self-determined manner. Harambee self-help projects supported by the government have established rural schools, health centers, water projects, cattle dips, bridges, roads and other infrastructure throughout the country. Harambees have been successful because Kenyans understand the benefits of shared responsibility and contribute generously towards the cause. People develop a sense of ownership and pride in the project and hence stay engaged in the longer-term. At the same time, harambees have been misused by unscrupulous people for personal gain. Socio-economic development projects that attempt to raise seed funds in this manner are particularly viewed with suspicion. When a person dies far away from home, the costs of transporting the body back to the rural home are so high that a harambee is essential to raise the necessary funds. It is also a convenient and elegant way for the family members and friends to contribute towards the funeral expenses.

It was nearing sunset when the preliminary planning was completed and the funeral committee was recruited by phone. Every single person graciously and proudly accepted the request to serve on the committee. They expressed their condolences and solidarity with the Obongo family.

---

[1] Mwaalimu = Teacher (Kiswahili)

The budget for the funeral was set at KSh. 500,000. Off this amount, KSh. 150,000 would be spent in Nairobi for transporting the body and the mourners while KSh. 350,000 would be spent in Kochia for the burial, various rituals, and feasts. Obongo was hoping that the harambees would yield half of the budget, and maybe more if the professor gave an inspiring elegy in Nairobi and Okello's music system worked well in Kochia. After Okello and Sister Phoebe headed home, Obongo spent the next two hours sitting outside his house and looking into the horizon remembering his father and reflecting on the fragility of human life. Yesterday, at this hour his father was alive.

"If only…if only he would have heeded my advice and returned home as planned. This entire tragedy would have never happened and we would be here together enjoying our dinner and celebrating the good news about the pension funds," Obongo was muttering to himself when Janet came out of the house and inquired if he had heard anything about the pension on the radio. Obongo, completely absorbed in his melancholy, did not respond to Janet.

The silhouette of Rev. Ndiege walking towards his homestead brought Obongo back to the moment. The appropriate time for announcing an elderly man's death was after sunset. In the olden days, people would learn about someone's demise by hearing a woman's long quivering wail followed by the sound of drums. Nowadays, a phone call was adequate. Obongo picked up the phone and the list prepared by Janet and got to work. He had completed five phone calls when Rev. Ndiege was at his doorstep. The Reverend hugged Obongo and explained how he learned about the old man's demise from Okello. Everyone gathered around the Reverend as he led a short prayer in the flickering light of the kerosene lamp. The Reverend's praise for Obongo Sr. drew tears from the family members.

"God is with you during this difficult time," the Reverend reassured the family. "Have you set the date for the burial?"

"Not yet," Obongo said. "Professor Onyango will be organizing the harambee in Nairobi next Sunday. Maybe the burial can be held the following Sunday?"

"OK. Would you like me to organize the harambee in Kochia? I stopped organizing fundraisers three years back but it would be an honor to lead the harambee for Mzee Obongo."

"Yes, Reverend," Obongo joined his hands and bowed his head, "it would be an honor for our father and our family if you would lead the harambee and officiate the burial." Obongo was overcome with piety and humility. The Reverend was an extremely charismatic speaker. His words could move people to action. The story of how he had built his church in one long day by asking his congregants to come with one brick each was a legend, not just in Kochia, but the whole of Nyanza.

"Please accept this goat as a gift from God." The Reverend carefully placed a kid in Janet's youngest son's outstretched arms. "This goat was gifted to the church this morning by a young man who was blessed with his first child yesterday night. The circle of life moves on," the Reverend professed as he headed out of the door promising to come back the next day.

Several neighbors and relatives had gathered at Obongo's house and supper preparations were underway. The dero[1] was half-full. Obongo's first-born son, Owiti, was tasked with arranging for the groceries and meat. The groceries had been ordered and were expected early next day. Obongo was one of the most respected and well-known citizens of Kochia. Along with his wife Janet, he had strived for over twenty years to develop the Empower Kochia CBO and launched several projects to improve the quality of life for the people. Very many people were expected to visit his homestead over the next few days to offer their condolences. It was customary to serve the visitors a complete meal with chicken, fish or beef, regardless of the time of the day they arrived. Obongo would become the laughing stock of Kochia if any staple foods like ugali, sukumawiki or maharagwe[2] were served. "Wadhi eliel K'Obongo to waa gi dhowa nono[3]," people would say.

Hence, arrangements were made to have a regular supply of Tilapia fish, goat ribs, beef and chicken over the next two weeks. Provisions of rice to make pilau[4], wheat flour for chapattis, and corn meal for ugali, were also being arranged.

Two of Obongo's paternal aunts were the first to arrive the next morning. It was customary for the older women to arrive at the announcement of the death and stay until the burial was completed. They were responsible for welcoming all visitors and mourning with them. The next few days saw a steady stream of visitors all through the day. Some of the visitors brought corn meal or sugar with them as a contribution towards the funeral while others pledged a goat or a chicken or a fish.

"Not one of them came to visit my father, or even gave him an aspirin when he was alive, and now everyone is running here to show how much they care," Obongo was amused.

---

[1] Dero = Traditional Luo granary (Dholuo)
[2] Maharagwe = Kidney beans (Kiswahili)
[3] We attended a funeral at Obongo's homestead and were never fed. (Dholuo)
[4] Pilau = Rice cooked with meat and spices (Kiswahili)

Obongo kept busy meeting with the visitors while Janet, Sister Phoebe, and the other women spent most of the day in the kitchen preparing and serving them food. Flyers with the death notice and particulars about the Harambee and the burial were put up on the major thoroughfares and shops of Kochia. A color advertisement was placed in the national newspaper in Nairobi. A bank account was set up to collect funds for the funeral arrangements. Friends and relatives that lived far away and could not afford to travel to Nairobi or Kochia deposited their contributions in the bank account. They could also send money instantaneously by using the M-Pesa service on their cellphones.

Ten days went by very quickly. The Harambee in Nairobi was held on Sunday morning after church. There were over a hundred people in the room - relatives, friends, or ex-colleagues of Obongo Sr. Just like him, several other teachers had stayed back after the rally to visit their kin and many of them showed up for the harambee. The ceremony started with an hour-long prayer service followed by an equally lengthy speech by Prof. Onyango that captured important events from the Mzee's life. The meticulously-crafted speech mentioned the Mzee's relationship with all the people that were expected to show up for the event. The Professor occasionally swayed from his prepared speech to ensure that he recognized every individual in the audience. Finally, a formal request for contributions was made. A table draped with a spotless white cloth and three chairs were set up on the podium. A small basket was placed on the table, right next to a photo of the old man. A hard-bound book was placed for attendees to leave their condolence messages. People would walk past and thank the professor for organizing the harambee. They would register their name and contribution amount in a notebook and drop their funds, either open or in an envelope, in the basket. Each of them would also leave their condolence message in the book and indicate whether or not they would be joining the official cortege to Kochia for the burial. When the event finally ended in the late afternoon, the contributions in the register added up to a respectable KSh. 70,000.

On the same day, another harambee was held by Rev. Ndiege at his church in Kochia. Mzee Obongo was one of the first teachers in the region. Teachers, just like doctors, were amongst the most respected people. For the citizens of Kochia, this was the end of an era. An era that commenced with independence from Great Britain, witnessed the gradual establishment of primary and secondary schools, and gave birth to a new educated nation. Obongo Sr. and his colleagues were the first champions in the rural areas that sparked the fire for learning, for reading and writing, and participating in a thriving community. Hundreds of people came over for the harambee. Although the proceedings were similar to the event in Nairobi, there was a more pronounced display of emotions. The people sobbed and wailed during the prayer service. Rev. Ndiege's speech on Mzee Obongo's life was punctuated with cheers and moans from the audience. There was a stampede towards the podium when the request for funds was made. In the true spirit of a harambee, everyone contributed something. Depending on their socio-economic standing, some contributed 2,000, some 200 and some 20. Attendees who could not contribute any funds brought in a chicken, cabbages, or sukumawiki from their farms. The harambee went on till late evening. Okello had to run to Imboyo market to pick up a new notebook for the condolence messages. The shopkeeper refused to accept money for the book. After completing the formalities of the harambee, the people settled down in the church compound and waited for supper to be served.

A notable absentee at the harambee was the local Member of Parliament (MP). The Elections Act of 2011 prohibited anyone aspiring for political office from participating in a fundraising event not connected to their political campaign eight months before the election. The Independent Electoral and Boundaries Commission (IEBC) monitored all harambees and fundraising events. This law was frequently used by politicians as a convenient excuse to avoid contributing funds to a harambee. Obongo Sr.'s funeral was a major community event and hence a great opportunity for the local MP to keep his name on the people's mind. Also, irrespective of the law, the MP's absence would not be viewed well by the people of Kochia.

"The law prohibits me from contributing funds to the harambee, but it does not prohibit my wife from participating in the event and providing supper for everyone!" The MP chuckled when he accepted Rev. Ndiege's invitation to the harambee.

Accordingly, the supper for the harambee was provided by the MP's wife. It is said that one cow and three goats were slaughtered for the feast. Rumors abound that chang'aa, the local brew, made an appearance later in the evening. Many people turned up just to partake in the festivities. Some left after supper with a smile on their face while others had to be carried home by their friends later at night. It remained a major topic of public discussion whether Obongo's stature, the Reverend's leadership, or the sumptuous feast led to the success of the fundraising effort. The next day, when all the funds were added up, there was a sense of relief in Obongo's homestead. In a region where the average monthly individual income was KSh. 5,000, the harambee yielded a staggering

Harambee for Mzee Obongo

KSh. 150,000. Obongo called all the members of the funeral committee, and personally visited the Reverend, to offer his heartfelt gratitude.

"If only the elections act was not passed by the government, the MP would have contributed his funds directly to the funeral rather than spending his money on the food. I am sure that the feast set him back by atleast KSh. 50,000, or maybe more," Obongo thought to himself. He was not sure whom the law helped more, the MP or himself, and whether the law reduced corruption or unwittingly facilitated vote-buying.

Exactly one week was left for the burial. Obongo was engrossed in recouping funds from debtors and applying for loans to meet the ongoing funeral expenses. The harambees were very successful but raised less than half of the necessary funeral expenses. Obongo sought loans from family members, informal lenders, Savings and Credit Cooperatives (SACCOs), and anyone else who would not ask for collateral. He was very confident that unlike some of his neighbors, he would not have to sell any assets or mortgage his small plot of land. Obongo ached to know whether he would receive his father's pension funds. Janet's constant nagging on the matter was aggravating his anxiety. The pension funds would settle his financial challenges in one instant. There had been no more news since the official statement on the day of his father's passing. Obongo had been religiously tuning his radio to the daily news but there wasn't a single reference to the teacher's backlogged pensions. He also spoke to his father's friend who had organized the rally in Nairobi but received no information. Everyone suggested that he should be patient and wait for further news.

The cortege was set to leave Nairobi for Kochia early in the morning on Saturday. On Thursday night, Obongo and Okello set off for Nairobi. Prof. Onyango received them early Friday morning and treated them to a modest breakfast in one of the tiny restaurants on River road. Obongo insisted that he would like to meet with the hearse operator and visit the morgue before heading to the Professor's residence and resting for a short while.

"Sawa sawa[1]. Why don't you stroll around for a few hours and then we will link up right here at 10 AM to go to the hearse company? Be careful, you are in Nairoberry....oh, I mean Nairobi." The Professor warned as he dashed off to attend a meeting.

Obongo and Okello waded through the rush-hour pedestrian traffic in the central business district of Nairobi.

"I fail to understand how my father stayed here for three weeks. I am

---

[1] Sawa sawa = OK (Kiswahili)

afraid to even be here for one day." Obongo confessed as he tried to keep up with Okello's pace.

Okello, who had lived in Nairobi earlier, was comfortably darting in and out of traffic and occasionally slowing down to give Obongo an opportunity to catch up. By the time they met up with the Professor, Obongo was exhausted while Okello was raring to go on another brisk walk through the markets. The matatu stage for Thika road was close by and the thirty-minute journey was devoid of any accidents.

"Hello, I am Blessed," a short, wiry young man with a ear-to-ear smile declared as the three of them entered through the glass door of a brand new office.

"We are also blessed," Obongo stuttered, much to the amusement of the young man who led the way to his plush air-conditioned office.

"Good Morning! I am Blessed Wamiti, the Managing Director of Blessed Angels Funeral Company. The professor texted me this morning and I have been waiting for you," the young man said to Obongo and Okello, and then extended his hand towards the professor.

"Good morning, Blessed," the professor responded, and then noting the puzzled expression on Obongo and Okello's face clarified. "Gentlemen, our friend here, whose good name is Blessed Wamiti was one of my students a few years back. He has just returned from his studies in the US to start this funeral company. We will be using his services for the funeral."

"Professor, is he the driver of the hearse?" Obongo asked in a matter-of-fact manner.

"We are not a hearse company, we offer end-to-end funeral services." Blessed was piqued. "And we will be providing you excellent service for Mzee Obongo's final journey on Saturday and Sunday; the coffin, the Angel Mobile   our brand new funeral car for the coffin – and three of our newly remodeled vans to carry the mourners back and forth. We will provide everything!"

Blessed stood up and started walking behind his guests' chairs. "And as a special deal for the Professor, we will be providing an upgrade on the coffin and a free bottle of water for our guests on both days."

The Professor was particularly pleased. Okello was amused by Blessed's company – the swanky office, comprehensive and courteous service, and the options available to customers. He looked forward to learning more about the company's operations.

"Here are the details of the services we will be providing for this event." Blessed passed a black leather folder towards Obongo. Okello opened the folder for his friend, and watched him pick up and carefully peruse through the three-page invoice. Obongo choked when he read the price tag of KSh. 200,000.

"Would you like to discuss any of the services?" Blessed broke the silence in the room.

"I would like to discuss the cost," Obongo said with incredulity in his voice. "I have been told by my friends that such a service should cost 100,000. And then, we need some money for the mourners' meals and drinks. Your hearse is just too expensive."

"You see, first of all, as I explained earlier, we are not a hearse operator." Blessed tried hard to control his temper. He invited his customers to a soda. Obongo refused to touch it. "For just 25,000, you can transport a body in one of those large trucks used by the laborers," Blessed said. "A truck leaves Nairobi for Nyanza every Saturday. I can call them for you if you want. Or you can get a regular hearse for 40,000. We are providing you a special vehicle that will take you all the way home and will stay there for two days. Your father will really enjoy the journey. As you know, our people consider it unlucky to drive a hearse," Blessed continued, "It is difficult and expensive to find a reliable driver. And then, the price of petrol has shot up so much since elections are around the corner. Have you seen the coffin we will be providing? Let me show you!"

Blessed pulled out a folder and pointed at photos of a black coffin with a shiny white satin lining. "A regular hearse operator will not provide you a coffin. You have to go shopping for that separately. Do you know how much they cost? It is at least 30,000 for a nice one. Imagine, just imagine. All the guests at the burial are going to be impressed when this coffin emerges from the Angel Mobile. In fact, we are giving you an upgrade on the coffin just because you are here with professor. Your coffin will have a pillow, extra sponge, satin lining, a big red bow as well as the deceased's photo on the outside. It will be a good quality color photo." Blessed's passion for his services impressed the professor and amused Okello.

Obongo was getting impatient with the endless rambling but he bit his lip and tried to decide whether he should accept the service or not.

"Then we will have three of our brand new vans for the mourners. We will be providing a bottle of Highlands water to every guest. There are ten comfortable seats in each van and a TV and DVD player as well. You just inform me which movies your guests would like to watch and I will make sure the driver…"

"Why don't you just charge us 150,000? That fits our budget," Obongo interjected.

"Unfortunately, we cannot do that Mr. Obongo," Blessed said. "However, what we can do is offer you two vans instead of three and bring the cost down to 170,000. Let me assure you that is a very reasonable price and the very best we can do."

Obongo turned to the professor for guidance. The professor shrugged and smiled. Okello nodded his head in agreement.

"Don't worry Mr. Obongo, I assure you that you will be so pleased with our service that next time..."

"OK. It is OK. We will pay you the said amount. How much advance do you need?" Obongo could not tolerate Blessed's voice anymore.

"We need the full payment before the cortege leaves. We don't do business on credit."

"We have 130,000 now but can pay you the rest by Monday," Obongo offered. All three of them reached into their bags, pockets and socks to retrieve the cash and place it on the table. Blessed straightened every individual note and leisurely arranged them into 13 little bundles with ten notes each.

"Professor, can you assure me that the funds will be received by Monday morning?"

"The funds in question are the proceeds of the harambee. They are, in fact, at my residence. I propose that you come with us right now and collect the money."

"I would be delighted to...and that way you can also experience the van that we will be using tomorrow. Would you like to pick a movie from the stack over there? We also have Nigerian movies..."

Before Blessed could complete his sentence, Obongo had chugged down his soda and stormed out of the door.

"My brother is very tired from our journey," Okello tried to cover up for his friend's brusque exit.

Blessed talked incessantly for the next hour as they traveled through the late morning traffic on Thika road to arrive at the Professor's house.

"Remember, only ten passengers per van, Gentlemen! We must follow the rules." Blessed's voice reverberated in their ears for hours after he had left happily with his money.

"I am convinced he has acquired three old matatus that operated on the Rongo-Homa Bay route and painted them blue and yellow. But, he is a very good businessman," Okello speculated. "With more people like him around, the funeral business will soon become a part of the hospitality industry."

Obongo didn't respond to Okello's musings, and had very little conversation with the Professor or his wife. He spoke to Janet briefly, responded to phone calls from banks where he had applied for loans, and then went to sleep. He was tired and fatigued from his physical exertions and financial tensions over the past two weeks. There was no solution to his financial woes in sight either. He woke up in the evening for a few hours, had supper, and turned back in.

The funeral car and vans arrived at the Professor's residence at the break of dawn on Saturday morning. The guests started arriving shortly thereafter. A few of the young people were given money for bus fare and food and dispatched by the morning bus to Kisumu. They were to then take a smaller bus to reach Kochia in the early evening. The cortege completed formalities at the morgue and started their journey west. Okello joined the mourners in one of the vans while Obongo and the Professor sat next to the driver in the Angel Mobile. It was certainly a very comfortable ride. Obongo was relieved that Blessed was not the one driving the car for the next nine hours. Interacting with Blessed had been a very unique experience for him - amusing and irritating. He had spent the previous evening making various calculations of the funeral expenses and concluded that this service was at least 35,000 Shillings more than what he would have paid for the coffin and services in a piecemeal manner. He rationalized the cost against the nice-looking vehicles, fancy coffin, and the little touches like the DVD players and the bottles of water. The vehicles stopped several times for short breaks and Obongo was delighted to hear the mourners' rave reviews about the proceedings so far. The last few kilometers were particularly difficult for the funeral car. A short distance before the Obongo homestead, the car engine miraculously stalled. The drivers used this opportunity to quickly clean up the dust from the vehicles and restore their lustrous shine.

All of Kochia was waiting for the cortege to arrive. Odhiambo had helped set up tents with tables and chairs outside Obongo's home. Children were watching a Hollywood movie on the TV in one of the tents. A large tent served as the kitchen while a series of small tents with blue plastic covers were set up for guests to rest at night. Loud gospel music was blaring from the gigantic speakers that Okello had set up before leaving for Nairobi. A diesel generator was used to power all the electronics while a few rented car batteries powered the LED lamps. A crowd of over a hundred people greeted the funeral party. The coffin was ceremoniously carried and placed next to the door inside Obongo's house. An oil lamp was lit next to the coffin. Inside the house, stools for relatives and church members filled every little room. The mourners started entering the house to bid farewell to the old man. They would go straight into the house without greeting other people, and then pray, sing, or cry in their own way. After a while, they came out of the house, greeted other people and joined them over a cup of sweet milky tea. This went on until the sun vanished into the glimmering waters of Lake Victoria. Supper was served to the mourners who had converged from Nairobi, Kisumu and all over Nyanza. There was a lot of singing and dancing. People were particularly impressed by Okello's music system.

The rightful place for the grave was an important decision to be made by the deceased's male kin and church members. After a prolonged discussion, the Rev. Ndiege, Obongo and Okello marked the exact location of the grave with chalk powder. In the olden days, the grave would be dug in the daytime.

"Our young people have become very weak now. They insist that it is too exhausting to dig in the daytime," an elder lamented.

The *kunyo*, or grave-digging, started around 10 PM and continued past four the next morning. The hard rock made it very laborious and tiring to dig. The young and middle-aged men took turns digging the grave, dancing, and imbibing great quantities of chang'aa that was prepared specifically for this event. The young women were advised to stay away from the homestead. Men with pregnant wives were not allowed to dig the grave for fear that they might give premature birth.

Finally, the big day arrived. The burial ceremony, called *iko* in Dholuo, was scheduled to commence at 2 PM. Most of the churches started their services early and were done by mid-morning. By 11 AM, Obongo's homestead resembled a fairground. People were socializing with their friends and relatives. Rambunctious children could be seen running around and playing. The young men decided that they had just enough time for a football match and headed to the field at the primary school, promising to return by 2 PM. Two cows and four goats had been slaughtered earlier in the morning for the hundreds of people expected at the burial. The women were busy boiling, roasting, and frying the meat. Accompaniments like ugali, chapatti, sukumawiki, and rice were being prepared. Special food requests of chips, cassava fries, and fish, ensured that the women had ample work to do. Wails of sorrow, guffaws of laughter, spirited discussions, and heated arguments filled the air around the homestead.

"Do you know who owns these vehicles that brought you people here from Nairobi?" Odhiambo addressed the small crowd around him. "Kikuyus! Each and every vehicle! This one, that one, that one...every single one is owned by a Kikuyu!" "EVERY SINGLE ONE," Odhiambo enunciated each word and walked around asking everyone: "Do you know who was driving the matatu that killed our teacher? Can you guess?"

The people of Kochia loved Odhiambo's hysterics on his favorite topic – bashing Kikuyus. He could be found at every community event ready to hold Kikuyus responsible for ruining the country, corrupting all Kenyans, and targeting Luos. While he did enjoy a few ardent supporters, the vast majority of the bystanders did not concur with Odhiambo's rants. Nevertheless, he provided ample entertainment that made his popularity soar. The topic of Odhiambo's next tirade was the subject of speculation before, and discussion after, every community event.

"Which self-respecting Luo will drive a hearse? Our brothers, the Kikuyus, will drive a hearse and charge you ten-times the money for it. That is, if they don't crash the vehicle and live to collect the money. But, here is the interesting part. Even if they crash the vehicle, the Kikuyus will never perish. Where as, all the Luos, I repeat, all the Luos will be gone! But these Kikuyus are very intelligent people. They don't want us all to die. In fact, they want us to have very many children. They want us to multiply very fast, just like rabbits. Do you know why? Do you know what the reason is?"

"No! No! No!" Odhiambo repeated every response from his swelling audience and turned it down.

"The answer, my friends, is very very simple." Odhiambo was an expert at building up the suspense. "Every time a Luo dies, a Kikuyu man makes money. If more Luos are born, more Luos die and more money is earned by our brothers."

The people clapped and cheered, thereby encouraging Odhiambo to his next performance. While Odhiambo was busy entertaining the crowds, a more serious discussion was ensuing in one of the tents. Sister Phoebe had asked a group of mourners if they were pleased with the hospitality at the funeral.

"There are few people in Kochia, or even Nyanza, that are capable of commanding such community support and organizing such a grand funeral," someone remarked to the concurrence of others.

"I have heard so many stories of funerals that result in the next of kin losing their home, land, livestock and ending up in debt that takes them years to repay."

"I know someone that committed suicide under pressure of debt."

"My cousin's fishing boats were confiscated by the police. Then his mother expired. The funeral was very ordinary - the mourners were fed sukumawiki and ugali. Our people were anything but kind to him. He became the laughing stock of the region and ultimately lost his mental balance."

"That is very bad. Everything has become so expensive now. What are poor people to do?"

"In the olden days, the neighbors and relatives would all come together in solidarity with the family of the deceased. Meals as well as all other expenses would be shared.

"Very true. When I was young, a badly organized funeral reflected poorly not only on the family, but the entire community."

"In my days, the feasting and dancing were meant to honor the dead and reinforce the continuity of life. Nowadays, our young people get so drunk. They get into fights and trouble the women. Yaai yai yai! They have forgotten that it is a funeral, a sad and sacred time, a moment for reflection."

"The way harambees are happening nowadays in some poor communities in Kisumu and Nairobi is very disturbing," Peter Omondi said. Peter was a social worker who conducted HIV/AIDS counseling in the slums of Kisumu.

"Have you heard of disco matangas?" He asked the curious and attentive group. Most people had heard the words before but did not know what exactly they meant.

"Disco matangas are parties held by the family of the deceased to raise funds for the funeral. They are generally held at night with loud music, singing, and dancing."

"How do they raise money though?" An elderly lady sitting across from Peter asked.

"Many different ways. The family will host bidding games and the highest bidder will receive something," Peter explained.

"So, they are auctioning their belongings. At least that will fetch more money than selling it in the market!"

"No. You all don't understand. The people are often bidding for dancing with the women. Sometimes the music organizer, I mean the DJ, will bring in girls to participate in the fundraising. The highest bidder gets to dance with the girl...or spend some time alone. Many adolescents participate in these parties and have casual unprotected sex with multiple partners."

"That explains how the HIV epidemic is spreading quickly amongst the young people."

"The boys will often buy some chocolates, chips, or cosmetics for the girls as a down payment for sex later on. There are very many instances of forced sex and even gang rapes at disco matangas," Peter said to the astonishment of the group.

"So, what are you doing to address this problem?

"Several things. First, we are dissuading older men from engaging with the young women. We are educating parents as well as youth about risky sexual behavior. We have been actively tracking and distributing condoms at such parties in Kisumu as well as Nairobi."

Elizabeth, who was quietly listening to Peter's explanation of disco matangas, spoke up, "Funeral customs contributing to the HIV epidemic is not a new phenomenon. What about the practice of wife inheritance? I cannot make up my mind whether it is a good thing or a bad thing!"

Everyone in the group shuffled uncomfortably in their chairs. This was a particularly thorny topic. In Luo customs, when a man died, his widow and children's responsibility was taken over by another man in the family. This way the woman and children were protected and cared for. Although having sex with the widow was traditionally a taboo, it was impractical and impossible to stop a man from having sex with his inherited wife. If the widow refused to remarry, she would be ostracized and the children would starve. Their land would be snatched away. There was no option but to remarry. This would pass on HIV to her inheritors, thus perpetuating the vicious cycle. Some widows agreed to remarry just to stay close to, and die on, their own land. An ostracized woman would often be on the receiving end of the worst insult – being denied burial in her homestead or her village. Also, this was often the only reliable way to ensure that the land and property ultimately transferred over to the children upon her death. The group spiritedly debated the few benefits and umpteen problems caused by wife inheritance until the drums indicated that the burial was about to commence shortly.

Sister Phoebe excused herself from the group and walked over to Obongo's home. Reverend Ndiege, Obongo and Okello were discussing the burial rituals and sipping their tea. They welcomed Sister Phoebe in their midst.

"Reverend," Sister Phoebe said, "I understand that you will be officiating the burial. I wanted to request you…"

"Okello has already conveyed your request to me," the Reverend said, "and in my speech, I will certainly emphasize frugal funerals."

"Thank you Reverend," Okello said. "Even after the successful harambees in Nairobi and Kochia, and the contributions he has received from well-wishers, Obongo is indebted by more than 400,000 Shillings to a host of different individuals and banks. How can a person with an average monthly income of 15,000 Shillings from ad-hoc jobs and livestock afford such debt?"

"I am considering taking up a job as a construction worker in Kisumu for a few years," Obongo said. "I will surely come home every

Reverend Ndiege Conducting Mzee Obongo's Burial

two weeks to continue working for our CBO. Janet is also thinking of doing a part-time job to contribute towards the loan payments."

"Please don't go to Kisumu," Sister Phoebe urged. "We really need you here in Kochia. Okello, Reverend, please do something! We need to find a way to keep our friend here!"

"I don't have an option," Obongo lamented. "If my daughter was born a few years earlier, I could have arranged her marriage and used the dowry to reduce my debt. If my father's pension funds come through, then all my problems will be solved immediately. But there is no good news about that either. I don't even know if my family will qualify to receive the pension now that father has passed away."

"Reverend," Sister Phoebe said after a long silence. "Peter Omondi was telling us about disco matangas and how HIV is spreading due to funerals. Then Elizabeth brought up the issue of wife inheritance."

"I am not talking about all that," the Reverend interjected. "I agree with you on frugal funerals but I do not support people questioning our culture and traditions. The traditions have withstood the test of time and they are just as applicable today as they were in the past."

"But how is wife inheritance relevant today? We know that it is leading to the spread of disease."

"When the wife is inherited, she is cared for by her new husband and is unlikely to engage in immoral activities with other people. The solution is very simple. If the wife is HIV positive, she must not sleep with her new husband. As for disco matangas, such activities are immoral and illegal. This is an issue for the police. I think that people who break the laws of God must also be considered criminals by the state."

"Reverend," Sister Phoebe challenged the man of God, "declaring something immoral or illegal does not mean that the problem is solved. Our responsibility as community leaders is to work with the people and find practical solutions to these complicated problems."

"No," the Reverend roared, "that is not my job. I can help people find the right moral way to live their life and the government can guide them in the right way by instituting laws. If people choose to break the laws of God and the laws of their country, then there is nothing else that can be done to save them from peril."

The Reverend's strong statement signaled the end of the conversation. The group finished their tea in absolute silence, waiting for the Reverend's signal to step out for the burial. The burial commenced with a prayer and a long speech by the Reverend. Family members and friends then took over the megaphone and recounted memories of the old man. They talked about his kindness, his jovial nature, and his leadership in promoting primary education. Two hours passed by. The heat and hunger were exacting their toll on the crowd. As the speeches dragged on, people scouted for shade and settled down to have their own conversations. The MP's wife delivered a long elegy on her husband's behalf. Finally, the actual burial was officiated by the Reverend. As per Sister Phoebe's request, he preached about humility and frugality at funerals. Sister Phoebe was not impressed by the Reverend's half-hearted attempt that conveniently avoided any discussion on cultural and religious traditions.

"If the Reverend encourages people to question funeral-related traditions, they will also question other religious practices," Sister Phoebe mumbled under her breath. "The Reverend certainly does not want people questioning him or his monthly tithes."

"Sister, don't give up hope." Okello walked over to her and held her arm. "Didn't I tell you that if we want to bring about social change in our community, we have to rethink our approach?"

"Yes, Okello." The nun agreed. "I understand the Reverend's compulsions and I understand Obongo's. I do not blame them. When such educated champions are unable to stand up and change their ways, what can we expect from the common people? Tch tch, we need to become more practical and more realistic. Teaching, preaching, and pleading is not going to change anything."

"We have to be innovative. We need to take direct and very practical action, Sister. We will work together." Okello promised.

"Bega kwa bega[1]," Sister Phoebe affirmed.

In the fading light of the setting sun, the coffin was lowered into the grave. Following the Reverend's lead, family members covered the coffin with fistfuls of soil. The youth used spades to put the rest of the soil in, and over, the grave. Two sticks were used to make a temporary tombstone. A cement structure with a marble tombstone would be finished up the following week. The sumptuous feast was enjoyed and praised by everyone. The immediate family and other relatives stayed inside the compound for a week. A host of rituals were held over the next few weeks that included the *tero buru matin* that symbolizes accompanying the dead person's spirit to the former background and a shaving rite called *liedo*. After the *liedo*, the mourners headed home in ascending order of age, only to return to Obongo's homestead a few weeks later for the *yaodhoot* ceremony. *Yaodhoot* literally means "opening the door" and this event marked the start of a new life for the Obongo

---

[1] Bega kwa bega = Shoulder to shoulder (Kiswahili)

family. Another feast was held for family members in order to please the spirit of the Mzee. The relatives were certainly pleased while Obongo's debt kept on growing.

The *tedo*, a meal for the deceased, was held in the presence of several family members on the day after the *yaodhoot*. Traditionally, the deceased's children would return to their natal home and share the responsibility for cooking a symbolic meal for the parent that had passed away. The *tero buru maduong*, or the big buru, is another ritual that builds on the previous small buru ceremony and symbolizes going to the battleground with the spirit of the deceased. Another large feast, comparable to the feast at the burial, was held. Finally the *tera cholla* ceremony was held to mark the end of mourning. Since the old man's wife had died at childbirth, widow-related rituals were not relevant. The *keyo nyinyo* that involves dividing the articles left by the deceased was very simple since Obongo was the sole inheritor. The *rapar*, or remembrance ceremony was held a month after the funeral and involved a night of singing and dancing followed by a feast on the following day. A few days after the *rapar*, Obongo's mother's family hosted another feast called the *budho*. The mother's family arrived after sunset and stayed up all night. A feast was held in Obongo's house and then they returned home. After three months and expenses adding up to over 700,000 Shillings, the ceremonies and rituals for the Mzee's funeral concluded. Kochia was impressed with the grand send-off to their respected teacher.

Obongo had a strong conviction that his father's pension funds would ultimately come through and that magic moment would be the solution for all his financial problems. However, over the past few months, the government had taken no action towards releasing the funds. As hopes of receiving the pension waned, his fiscal worries grew. Alongside her duties as a health worker, Janet started working at an M-Pesa kiosk. This added about KSh. 5,000 more to the family's monthly income. Okello hired Owiti to help him with his rental business. Obongo went to Kisumu twice but was not successful in finding reasonable work that would let him repay the loans faster. He realized that he would make just as much money in Kochia and Homa Bay, especially after considering the rent, transportation and living expenses he would have to bear in Kisumu. Obongo decided to actively engage in farming goats and hens. In a few weeks, his younger children took deep interest in caring for the animals while Janet realized that she could sell the milk and eggs at her M-Pesa kiosk. Obongo was now able to invest his time in a variety of jobs in Homa Bay. He would help organize workshops, aggregate research data, or connect people and facilitate business deals. This allowed Obongo to earn decent money while expanding and strengthening his social network. With the entire family engaged in income generation and tightening expenses, Obongo was able to pay back about KSh. 30,000 every month.

"So, Okello," Sister Phoebe said during one of their regular meetings, "as you suggested, I talked to many people at the funeral. They said that they were proud of their culture but wanted to do away with the traditions that leave them economically crippled. Every single person expressed that they wanted some degree of reform. At the same time, they felt powerless and lacked confidence to stand up for themselves."

"Yes Sister," Okello concurred, "our people expect their religious, community and political leaders to help them navigate these cultural challenges. Without leadership, things will remain the same. But if we champion new ideas, I am confident that people will respond and support us."

"I thought of at least one practical solution," Sister Phoebe said. "The funeral expenses will be substantially less if our leaders sanctioned the burial at the place of demise rather than insisting on a funeral in Nyanza. That will automatically eliminate the need for the twenty other events at home, and the feasts, and the loud music, and the revelry. I know that is difficult but there are many precedents. In the past, our elders and religious leaders have introduced new rules and given directives that have been accepted by the people. You said that we must look into our culture for solutions. Isn't respect for our elders and religious leaders an integral part of our culture?"

"Conducting the burial at the place of demise will substantially reduce the two major expenses –transportation and food," Okello agreed. "But the problem is that no religious leaders will support and issue such decrees. It is very risky for them. You saw how the Reverend clearly refused to go against tradition."

"The Reverend has sway over many people, but not all the people. We just need one religious leader to take the lead, just one. Then the others will follow."

"I think it is a good idea but it is completely beyond our control. Even after trying for many years, we might fail to convince our leaders. This is a very slow solution."

"Why don't you give me some specific ideas then?" Sister Phoebe chided Okello.

"Well, as you proposed, we must try to convince religious leaders." Okello smiled. "But let us not forget that you are a religious and community leader too! The residents of your HIV home, as well as the patients in the communities, have immense respect for you. We can start by focusing on them."

"But they are the poorest people in our community. Their funerals are already simple and inexpensive."

"Change does not have to begin at the top of the social ladder. It would have been radical for Obongo to host a frugal funeral. It is much more practical to start with your terminally-ill patients. We can reduce costs further and, more importantly, introduce new approaches to hosting respectful funerals without the fanfare, financial ruin, and spread of disease."

"Surely," Sister Phoebe nodded, "my home for HIV patients is always open to new ideas. Right now, every funeral costs KSh. 30,000 and very little comes from the residents' family. If we can reduce the funeral costs, our donations can be used for improving the lives of the current residents or providing services to HIV patients in this area or conducting health awareness and prevention campaigns."

"Don't start spending the money just yet," Okello teased, "but I feel confident that cutting your funeral expenses in half is an achievable goal."

Thanks to the funeral, Okello's music system renting business expanded rapidly. Obongo's son Owiti was hired every weekend to set up and operate the music system. No wedding, funeral, political rally or church function was complete without music served up on Okello's music system and gigantic speakers. Okello launched a successful battery renting enterprise that garnered most of its business from weddings, funerals and crusades. People would rent charged car batteries to run lights, TVs, radios, or to charge their cellphones. Okello had learned several lessons from the Blessed Angel Funeral Company. He established a good relationship with its namesake founder, who enjoyed communicating with Okello just as much.

"End-to-end operations," he could hear Blessed's high-pitched voice in his ears every day. "Our customers don't want batteries, they want parties." Okello would often remind the three young men that worked for his rental business. In a few months, Okello had purchased radios, lights and a few TVs to rent out along with the batteries. In three short months Owiti started working for Okello on a full-time basis, managing all the rental businesses.

Okello invested the profits from his rental businesses into prototypes of inexpensive and environment-friendly cardboard coffins. The wood coffins weighed over 75 kgs and cost at least KSh. 15,000. The nicer wood coffins went for KSh. 30,000 all the way up to KSh. 100,000, depending on the design and additional features. Okello resolved to build cardboard coffins that weighed less than 10 kgs and could be manufactured under KSh. 5,000. Unlike the conventional coffins, such coffins would be free from chemicals that seep into the ground and cause pollution. They could be folded and reassembled easily, thus making them easier and less expensive to transport.

"Even if I am poor, I do not want to be buried in a cardboard coffin. I don't want my family members to just throw me away," an elderly lady had said when Okello had explained the idea to her.

Okello and Sister Phoebe came up with an ingenious solution to change the perception of these coffins. They painted the coffins white, took them to the HIV hospice and invited the residents to write their favorite Bible quote on it. Now the coffins were just as beautiful as the wooden ones, had religious significance, and were cheaper and lighter! Finally, instead of calling them cardboard coffins, they were christened "Bible Beauty Coffins."

"I like this idea very much." Reverend Ndiege approved the cardboard coffins. "They support our traditions and religion. They provide some income to terminally-ill patients, and they are better for our environment." The Reverend shared his favorite Biblical quote to be included on the coffins. He agreed to officiate funerals of residents from Sister Phoebe's home free-of-cost as long as they agreed to use Bible Beauty Coffins. On Sister Phoebe's insistence, he agreed to support a new rule that there would be no food at "Bible Beauty funerals". The funeral costs were thus reduced from KSh. 30,000 to KSh. 8,000. These funds were directly recovered from the harambee held at the funeral, with the rest of the harambee proceeds being used to support HIV prevention activities. Sister Phoebe and Okello were both convinced that this was a valid approach to reducing funeral costs, alleviating environmental damage, and engaging the hospice residents in income-generating activities. The gradually increasing demand for the cardboard coffins further validated the appropriateness of the solution and its potential for larger impact.

Okello was able to manufacture the coffins for KSh. 4,000 and sell them for a thousand more. After paying KSh. 400 to the residents for painting and writing the Bible verses, he was left with a trivial profit of KSh. 600. Bringing down the manufacturing time from eight hours to two hours was one of Okello's biggest challenges. Several other issues needed to be addressed before the coffin business could be officially launched and made economically sustainable. Refining the coffin design, conducting strength tests, setting up a manufacturing facility, establishing the supply chains for raw materials, and getting regulatory approvals were a few of the big tasks. Okello and Sister Phoebe worked day and night on the technical and business aspects of this new venture, which they hoped would someday change the face of Kochia.

"Now, I have completely understood what you meant by championing a new identity," Sister Phoebe said after the twentieth coffin was lowered into the soil. "Every day, when I return home and greet the residents, they proudly tell me how many coffins they painted that day, and how many Bible verses they managed to write on each coffin. Every single resident, from the cook to the painter to the laborer, considers himself or herself a businessperson! They tell me that, 'we are a different kind of businesspeople. The money helps with our few needs and wants but we don't do this work for the money. Our reward is the social good that accompanies the use of our product, and the peace of mind that the mourners will feel when they see the remains of their loved one enveloped in the beauty of the Bible.' No one can tell that these people are terminally-ill. They have a new life, a new outlook, and a new identity just because of this project. I am also happy that I don't have to buy them airtime anymore. They proudly buy it themselves and speak to their friends and family often."

"It is definitely a different kind of business, isn't it?" Okello returned Sister Phoebe's smile with an ear-to-ear grin. "There is a lot of profit, but only some of it is in Shillings, the rest of it is paid to us in many other currencies."

#4

Odhiambo's Journey to God

"I am very grateful to God for the increase in traffic accidents around Nairobi. The Thika road is really the highway to heaven – for passengers and for preachers." John Ouma laughed as he sipped his beer outside Odhiambo's home. "Everyday, I make at least 1,000 Shillings," he turned to his cousin and whispered, "and sometimes as much as 3,000."

"That's how much money I make in two weeks and sometimes in one full month," Odhiambo admitted. He was astonished with the amount of money his cousin was earning in the city. They had grown up together in Kochia. Then, five years back, John had moved to Nairobi in search of a job. He started off as a laborer in the industrial area of Nairobi but in a few months got promoted to a salesman position. His clear voice, excellent conversation skills, and friendly demeanor caught the attention of one of his customers – a pastor who was building his own church. The two quickly became friends and John realized that his calling was not in the steel markets of Nairobi earning a monthly salary of KSh. 5,000. John did a series of commission-based jobs for the pastor while learning the tricks of his trade. Once the church construction was complete, he started preaching on a full-time basis in busses around Nairobi.

John was considered one of the pioneers of bus preaching. His stature and extensive professional network gave him access to preach in the busses traveling from Nairobi to northern destinations like Nanyuki, Meru, and Garissa. Business was slow at first. John would enter the bus near Muthaiga roundabout. He would preach loud enough for the passengers to hear him over the roar of the engine and the blaring music. He had a standard routine that started with a Bible verse from Psalm 125. "Those who trust in Jesus are strong like Mount Zion, which can't be moved, but remains forever. Kenyans that trust in Jesus are like Mount Kenya – Jesus makes us strong and He protects us when we need his protection. Do you know how many accidents happen on Thika road every day? Do you know how many passengers like you die every day in bloody accidents? Over fifty people, I repeat, fifty people die every day on this road. Why? Because they do not pray to God – they do not pray to Jesus Christ. So, let us live to be old and strong like Mount Kenya. Let us pray to Jesus to protect us." John would then say a small prayer and walk back and forth in the bus collecting money from the scared passengers. Most passengers would just ignore him, while others would give him 20, 30 or 50 Shillings.

With the construction of the super highway, the number of accidents on Thika road started increasing rapidly. John's sermons became more profitable. He would give details about accidents and scare the passengers until they would be willing to part with their money. He learned that it was more effective to first preach to the entire bus and then say prayers four or five times down the aisle. Passengers responded better to his personalized prayers and the Shillings flowed out of their pockets faster. Sometimes he would target college students and almost force them to fork out cash towards prayers for good luck in their journeys.

"I have been summoned to go and preach the gospel in the service of God to our soldiers fighting in Somalia." John would appeal to the patriotism of young men to reap rich rewards. He would pass a crumpled 100 Shilling note to the bus conductor to have the music system turned off for the thirty-minute prayer service. A particularly profitable journey earned the bus conductor an additional tip from the preacher. He would alight the bus at Kenyatta University, 16 kms away, and wait for busses going in the opposite direction to Nairobi. The same sequence would be repeated with additional prayers to request protection from God against the thugs and muggers of Nairobi. On any given day, he would return home late at night with at least a thousand Shillings, typically much more. John's monthly income of KSh. 60,000 was twice the typical salary of a nurse and was comparable to a university professor's salary.

Odhiambo was very impressed with John's professional accomplishments, even a tad bit jealous. They were peers in school and Odhiambo always earned better grades than his cousin. If John could cut out such a nice life for himself, so could he. Odhiambo was an excellent storyteller and always in-demand during any family or community event. "Easy come, easy go," he said to John. "The Kikuyus have all their nexuses in Nairobi which are the source of their ill-gotten wealth. They want redemption for their sins. Why should we not give them an opportunity to share their wealth with us and show them the road to Jesus?"

Odhiambo resolved to become a preacher, whether it was in Nairobi or Kisumu or Kochia. John had invited him to Nairobi and promised to help him become a bus preacher. He thought it would be wise to talk to his friends in Kochia before leaving his family behind and heading off to the big, bad city. The first person to consult with was Reverend Ndiege. Odhiambo spent a small fortune on a brand-new Bible in a black leather case with a shining gold cross on it. If he wanted to be a preacher, he must also dress like one. He dawned his best Sunday clothes and sprayed the red perfume that his cousin had recently gifted him. The buttons on his jacket wouldn't close and the tie ended a few inches above his belly. As he walked towards the church, he returned the stares of puzzled bystanders with a big smile and a slight bow. He made the sign of the cross several times and was quite pleased with his smooth moves.

The Reverend was preparing his next sermon on his old clunky computer in the little office behind the church. He was surprised to see Odhiambo in his comical outfit with a Bible in hand. The Reverend carefully placed the keyboard on top of the tiny monitor and turned towards his visitor.

"Odhiambo, I am delighted to see you in church. Have you lost your way or have you found it?"

"Reverend, I think I have finally found my way to Jesus."

"That's very nice but you are three hours late for the morning service."

"Reverend, there is something else I want to say. I remember attending your first sermon when you started your church in Kochia. Under the big fig tree, you told us how the voice of God led you to Kochia. On that day, I did not understand…"

"Odhiambo, I am in the middle of some important work. Can you please get to the point?"

"Why not? Yesterday night, I heard a voice telling me that I should start preaching the word of God. The voice belonged to my brother, John Ouma. He is now a very powerful preacher in Nairobi and has saved countless souls from accidents. I have decided to become a preacher too and dedicate my life to God."

"This is completely absurd." The Reverend jumped out of his chair. "Odhiambo, what do you know about the Bible? What do you know about the life and lessons of Jesus Christ? How in the world can you become a preacher?"

"John will help me become a bus preacher in Nairobi. He suggested I learn a few verses from the Bible. Can you tell me how I should go about doing that?"

"Don't waste my time and don't waste yours. All those street preachers and bus preachers are conmen. They fool ignorant people to enrich themselves. If you want to become a preacher, go and study at a Bible school and you will some day become a respectable pastor of a respectable church."

"Yes, Reverend. I want to become a good pastor. I have heard of Bible schools in Kisumu. Okello has lived there for some years. I will talk to him right away. Is there anything else I should do?"

"Start attending church regularly and pay your tithes on time. It is the responsibility…"

Odhiambo had marched off long before the Reverend stopped mumbling and resumed his work. Odhiambo was quite excited when he calculated how much money the Reverend earned from the 300 members of his congregation, even if only half of them paid their tithes responsibly.

Over the past few decades, countless Bible schools had sprung up in East Africa to meet the growing demands for formal religious education. The established public and private universities offered graduate and post-graduate degrees in theology as a stepping-stone towards a career in ministry. At the same time, hundreds of private Bible schools offered educational programs that ranged in duration from a few weeks to a few years. The expensive schools boasted collaborations with universities in the United States, exchange programs in Europe, and internships in rural and urban areas across East Africa. Graduates of the universities took on leadership roles in large churches and their associated organizations. At the other end of the spectrum, Bible schools in rural areas and urban slums operated in tiny poorly-lit tin shacks with students learning the gospel and ministry from uneducated teachers, many of them graduates of similar fly-by-night operations. These were more akin to vocational schools and churned out pastors of small local churches and preachers that plied their trade on streets, busses, matatus, or any other place where people congregated. Collectively, this was a multi-million Shilling industry that provided employment and entrepreneurship opportunities to a multitude of East Africans.

Okello was working on his cardboard coffin project when Odhiambo walked into his workshop. After a brief exchange of greetings, Odhiambo explained to him the purpose of his visit. Okello offered the aspiring man of God a chair and continued working on his test jig for conducting load tests on coffin prototypes.

"So, my first question for you is whether you want to help people or you want to make money?" Okello asked.

"Okello, you are a good man and a businessman. So I hope you will understand. I want to make money while helping people."

"If you want to become a real pastor like Reverend Ndiege, you should go to a good university. You have finished Form 4, but that was over fifteen years back. I am not sure if you will get admission now and I don't know how you will pay the fees. Your other option is to go to a private Bible school and sign up for one of those short-term courses. There are plenty of them in Nyanza and you won't even have to travel to Kisumu for that. However, if you just want to make money, go to Nairobi and shadow your cousin for a few days. That way, you will learn all the practical aspects of running your own business."

"How can I learn all the Bible verses like John asked me to? This book is so fat and there are no pictures in it either."

"Tch tch, Odhiambo, you only need to memorize two or three verses and the other things you have to say. Then just start working in the busses. Practice will make you perfect." Odhiambo was relieved that he didn't have to memorize the entire Bible.

"What have you planned for your family here in Kochia? Who will take care of your elderly parents and children? Who will look over your wife – isn't she expecting a baby?" Okello asked.

"Indeed, we are expecting our fourth baby. I do not want to leave Kochia but how can I become a preacher here? Even if I become a preacher, our Luo people - they just won't spare any change."

"If you want to make money, there are many ways to do that. That is a different conversation. Why don't you go and talk to the preachers at the matatu stage in Homa Bay? See what opportunities are available closer to home."

"That is very good advice. I must do that. If I can stay in Kochia and become a preacher, everything will be perfect. My problem is that I cannot stay away from my children for long."

"Come back and we will talk about your options. Meanwhile, I will discuss your newfound love for religion with Sister Phoebe. She might have some ideas too." Okello waved him goodbye and continued his work. Someday, I will write a twenty-page textbook for aspiring bus and matatu preachers. It will sell like hot cakes, he thought to himself.

Odhiambo had a modest lunch of roasted corn and two slices of juicy pineapple on the matatu as he headed to Homa Bay. The bus station was as chaotic as ever, replete with confused travelers, boisterous conductors, persistent touts, and countless goats stretching their limbs after another uncomfortable journey. The preachers were dressed in suits and ties and walked around with a Bible in hand. Some of them wore an orange headdress to indicate their affiliation with a particular denomination. Odhiambo initiated a conversation with an emaciated young man with big eyes and an ear-to-ear smile.

"You see, I protect innocent travelers from the dangers that lurk on the roads," the young preacher proclaimed. "My prayers cover accidents, traffic jams, drunk drivers, demonic powers and curses."

"Ayyyyy, that is very good. Do you pray for every passenger?"

"You see, we pray for every vehicle and since the passengers are in the vehicles, you can say that we pray for every passenger."

"I don't understand. Who is 'we'?"

"You see, I belong to a group of preachers. We take turns conducting the prayer service. That way there is no problem – no fighting. I just finished my turn and need to wait for about 30 minutes now." The preacher looked around furtively. "But, if you want, I can do a special prayer for you?"

"NO NO NO! Please don't pray for me!" Odhiambo hastily covered his shirt pocket and pushed the fifty Shilling note deeper. "You see, I am also planning to become a preacher like you and so I came here to meet my fellow comrades."

"Where are you from?" The preacher demanded.

"I am from Kochia and my name is Odhiambo."

"You see Mr. Odhiambo, I don't care where you are from but there are enough powerful preachers in Homa Bay. We have successfully protected all the passengers from bad things. We don't want any self-proclaimed preachers like you to spoil the peace with the devil and his friends. We will not permit you to operate here." The preacher's tone was getting louder and more agitated. A few curious people stopped whatever they were doing and started walking towards Odhiambo.

"I think there is a misunderstanding. I don't want to preach here. I just came to learn…"

"Here…this is your matatu." The angry preacher led Odhiambo by the arm and forced him into an already full vehicle. He slammed the sliding door shut, gave the driver a hundred Shillings and roared, "Take this man to Kochia and make sure he doesn't come back."

Odhiambo was livid with anger and fear during the 45-minute journey home. In his younger days, he would have put up a fight. Now he had three children with a fourth one on the way – he was too old to fight.

A Matatu Preacher

"These matatu preachers are a rowdy lot. You must be pleased that I am back home alive," was all he said to his wife as he sat down in his favorite chair.

"Tomorrow, I want to go to Homa Bay for Bishop Mwangi's crusade. Why don't you take me there?" his wife urged.

"No – I am not going to Homa Bay and neither are you. It is not safe," Odhiambo said, much to the amusement of his wife. He had seen posters about the crusade all over Kochia and there was excitement about it in Homa Bay too. He wanted to experience the crusade first-hand too but was terrified of running into the preacher and getting beaten up.

"Won't you take me to seek blessings for our unborn child?" His wife nagged him until he finally relented. They set off for Homa Bay mid-morning the next day. Much to the chagrin of his pregnant wife, he made her alight two stops before the bus station and walk on a circuitous route to the crusade venue.

Loud gospel music greeted Odhiambo and his wife in the large field where the crusade was to be held over the next three days. The crowd swelled from a few drunkards and elderly ladies in the morning to over 400 people by early afternoon. When microphone testing commenced at 4 PM, there was no room to move. People had climbed on the rooftops of the few one-storey buildings in Homa Bay while others struggled for a premium spot on the trees and electricity towers. This was a special crusade featuring an American preacher alongside the famous Kenyan pastor, Bishop Mwangi, from the Moneymaker church. The first day of the crusade was tailored towards pregnant women and new mothers.

This is a disaster waiting to happen, Odhiambo thought to himself as he surveyed the countless pregnant women and devout mothers hoisting their children as high as they could in hopes of attracting more blessings from the pastors. As he turned towards the podium, he spotted Owiti testing the microphones. Owiti was Obongo's son who now managed Okello's audio system rental business. Odhiambo grabbed his wife's arm and pulled her through the crowds. As he reached the bamboo barrier, he screamed and gesticulated until he caught Owiti's attention. Owiti waved back and then turned towards the podium to speak to his boss.

"What are you doing here, my good man, and that too with your wife? Don't you know how unsafe such events are?" Okello ran over and scolded his friend. "Just last week, four people were killed in a stampede at another crusade! How can you be so irresponsible?"

"I told her but she insisted," Odhiambo stuttered. "Now, she is very tired and wants to rest but she refuses to return home. She wants to see the preachers and the crusade."

"Now that I think about it some more, I am glad you came. Come over to this side." Okello requested the guards to let the couple towards the podium. There were several rows of sofas and benches on both sides of the podium for the important people – government officials, church elders and major donors. Okello had originally planned on selling off his two VIP passes – they would fetch him at least KSh. 2,000 each. Instead, he gave the passes to Odhiambo, and walked them over to the red-carpeted VIP enclosure.

"The program won't start for at least 30 minutes. I suggest that you listen to the Bishop for an hour and make your way home before sunset," Okello advised. He asked one of his employees to run to the concessions and bring mayaai chips[1] and two sodas for his guests. Okello then ran backstage to finish testing the audio system so that the crusade could commence.

Odhiambo and his wife peered at the mass of humanity on the other side of the barrier. They thanked God for sending Okello over to rescue them from the madness. The praise and adulation team started singing religious songs to entertain the crowds and get them fired up for the Bishop's act. The spontaneous crowd clapped, shouted, swayed and danced to the music. This was an outlet for their repressed feelings. For a few hours, they forgot their problems and tensions in the warmth of the close-knit community nourished by the words of hope and purpose in the melodious songs. Women and youth, long ignored by the oligarchic traditions of the church, were drawn to the crusades because it helped them overcome their perceived disenfranchisement and alienation. The youth craved for social support and opportunities to earn honest livelihoods, build their own homes, get married, and have babies. The crusades gave them a chance to belong to, and identify with, others in similar predicaments. The Bishop's ideologies and approaches to life, livelihoods and religion resonated with some of them. If the Bishop had achieved so much power and wealth, why could they not follow in his footsteps to be successful as well?

Just as the people were starting to tire from the dancing, the megaphone blared to life and a church official proclaimed, "Today is a new beginning for Kenya, a new beginning for Homa Bay, a new beginning for the entire world and all of creation, a new beginning for you. The Holy Spirit will be speaking through Bishop Mwangi. The sun will rise again to signify the dawn of a new day in our lives." The Bishop

---

[1] Mayaai chips = French fries with a fried egg on top (Mayaai = Egg in Kiswahili)

arrived on stage, cheered by hundreds of his followers. For the next fifteen minutes, he proclaimed a new dawn.

Odhiambo looked at the sky – it was almost sunset. He wanted to avoid going to the bus station, especially after dark. In his trademark hoarse voice, the Bishop recited several verses from the Bible and explained their meaning. He preached about sexual fidelity and the dangers of smoking and drinking. He assured the people that if they pray with him, they would be freed from the bondage of poverty, unemployment and disease. They would be able to pay their children's school fees and send them to college, shop at supermarkets and drive cars, host lavish weddings and funerals, and even uproot corruption and tribalism from the Kenyan government. I may have wasted my life by not going to church. I could have been a very successful man, Odhiambo thought to himself, but I am sure even Jesus Christ cannot remove Kikuyus and corruption from the Kenyan government.

The Bishop started calling groups of people to be reborn and blessed. The conversions would commence with the VIPs. Taking a cue from their neighbors, Odhiambo and his wife stood up. A church official was distributing orange headdresses with information about the crusade printed on them in black ink. Odhiambo was not sure if he should take the headdress or not. He observed that about half the people were picking them up and putting them on, while the others just waved the person by. "There is something fishy going on here. If these headdresses were free, they would all be gone by now. But, I don't see any money being collected either," Odhiambo wondered. After considerable deliberation, he decided to take a calculated risk. He had seen vendors in Homa Bay sell similar headdresses for a hundred bob so he figured that these could not be much more than that. He extended his arm to take one for his wife.

Just as he was about to touch the orange cloth, he felt a sudden jerk on his arm. "Do you want to pay 2,000 Shillings for that worthless piece of cloth?" Okello jumped in and waved the church official by.

"2,000 Shillings! But no one is collecting money. I think they are free."

"Nothing in this world is free; certainly not at a crusade of the Moneymaker church. The Bishop will shortly declare that all the worshippers are reborn and he will ask for donations to advance the work of God. The minimum sadaka[1] for the VIP stand is 2,000 and they will shame you in front of everyone if you don't fork out the cash."

---

[1] Sadaka = Religious offering

"Why don't they just tell you the price before you take one?"

"Then, I think, there will be no takers! Why don't you ask the Bishop yourself?" Okello gave a devilish grin. "Yesterday, when I was talking to him, the Bishop expressed that he was looking for partners to lead branches of his church in Nyanzaa and beyond. The first person I thought about was you, Odhiambo. The Bishop wants a new beginning for Kenya. He wants to save more people from the bondage of sin. He wants to make money and help his brethren make money. It seems like your interests align with the Bishop's. Would you like me to set up a meeting with him?"

"You mean, the Bishop will agree to meet me in person?" Odhiambo was star-struck.

"Indeed! We can talk about the possibility of you starting a branch of the church and becoming a pastor. I will speak to him tomorrow morning and try to get an appointment for next week," Okello promised. "And by the way, I talked to Sister Phoebe and she wants to meet you too."

The crusade continued just the way Okello had explained. Groups of people would stand up, wear the headdresses and be declared reborn by the Bishop. Songs with fervent dancing by the attendees were interspersed with the Bishop's sermons and conversions. Odhiambo's wife begged her husband to go home. He promptly refused.

"This is the biggest opportunity of my life. If everything goes as planned, I don't have to go to Nairobi. I can be here with you and the children, have my own church, and we can live a comfortable life," Odhiambo insisted. "Don't you think it is important for me to learn everything about the crusade and the Bishop before the meeting? And besides, Okello can drop us home. It is too late to go to the bus station now. I will definitely get beaten up." His wife had already succumbed to the day's adventures and was fast asleep with her head on his shoulder and her hands on her belly.

It was past 8 PM when the Bishop introduced the American pastor and praised his healing powers. Faith healing and miracle services were a mainstay at crusades by influential pastors and preachers. Such cures for ailments ranging from AIDS to infertility to blindness were very popular because health care was beyond the reach of many ordinary people. While women from lower socio-economic classes formed the majority, people of every age, gender, ethnicity, socio-economic status, religious affiliation and academic level attended crusades and partook in faith healing and miracle services. The American pastor specialized in curing people with HIV/AIDS. Today, he was to conduct special miracle services for infertile women, pregnant women, and mothers with post-partum health problems. The women who wanted to be healed had assembled in the specially barricaded area in front of the podium, flanked by the VIP enclosures on both sides. This special enclosure was further divided into sections with the help of nylon ropes. The KSh. 1,000 ticket gave the women standing room towards the back of the enclosure. Every additional KSh. 500 moved the patients a few steps closer to the podium, and then, for KSh. 8,000, the patients could share the stage with the American preacher.

There were emotional testimonials from patients who had been healed by the great preacher. A tearful woman, clutching her crying infant in her arms, narrated how she failed to conceive for over seven years. Soon after the pastor healed her, she was blessed with a healthy baby boy. Another woman had several miscarriages before a miracle by the preacher resulted in the birth of twins. An HIV positive woman and her newborn baby were both cured of the deadly virus in just a few days after a personal miracle session. After many more testimonials that seemed to defy the science of medicine, the preacher started healing the patients. Screams of "Jesus" from the thousands of hyper-excited believers prevailed over the gospel music blaring through the gigantic speakers. The preacher touched the patients on their head to heal them. Three women were overcome with delirium and broke into a fit of trembling and swaying that continued even after they were on the floor. The chanting from the crowd got louder and faster as the preacher healed people in the front rows with his own hands and dispatched his assistants with a blessed Bible to heal the throngs in the rear sections. Odhiambo's wife was woken up by the feverish chanting and intense, almost surreal, atmosphere.

"I don't think I have the power to do any miracles or heal people," Odhiambo humbly admitted to Okello. "I don't think I can become a preacher like Bishop Mwangi."

"You don't have to do crusades and heal people. You can be the head pastor of a branch of Bishop Mwangi's church," Okello suggested. "You will likely have to take care of the church facilities and deliver the sermons."

"So, I don't even need to learn the Bible?"

"I guess, you don't need to, but you should. Remember that people might ask questions or come to you for personal counsel. You cannot blame the Kikuyus for all their problems." Okello grinned.

"If my boss is a Kikuyu, I better be careful with what I say." Odhiambo smiled back. He shuffled in his seat a few times, turned around to say something and stopped.

"Is there a problem – what are you thinking?"

"I am very moved by this crusade and am convinced that religion can help our brothers and sisters live better lives. I have heard of very many miracles but some of the stories we heard today are a little hard to believe. I have been trained as an HIV/AIDS care provider and we have been told again and again that there is no cure for HIV. Do you think that the preacher can really heal these people?"

"I don't know if the preacher can heal patients. What I do know is that the woman with the baby works for the Bishop and so does the woman whose HIV was cured."

"My dear Okello, is that true?"

"As true as the fact that the three women who were having a fit were sneakily made to smell some medicine, which caused their delirious screaming and trembling."

"Shouldn't the Bishop be behind bars? This is outright fraud."

"Speak softly my friend. You will get both of us in trouble. Don't you know how well-connected the Bishop is? He knows everyone and everyone knows him. They condone his deeds. Some think that the overall impact of his work is positive while others are too afraid to touch him. There are also some politicians and policemen who believe in his powers of healing and conducting miracles."

"I agree that there are some positive results of his crusades – I can see it in the fellowship that has formed right here. It is very moving. I saw several young men resolve to give up smoking and drinking. I saw women share their knowledge on traditional medicine with their peers. But, what about the patients who should actually have gone to the doctor instead of coming here? Does the preacher take responsibility for healing them? Does he guarantee it?"

"Why don't you ask the preacher when you meet him?"

"Yes, I will. But you will have to come with me Okello. I cannot go alone."

The crusade ended with testimonials to encourage the people to come back for the next two days. The miracle healing sessions on the second day focused on curing people with HIV/AIDS while the third day was dedicated to miracle services that enabled people to get rich quickly. In a place where the HIV prevalence rate was over 15% and there was abject poverty, both these miracle services were in high-demand. The crowds started dispersing around 10 PM. Most people walked home while others were too tired or too drunk, and had to be carried home. Matatus gouged the passengers by charging three-times the regular fare. Those who lived far away and could not afford the matatus went to sleep at the crusade venue. It was almost midnight when Okello dropped his friends home.

"Should I go back tomorrow?" Odhiambo asked while shutting the door of Okello's rented matatu.

"I am glad you were there today and saw everything that happened. You are a very intelligent person, Odhiambo, and I want you to make your own decision. I am afraid I cannot give you my passes for tomorrow or the day after as they will earn me a small fortune." Okello smiled and drove away into the night. He was pleased with the day – everything worked out well on the business side of things. Odhiambo's surprise visit to the crusade was a godsend – it eased a few hurdles in channeling the aspiring preacher's energies in the right direction.

Odhiambo decided not to attend the crusade for the next two days. He texted Okello and requested a meeting at the earliest. He spent most of his day and night replaying the crusade in his mind - the Bishop's sermons, the planted testimonials, the zealous and gullible people, and his conversations with Okello. His head hurt from the mental stress. Three days went by before Okello wound up his business with the crusade and went over to his friend's homestead. They pulled up two chairs under the tree.

"Okello, all I have been doing for the last three days is thinking about the crusade. A few days back, I had made a decision to become a preacher as a way to earn money and help people. The crusade helped me confirm my decision. But it also brought up several questions in my mind. Do you think what Bishop Mwangi is doing is fair?

"Some things are fair, and some, like the planted testimonials and miracle healing, are not."

"How does the Bishop view his own church and its work?"

"I don't know. Ask the Bishop when we see him tomorrow morning. He is heading to Nairobi tomorrow and then to America. It wasn't easy but I have secured a meeting with him tomorrow morning at 8 AM. And then at 3 PM, we will be meeting with Sister Phoebe."

"Very well. Let us talk some more after we see the Bishop tomorrow."

"See you a five tomorrow morning. Be careful what you say and how you say it," Okello warned, and headed home.

The duo left home early morning in Okello's rented matatu to reach the Moneymaker church on the outskirts of Kisumu at 7:30 AM. Sharply, at the appointed time, they were invited to the preacher's plush office in the church complex. The Bishop was very personable and charismatic in his style.

"Okello, my dear friend, you are the reason the crusade in Homa Bay was so successful. People don't come to listen to me. They come to listen to the music and words from your megaphone and speakers. So, thank you!"

"That is very nice of you to say. I think the people loved you and the American preacher. Thank you for making me a part of your work."

The Bishop got straight to the point. "We don't have much time – let us talk about business. The purpose of this meeting is to discuss how your friend here can start a branch of my church?"

"Yes, Bishop, I want to know more about you, and the church, and what it means to start a branch of your church." Odhiambo went on to provide a brief bio sketch and explained how he found his calling for God. "…but I must admit that I am no man of God like you and I know nothing about the Bible. But my friend here will tell you than I am an honest and hardworking man. In my heart, just like Okello, Obongo and countless others, I want to help my people. I am not sure yet if I want to become a preacher. There are very many things I want to ask you first."

"Thank you Mr. Odhiambo, or should I call you Pastor Odhiambo? Let me assure you that not knowing the religious texts is not a disqualification. I suggest that without further delay, you put your questions to me."

"What denomination does the church belong to? What doctrine do you follow?"

"We just follow the Bible. Our denomination is the Moneymaker church – an independent evangelist organization. When necessary, we work with other denominations. For example, the American pastor is from a Pentecostal church and we are working together to conduct miracles and save souls in Kenya."

"How did you come up with this name for your church?"

"Moneymaker - that is what our country needs! In the Central region of Kenya where I come from, we grow lot of tomatoes. The Moneymaker tomatoes are the most profitable ones. If we have Moneymaker tomatoes, Moneymaker water pumps, why not Moneymaker churches?"

"Do you want the church to make money…or do you want your members to make money?"

"Jesus loves his followers and wants them to make money. I want my flock to do away with poverty and live a happy life. The church needs to make money too, but the church belongs to the people, doesn't it?" Odhiambo was not pleased with the roundabout response but realized there was no point pushing the question.

"Bishop, I am really impressed with your power of healing sick people. I have been conducting home-based care for HIV/AIDS patients. We have been told that there is no cure for HIV. But you have cured so many people from the deadly disease...I am trying to say...,"

"Don't worry Odhiambo. I get that question all the time and I like answering it. I do not heal people, Jesus heals them. I am simply doing the Lord's work. While most patients are healed of any disease they have, some patients, do not get cured." The Bishop leaned forward in his chair. "The handful of patients who are not cured are the ones who do not have faith in the Lord. You must have faith – deep down in your heart. You must love Jesus very deeply and Jesus must love you. Otherwise you cannot be healed."

"So, when you charge people so much money, do you provide a guarantee that they will be healed?"

"We don't charge people money, our healing and prayers are completely free of cost. The patients give donations to the church to advance the work of God. I cannot guarantee that patients will be healed because there is no way for me to know if they really have deep faith in Jesus."

"Is it essential to request so much money in donations? I am worried that our people are poor and giving so much money just pushes them further into poverty."

"Odhiambo, if you want to become successful in anything, you have to understand that everything costs money. Do you know how much we paid your friend here for the audio system? How much I paid for stage construction? Wages of the 75 workers? Do you know how many thousand dollars the American pastor charged for just three days? Our people are poor, but how will they get wealthier if they are sick? If they spend some money and become healthier – physically, socially, and spiritually, they will end up making more money. What is the harm with that?"

"Bishop, are you trying to say that this church is a business?"

"Odhiambo, you have to understand the basic principle of the Moneymaker church. Jesus wants his flock to be wealthy and happy and he also wants the church to be able to stay alive and grow. If the church cannot grow, how will it save more souls?"

"So, how can we set up a branch of the church in Kochia?" Odhiambo inquired.

"First of all, my dear friend, you have to understand how to run a business. You will have to manage all the facilities of the church – the

Bishop Mwangi and the Moneymaker Church

chapel, the offices, and the shop. You will have to deliver the sermons which I will send you every week. Let me give you a tour of the facilities while we talk." the Bishop stood up and led the way.

"Won't we have to put up a church in Kochia first?"

"Indeed. I want us to be equal partners. I will pay half the costs and you will have to come up with the other funds."

"How much will it cost?"

"At least one million Shillings. If you don't have the money to invest, I will pay for it completely. But then, you will be a salaried employee with additional commissions based on sales," the Bishop said as he opened the door to the church shop."

"I have never seen a church with a shop like this," Odhiambo mumbled as he stared at an elaborate "Menu of Services" painted on one of the walls. Headdresses of different colors hung from one corner. A series of shelves adorned one of the walls. One shelf was lined with bottles of red liquid in different sizes. Another shelf had laminated pictures starring the Bishop, Jesus Christ, and several poses with both of them together! There were printed t-shirts and caps and row after row of religious books.

"What is in these bottles?" Odhiambo wondered.

"Oh, those are sacred anointing oils – for jobs, protection from black magic, catching more fish, better harvests, lightening skin, strengthening your manhood, and many more. They are also guaranteed to work for those who have deep faith in the Lord." The Bishop said in a matter-of-fact manner.

"If I am understanding you correctly, my responsibilities are taking care of the shop and delivering the sermons?"

"Yes, and managing the account very honestly."

"You said that you will be writing all the sermons and I am supposed to deliver them in the church. Can I change the sermons to meet the needs of my people? I am very good at engaging people through stories."

"No, you cannot. All my churches receive sermons that I have written. In fact, Okello and I have been talking about how we can have TVs in all the branches so that the people can watch me live from my main church here."

"What if people come to me for counsel or advice? I won't know what to tell them."

"That is easy. We will provide you one-day training on counseling your people. The solution to every problem can be found in the anointing oils and headdresses, which can be purchased from the shop. While some products are in the shop year-round, others are seasonal. For example, very many young people will come to you during the annual exams. The solution to their exam-related problems is the specially-anointed pens and pencils that we will send to your shop."

"I think I completely understand how this works. I am sure I can fulfill these responsibilities. What is the salary like?"

"When you are sure about working with me, come back and we will talk about the details. Just so you have some idea, the pastor at the branch in Busia receives a monthly salary of 4,000 Shillings and 20% of all sales from the shop. He makes a very decent living. In fact, I anointed his new car last Sunday."

"OK. When can we start the church?"

"Building the church will take a few years. First we need to assess the feasibility of having the church in Kochia. We will start with a small church shop and then build the church around it over time. We can find a place to rent out as early as next month. I will even pay the rent for three months."

"So Bishop, I have been thinking about how our people are getting divided and sub-divided into more and more denominations. Instead of coming together, these denominations are competing and fighting with each other. I really want to see people stop fighting and come together irrespective of their denomination, tribe, or even religion."

"Yes Odhiambo, I agree with you. I want all people of Kenya to come together too. We have to move beyond tribes and religion and denominations. That is why I decided to make the Moneymaker Church independent of any mainstream denomination."

"I am happy to hear that Bishop. You are a visionary. Can people from any denomination then come to the Moneymaker church and participate in various activities?"

"Very much so. But as I explained earlier, all members must be baptized into the church and pay their tithes in a timely fashion. The more they give to the church, the more they will get back."

"I think that answers all my questions Bishop. Thank you very much for meeting with us. We know you are a very busy man." Odhiambo and Okello shook hands with the Bishop and headed towards the door. They promised to reconnect and discuss the details about the new Moneymaker church in Kochia when the Bishop returned from his travels in two weeks.

"Odhiambo, I am impressed. You certainly came prepared to ask tough questions!" Okello praised his friend as they walked towards the matatu to start their drive back to Kochia.

"Yes," was all Odhiambo said. He stared out of the window until

Okello broke the silence thirty minutes later.

"What are you thinking? Are you going to take up the Bishop on his offer?"

"The Bishop's answers were very candid but I did not like the way he took refuge in "deep faith". I don't trust his handling of church finances either. I don't see how he is using the money for his people and I don't see how his people are benefitting from the church."

"Yes, you are right. He is running a business and most people consider it a very honest business. If you make an exception for the planted testimonials, everything he is doing is honest – just the way it has been done for centuries."

"Do other pastors use such devious ways to build trust in their healing powers too?" Odhiambo wondered.

"Actually, the Bishop's ways are not as glaring as some others. Last year, they caught a Ugandan pastor with electrical gadgets meant to shock people to the ground when he would lay his hands on them. The worshipper writhing and falling to the floor convinced his faithful congregation of his superlative healing powers."

"But won't people die if they are given electric shocks?"

"Not if they are light shocks. The pastor had even hired two engineers to design and manage the gadgets." Okello laughed. "And then there was the case where this preacher healed sick people after giving personal details about their lives to the astonishment of the crowds…but it was later discovered that his wife and associates would mingle with the worshippers to collect personal information before the healing session and transmit it to the preacher backstage with walky-talkies." Okello jogged his memory. "Then do you remember the scandal implicating Firepower Ministries? Hey…that one was very funny."

"Wasn't that the pastor who used prostitutes to pose as sick people and then he healed them?"

"Yes, the pastor's men would go and find prostitutes in the streets at night and prepare them for showing up in church the next day. This woman twisted her lips into a shocking contortion. When the preacher prayed for her, she quietly removed the rubber bands to regain her original form. She started jubilating and jumping around in joy to show that she had been healed. I have been told that the preacher made over KSh. 200,000 just that one day."

"Yes, but he was so stingy that he refused to pay the poor lady the promised KSh. 2,000. Of course she was bitter and lodged a complaint with the police and also went to the media. It was a serious embarrassment for the pastor because her story was told around the world."

"The funniest part," Okello said, trying to suppress tears of laughter. "When the police questioned the pastor, he was angry that they were interfering in God's work. His own people wrote up stories about his miracles in the newsletter but refused to let any journalists from the mainstream media cover the miracles by insisting that they were sent by the devil. Do you know that the ministry is still going strong and the pastor is as popular as ever?"

"Sometimes it is difficult to tell when religion stops and crime starts," Odhiambo lamented.

"or when crime stops and religion starts..." Okello jumped in. "Remember how the Mungiki gang mercilessly slaughtered thousands of poor people that resisted their extortion demands. The police, in their efforts to root-out the gangsters, killed thousands more. As the bloodshed continued, the embarrassed government caught the main man and put him in prison on minor charges. He was 'born-again' and came out of jail a prophet. He is now the pastor of his church and is being courted by politicians from every party."

"I heard that he is planning to run for Kenyan presidency during the next election: What an embarrassment!" Odhiambo groaned in utter disbelief. "But maybe that is the price for peace; I am happy that the Mungikis are now gone."

"These are deep-rooted problems, Odhiambo, that cannot be solved overnight. While the killings have stopped, extortion continues as usual in Mungiki strongholds. Our young people are unemployed. They are disenfranchised and until we find gainful work for them, Mungikis will keep emerging under different names all over the country."

The duo shared many more stories and laughed all the way home to Kochia. After a quick lunch of ugali and sukumawiki, they walked over to Sister Phoebe's home. Sister Phoebe was finishing up her daily visits with terminally-ill HIV/AIDS patients. She walked over to the visiting room of her quarters when she was informed about her friends' arrival. Okello made some tea in the kitchen while Odhiambo once again narrated his journey towards becoming a preacher. He did not shy away from recounting his adventure with the matatu preacher in Homa Bay and the long day at the crusade. Okello served his friends some tea and sat down on the wooden chair with his legs resting on the coffee table. Odhiambo started discussing the conversation with the Bishop. Sister Phoebe was visibly surprised and somewhat agitated with the Bishop's views and business strategies. Despite Odhiambo's pleading, she withheld her thoughts on the Moneymaker church.

"My opinion on the Bishop and his so-called church does not matter. Who am I to judge?" is all she said, in her characteristic unruffled manner. Odhiambo had been so earnest and detailed in his questions to the Bishop that even Okello was not sure what he was really thinking. While Okello was convinced that his friend had come too far to go back to his laidback way of life, he was not sure if he would work with the Bishop, head to Nairobi and team up with his cousin, or take his own independent route?

"Our people are poor – many have no food to eat; they are sick; they are desperate. Shouldn't we stop them from turning over their life savings and their rational thinking to this fraudulent preacher?" Odhiambo roared with anger.

"No, Odhiambo, I don't think we can stop them." Sister Phoebe comforted him. "Not until we can provide them with what they are seeking. Our people want jobs, they want to go to sleep without worrying about food for the next day, they want their children to get a good education, they want hope, and they want a sense of belonging. Can we provide them any of those things? And by the way, I also want you to realize that all the preacher's activities are perfectly legal. Unethical and immoral, maybe, but certainly he cannot be stopped by the legal system."

"Sister Phoebe is right. This is not about the Bishop and his church. As long as these basic problems remain, unscrupulous people will exploit the masses for personal gain," Okello chimed in. "...and I don't place the entire blame on the preacher's shoulders either. I think our people are equally responsible for this menace. They put aside their power to think when the preacher starts talking."

"Yes, Okello. Just like me, our people get dazzled when they see the power and money that the preachers have. I did not get blinded by the Reverend or Sister Phoebe – they have studied religion and worked with people for decades. Their daily lives, their problems and their lifestyles are very similar to mine and we all look up to them. But the Bishop and other preachers like him are different – they have become so rich and powerful overnight. So when simple people like me see them, they think, if this man can do it, why can't I? Then the preachers prey on human greed, aspirations and ambitions towards their nefarious goals." Odhiambo was very forthright in his analysis and not shy to admit his own shortcomings.

"What worries me is the amount of money changing hands and how much money is coming in from abroad. I have worked for several preachers besides the Bishop and seen first-hand how much money and support is being provided by a few unscrupulous evangelical churches in

America. They are exporting their culture wars and their intolerance of other religious traditions to our country. Did you know that the Bishop himself used to be a street preacher in Nairobi a few years back. The environment ministry slapped a ban on street preachers in a strange move to curb the noise pollution in the city. That's when the charismatic preacher met an American evangelist who was looking for a local partner to preach the prosperity gospel and superiority of his church over other denominations and religions. How could our desperate preacher pass up on an opportunity to spend a few months in America and come back to start his own church? The rest is history."

"I wish that these Americans would mind their own business and not interfere with our religion. I am a Christian and I have dedicated my life to Christ. But I think that such preachers and their churches are seriously undermining my faith. A few years ago we were poor and hungry but we did not fight over denominations and we did not fight over religion," Sister Phoebe lamented.

"When I was in Mombasa, many of my friends were Muslims and I used to work with the Asian traders who were Hindus. Everyone was so much more respectful. Even if we did not approve of each other's beliefs or lifestyle, we respected them and got along. We celebrated our festivals together and we attended weddings and funerals in solidarity. I can see it changing now..." Okello said.

"Yes, that is why I stopped going to church years back. My wife wanted to go to one denomination and my mother insisted on a different one. I was fed up with the regular arguments at home and decided that I would rather spend my time teaching and playing with my children rather than going to church."

"So, Odhiambo, what have you decided to do?" Okello jumped in. He was getting a little restless; Sister Phoebe did not enjoy engaging in such rhetorical discussions either.

"I knew you would ask me this question sooner or later today." Odhiambo smiled and rubbed his hands. "I think that I have made up my mind on what I will do with the rest of my life. That is, if I have your support, and support from Kochia."

"Both of us are with you, and I know that Obongo, Janet and the rest of Kochia will support you too, as long as you are not selling us anointing oils or photos of the Bishop with Jesus Christ," Okello teased. Sister Phoebe could not suppress a smile.

"When I came to you first, I told you that I wanted to help our people and make money at the same time." Odhiambo said, and turned towards Okello. "And I am grateful for everything you did to educate me. Over the last week, I have concluded that I am no man of God and don't aspire to be one either. I don't want to live away from my family or spray my saliva on people's faces to compel them to give me their money in the busses of Nairobi. I will not go to Nairobi. I want nothing to do with the Bishop's shameful business either. I am sick and tired of tribalism, denominations, religion, and other such things that create division amongst our people and stop them from working together to improve their life. Let me be clear, I am not against religion. I am against the misuse and abuse of religion for personal gain."

"So, will you go back to your normal way of life?" Okello asked with a hint of sadness.

"On the contrary, I have made some very specific plans and will start working on them soon." Odhiambo smiled. Okello and Sister Phoebe could feel the excitement and pride in his voice. He sounded just the way he started off every diatribe on the Kikuyus. Once he was on a roll, there was no point stopping him or rushing him. Both of them looked at each other and smiled. They sat back and motioned Odhiambo to bring it on.

"I want people to come together. I thought that if I build a church, only some people would come and then they would bother me with details of doctrine and denomination and ask me for miracles. Another thought that crossed my mind was to start a church for our cattle. After all, they are part of creation too and need to be shown the path to God. Surely they would not bother me about miracles and healing but I would have to walk very long distances to preach them and so I disbanded that plan. If I build a bar and then preach there, it would attract very many men but the women would be left out. Then I thought, I should build a night school for adults but I was afraid I would be shamed into taking classes at night. I considered a Bible school because I want to study the Bible too and it does not require much capital – just a bunch of Bibles and an honest preacher. The problem, as we have found out, is that learning the Bible doesn't help our people find jobs and feed themselves...and I don't want to commission more miracle workers or rowdy matatu preachers either. I thought about building another home for HIV/AIDS patients, just like Sister Phoebe's. There is a great need for it, but you see, it is difficult to make money there and it is very stressful. I cannot work with dying people; they don't appreciate my humor either.

"I thought about many other options but I concluded that there is only one way to bring all our people together – men and women, rich and poor, young and old, every denomination, every religion, able-bodied and disabled, everyone. I want to build something where everyone will come… and when they come, I want to help them in some little way, and make little money as well. I thought, so many of our children die every year because of diarrhea. Our food and water gets tainted with waste matter which leads to many problems. So, I have decided to build a public toilet. A beautiful, clean, and hygienic toilet where everyone will come and be one with nature. People will be healthier and more productive. They will do their business with dignity and privacy, and I will do my business with pride."

So unexpected was Odhiambo's narrative and decision that Okello and Sister Phoebe were stunned for a few moments…and then they laughed until they had tears in their eyes.

"Brother Odhiambo, your journey to God ended up in the toilet," Sister Phoebe teased, "but I am proud of your decision."

Odhiambo, the great storyteller of Kochia, gave a theatrical bow. "As you know, I have a small piece of land on the main road. The toilet block will be built there. There will be six toilets in the building and customers will be charged a small fee, just 10 bob, to use them. I have spoken to my neighbor who does construction work. It will cost about KSh. 50,000. I am hoping that both you and Obongo will help me find the necessary capital, and Okello can provide his technical expertise. Tomorrow morning, I will meet Godgift to talk to him about painting a nice signboard and putting it up at the earliest. And there is a young man I have in mind for day-to-day operations." An excited Odhiambo rattled off all the plans for his new project.

In a few short days, Obongo, Okello, and Sister Phoebe were successful in loaning him KSh. 10,000 each while the entrepreneur dipped into his family savings and took a loan to come up with the rest of the capital. The signboard, christening the "Moneymaker Toilet", was completed over the next week and the toilet started operating two months later. It was a huge success and Odhiambo started planning many more Moneymaker toilets across the region. Godgift's signboard did not contain a single spelling error. Odhiambo read that as a sign from God in support of his approach to helping people. The black leather Bible with the shining golden cross can still be found in a little glass box over the main door of the toilet block.

#5

The Message for Sister Phoebe

"Oh, my goodness," Sister Phoebe rubbed her eyes. "This is the moment I have been waiting for all my life. After all these years, God has finally sent me a message." She grabbed her phone, haphazardly put on her wimple, and ran from her tiny quarters towards the residents' dormitory at her home for HIV/AIDS patients. The sun was about to rise, a beautiful orange sliver over the majestic lake in the distant horizon. The morning light reflected off the tin-roofed huts, spread across the tiny farms, on the gentle hill-slopes of Kochia. She screeched to a halt, turned around, and said a quick prayer thanking God for the message and the new day. And then she ran again, through the quadrangle, across the potato farm, and pushed the door of the dormitory open. "God talked to me today," she screamed. "I have a message from God."

While most residents were fast asleep, others lay wide-awake, starring at the ceiling and waiting for another day to pass by. A few residents got up from their beds and crowded around the excited nun. Some startled residents sat up in their beds and Sister Phoebe walked around to show them the message on her phone.

"But, sister, what does this message mean?" an elderly lady asked.

"If God has sent me a message, he will also give me the wisdom to decipher its meaning." Sister Phoebe smiled.

"There is an empty coffin and then another coffin with a small cross inside it and then another large cross in the ground. I think God is reassuring us that after we die and are put in a coffin, we go to heaven," the woman croaked.

"Maybe, you are right," Sister Phoebe admitted, "but don't let it trouble you. Your health is getting better and you are responding very

Sister Phoebe Showing the Message from God

well to the medicines. You will live long."

"So, what do you think the message says?" the woman countered.

"I think that God is trying to say that at a funeral, it is the deceased person that is important. That person is already with Christ. With the big 'X', God is forbidding us from overemphasizing the coffin and the funeral rites. With this message, he is expressing his support for doing away with funeral rites that are hurting our society."

"Tch tch, why must God tell us that?"

"Just last month, God saw Obongo's father's funeral. God disapproves of it and wanted to send a direct message denouncing it. I will show the message to Okello and Obongo today."

Sister Phoebe leisurely visited the residents during her morning round. She religiously showed each one of them the message and gathered their thoughts on its meaning. Most of them interpreted it just the way the elderly woman did. I am at a home for terminally ill patients, which explains the morose meaning they gather from the message, Sister Phoebe thought to herself. I don't think God will send a message reassuring us. He wants us to take action, he wants us to right a wrong. She walked over to Okello's place and was disappointed to learn that he had gone to Kisumu for some work. She walked over to Obongo's homestead. As she entered, she observed that the Mzee's grave was now a concrete structure with a marble slab inscribed with a golden alphabet. A small light bulb hung from a wooden stick next to the tombstone.

"Is that a solar panel?" Sister Phoebe pointed to a black shiny object at the base of the wooden stick.

"Oh, Sister, when did you arrive?" Obongo turned around to find the nun curiously trying to see the dorsal side of the solar panel. "Yes, indeed, that is a solar panel to power this LED lamp at night. I thought it would be most appropriate to have one on my father's resting place. I just bought it in Kisumu yesterday."

"Hey, you are still obsessed with the funeral and the grave," Sister Phoebe teased him. "Did you go to Kisumu with Okello?"

"Indeed. Okello had to deliver three cardboard coffins at this facility to conduct advanced product testing. He requested me to go with him because the coffins are very bulky."

"I like the cardboard coffin idea very much. But aren't they supposed to be foldable?"

"Okello said that he is still working on making them foldable and easy to transport. The current model is not heavy but very bulky. The government office in Kisumu is helping Okello with advanced testing of the coffins, which is mandatory before he can start a factory."

"That is very nice. Very many of our people don't know about such facilities and services provided by the government. They just want to criticize the government all the time."

"Yes, they are very helpful people. They also showed me several new low-cost solar panels that convert light into electricity. Okello and I also went to the market and did some shopping."

"I see you bought this solar panel and lamp. Is it working?"

"You should come after sunset. You can read the tombstone very well from the light of this small lamp. There is a small battery that gets charged in the daytime and powers the lamp at night. In fact, the lamp stays on until sunrise."

"But, this one is doing something funny," Obongo said, holding up a gray plastic tablet. He opened it like a book to reveal a black solar panel shining in the bright scorching sun. "This a foldable solar panel to charge cellphones. The shopkeeper said that it will charge my Nokia phone in just three hours."

"That must be expensive!"

"Actually, no, it was just 1,000 Shillings. Right now I pay 30 bob to get my phone charged and I have to walk for two hours each way to reach Imboyo market. I get my phone charged every 2-3 days. I will recover the cost of this solar panel in less than three months, even earlier."

"If it works, I will get one too. Many patients have mobiles and they are always requesting me to get them charged. I even have to pay for half of them!"

"But, there is a problem. Sometimes it charges my phone and sometimes..." Obongo took a long pause and scratched his head. "And sometimes, it discharges my phone."

Sister Phoebe could not suppress her laughter. "This one is like my cow. Half the days she gives milk and I get good money for it. Then she falls sick and I spend more money on her medicines. Do you know when it works and when it doesn't?"

"Janet's phone was completely discharged and this solar panel did a good job of charging it. But now, I connected my phone, and it has discharged. I tried a few of my neighbor's phones too and sometimes it works, sometimes it doesn't."

"Well, you must ask Okello when he returns home." Sister Phoebe suggested.

"Yes, he will be back home tomorrow. Do you think this is a sign from God?" Obongo wondered.

"It could be..." She pulled out her phone from her pocket and thrust it in Obongo's face. "…But here is a real message from God. I received it just this morning."

Obongo studied the message carefully. "There is no sender of the message. Your phone is a simple one and does not even support photos like Janet's phone. It is impossible to have a message like this on your phone. It is indeed a message from God. This is truly remarkable!" Obongo shared Sister Phoebe's excitement.

Sister Phoebe then went on to discuss what the residents at her home thought about it and how she disagreed with them. Finally she asked, "What do you think it means? Do you at least agree that this is a coffin with the cross in it?"

"Yaai…and then you keep blaming me for being obsessed with coffins and graves?" Obongo joked. "I don't think that this is a grave at all. This is clearly a windmill. Don't you see the blades of the windmill on top and the lattice structure to hold the turbine in place at the bottom. The box on the side is definitely a big battery."

"Why should God send a picture of a windmill to me?" Sister Phoebe was stumped at the completely unexpected interpretation that Obongo put forth.

"You know, we inaugurated the signboard for the solar power project last year but since then there has been no movement at all. At that time, Okello had suggested that we install a windmill rather than solar panels."

"But why should God send that message to me and not to you?"

"Because it had been suggested that the windmill should be put up in your home rather than the currently planned site. Maybe God is trying to say that we should not rely on the SUV Foundation and other organizations. Rather, we should start working towards that goal ourselves."

"Yes, we should not rely on others. But, I have still not made up my mind about this message. Let me ask Janet what she thinks too!"

Obongo got back to testing his new solar panel while Sister Phoebe went into the kitchen to get another opinion on the message. Janet was busy cooking chapattis in the smoky little kitchen. She rolled up a hot chapatti, put a fork through it and presented it to Sister Phoebe. "I am sure you have not had lunch yet," she said. Janet was confident that she could read 'HIV' in the graphic message and was convinced that the message had something to do with HIV/AIDS but could not come up with a good explanation. After a brief discussion on the message, Janet started discussing her cellphone plans. She was going to give her phone to her daughter who just turned 16, and was planning on buying a new phone for herself.

Obongo with his Quirky Solar Panel

Two hours later, as Sister Phoebe was ready to leave, an exasperated Obongo was still struggling with his solar panel. A few of the curious neighbors had come over and situated themselves around Obongo. Half of them empathized with his struggle, while the others found it entertaining. The whimsical solar panel inspired metaphorical comparisons and anecdotes about matatus, local politicians, and male aphrodisiacs.

"Generally it works, but when you need it most, it fails you," there was great laughter in the homestead. The group agreed that their ad-hoc party was incomplete without Odhiambo. Immediate action was taken by calling the story teller of Kochia and inviting him to share his perspective on the solar panel and the message from God. Obongo was about to scold his boisterous guests when Chief Achieng from the Sustainable Utopian Village (SUV) Foundation walked in through the bamboo gate. Obongo smiled, waved at him, and got engrossed in his project again.

"Yes, I know what that is," Chief Achieng claimed. "It is a Chevrolet SUV at the finish line of the Rhino Charge. I was there last week – what a rally it was! A Chevrolet truck won the rally." Chief Achieng responded to everyone's puzzled stares with a hearty laugh. "You see, they are building a fence around the Aberdares National Park in Central Kenya, about five hours from here. To raise money for the fence, they host a race through the rough roads of the park. Teams pay a lot of money to participate in the race with their big trucks. This year, our director from America was here and he invited me and two other colleagues to see the race. The winning truck was made by an American company called Chevrolet, and its symbol looked like this," Chief Achieng said, pointing at the message.

"No, no, this message has nothing to do with a car race." Sister Phoebe was a little piqued, "Unless you think that God is sending us a message before dispatching a real truck to us? I had expressed the need for a vehicle to conduct home-based care in faraway places to the HIV workshop coordinator. She said that they were expecting a lot of funding for HIV/AIDS work from America and if that would come through, we would get a vehicle."

"I hope so. That will help you with your noble work. I would like to have a truck like that too. My SUV is good but not as good as that one."

"Even if you get a big truck like what the chief described, how will you pay for the petrol?" Obongo temporarily resigned from his battle with the solar panel and jumped into the conversation.

"Chief, I think that the message from God and my trouble with the solar panel are related. We should reconsider building the windmill at

Sister Phoebe's place. The message is clearly a windmill system – the blades, the turbine, the support structure and even the battery bank. God is so clear and detailed in his message and he even sent it to the most appropriate person," Obongo implored. "It has been almost a year now and we have made no progress on the solar power project."

"In fact, that is why I am here. I have been instructed that work on the solar power project will begin in two weeks. The funds have already been sanctioned and the engineers are working on the detailed plans. The project will be completed in a month's time," Chief Achieng promised.

"You bring us wonderful news," Obongo cheered. "But are you sure that solar power will work here? I have been trying to get this solar panel to work since early morning but it only works with some phones and not with others. I think I have wasted 1,000 Shillings on it."

"Only 500," Sister Phoebe quipped. "It works half the time, doesn't it?"

"I am worried about the solar panels too," Obongo's neighbor Jaramogi chimed in. "My brother lives in London and he sent us one million Shillings to install solar power at home for lighting. We hired a company in Kisumu to install the system. All of you were there for the celebration. At first, it was like a miracle. My children had reading light and their performance in school improved. I saved a lot of money on kerosene, radio batteries, and charging my cellphone. In fact, I was able to invest in six goats. The toxic fumes of the kerosene lamp were making my mother sick, but now, there was no problem. My wife was happy because there was light in the kitchen. After two months, one day the solar just stopped working. The company in Kisumu wants 5,000 Shillings just to come and have a look. The repairing charge is extra. I am fed up with my wife's nagging so I am trying hard to save up some money to get it repaired." Jaramogi was an active member of the Empower Kochia group. He was a Jua Kali and had his own little workshop in Imboyo market where he made shop shutters, gates, agricultural implements and other similar items from mild steel.

"The problem is that there are very few trained technicians to install and maintain solar power systems. Power systems, like most technologies, require routine maintenance. All equipment that SUV Foundation uses - solar panels, batteries, charge regulators, everything - comes from America or Europe. It is of very good quality. Also, this project will run for at least three years and, during this time, our engineers will conduct frequent maintenance," Chief Achieng reassured the group.

"One of my friends from Homa Bay was trying to start a business to process and refrigerate Tilapia fish near Ngegu. He has a small official income but a very good unofficial one." Obongo winked. "Two years back, he found a partner who was willing to invest in the project by providing the refrigeration equipment and expertise. The problem was how to power it. This is before the electric sub-station was set up in Ngegu. So our man goes to Nairobi and an agent convinced him that the solar panels will be able to power his plant. This man sold him the power system for 5 million Shillings and collected one million in advance. My friend paid up the money at the office and when he went back the next day for delivery, he learned that no company by that name even existed. He was conveniently relieved of one million Shillings by this conman. He lodged a police complaint but nothing could be done. Unfortunately, the story did not end here. He went with two friends to another reputable dealer with a big storefront. After they were convinced that it was not another fly-by-night operation, they paid two million Shillings cash and were immediately given delivery of 12 large solar panels. A million Shillings more were spent on the charging system, alternator and battery bank. They hired a truck to transport everything to Ngegu and found a technician from Kisumu to install the system. The technician confirmed that the solar panels and the other equipment were of very good quality and congratulated my friend on negotiating such a good wholesale price. The assembled system worked perfectly but there was one problem – it provided less than one-tenth the power that the refrigeration equipment needed. After consulting with a few other experts, including Okello, my friend finally abandoned the project. The technician helped him sell all the equipment to a dealer in Kisumu at a loss of a million Shillings. Since then, he has never set foot in Ngegu again. He gets violent if anyone uses the word 'solar' in his presence."

"Obongo, I have heard many similar stories. The basic problem is that there is a lack of education amongst our people on what solar or wind power can, and cannot, do. People try to operate water pumps, coffee roasting machines, refrigeration plants, leather presses, and similar machinery with solar panels. That is very impractical because most of these machines require a lot of power and the people will have to invest millions of Shillings and need a lot of space for the solar panels. However, solar panels are very good for lower loads like lights, radios, TVs, cellphones, and charging batteries," Chief Achieng explained.

"Our foundation has successfully installed solar panels at very many places. We have them at rural health centers for preserving medicines, at schools for lighting, and at cooperatives for drying food products." Chief Achieng continued, "in fact, we have had a solar power system at the primary school for a year now."

"It is not working since the last nine months," Jaramogi called out. "My children study there."

"Oh, really?" Chief Achieng was surprised. " I will certainly inform our engineers about it."

"I will be working at the school next week. Why don't we coordinate and get the matter resolved?" Sister Phoebe's offer was gladly accepted by Achieng.

"Chief, do you provide solar panels as a loan or a donation?" Jaramogi asked.

"Depends. The community projects, like yours, are donations. The community partner provides the land, operates the solar power business and takes responsibility for everything."

"What about the solar lamps? Do you provide those too?" Obongo wondered.

"We sell them to community members at the market price. You can always buy them yourself in Homa Bay or Kisumu or Nairobi."

"Why don't you subsidize the solar lamps for us? I understand that they cost more than 1,000 Shillings," Obongo requested. "Not all our people can afford them."

"We have found that if we subsidize them for certain groups, people resell them at the market price rather than using them. Also, it is unfair competition that stifles the regular dealers and they become upset with us."

"You can always take an informal loan from a friend or relative to buy a solar lantern," Sister Phoebe suggested.

"Many shops are already providing them on loan to known customers. For example, in Kisumu, several shops sell them for 1,000 Shillings cash or two installments of 600 Shillings each. Sometimes they will request the customer's ID as collateral but other times it is just on a trust basis," the Chief explained.

"How long do the solar lanterns last?"

"Generally two to three years – depending on the brand. There are several brands in the market – some have narrow beams and can see far. These are good for walking while others have spread-out light and these are good for use inside homes, especially for hosting visitors. The ones used indoors generally last longer than the ones used for walking. Some of them also need maintenance like changing the batteries. Sometimes the batteries are three-fourths of the cost of the lantern. This is another reason we don't subsidize the lanterns...people will buy the more expensive lanterns initially at subsidized rates but will not be able to afford the maintenance costs later. Then they will just abandon the lanterns – which is really a loss for everyone."

"So Chief, do you think that the message from God is indeed a windmill? Will you help us build a wind power system at my home for HIV patients?" Sister Phoebe asked.

"We don't have any such plans for now but I can present it back to our management. They know about your noble work and I am sure they will be supportive." The chief gave a candid response. He thought for a while and continued, "We have a few windmill sites but they have not been as successful as the solar power sites. Windmills require much more maintenance than solar panels."

"We have a water pumping windmill at Kochia and I have welded its broken parts together very many times," Jaramogi agreed.

"Windmills can provide a lot of power with a relatively small capital investment...but I am ashamed to say that in our country, the biggest advantage of wind turbines is that they cannot be stolen as easily as solar panels," Achieng admitted. "We have been forced to hire a security person at some of our sites and one poor fellow even lost his life in a daylight raid by thugs."

"That must be in central Kenya where the Kikuyus live. They love their plots and stocks and matatus and now...solar panels." Odhiambo pulled up a chair and joined the conversation, cheered on by the entire group.

"I was informed about Obongo's solar panel problem. Actually, I have a folding solar panel that my cousin, John Ouma, brought me from Nairobi. It works perfectly. Here, I brought it with me!" Odhiambo pulled out an identical solar panel from his bag and placed it next to Obongo's.

"I must have ended up with a defective piece, or maybe I don't know how to use it. It seems I will have to wait until tomorrow morning to continue testing." Obongo looked at the setting sun and lamented.

"You can keep my solar panel for now," Odhiambo offered. "I have brought another item to show Chief Achieng. This is a hand-powered light. You crank the shaft like this and the light comes on. No batteries, no solar, no wind, just use your hand. It worked very well for a few days and then just stopped working." Everyone took turns studying and testing the light but it would not turn on.

"I have heard of these lights but this is the first time I am seeing one for myself. I don't know what is wrong with it." Achieng admitted.

"I think these are made for Kikuyu hands. The light will work well when they are selling them to us...but as soon as we buy them and bring them home, they will stop working." Odhiambo hijacked the conversation to his favorite topic, Kikuyu bashing, for the next hour until everyone finally dispersed and headed home.

Sister Phoebe woke up at 4 AM next morning and stared at her phone for three hours. She was hoping to receive a follow-up message from God that would solve the mystery. That was not to be. Somewhat dejected, she got ready and headed out to Reverend Ndiege's church.

"Come with me," the Reverend said proudly and led her to the main gate of his church. "What do you see?" he asked, pointing at the church building.

"The church..." Sister Phoebe was not quite sure what response he was expecting.

"Look at the big cross on top of the church. It is in a box, just like the cross in your message. This is a very clear message from God – this is the front of my church. God wants you to join my church. We should baptize you at the earliest. You can still keep doing all your good work with HIV patients. I might also be able to provide you some financial support...but of course you will have to recognize our church clearly." The reverend broke into an excited frenzy and put Sister Phoebe in an uncomfortable predicament.

"Reverend, maybe you are right. I can see that this message looks like the front of your church."

"It is the front of my church. There can be no question about it."

"Ok, but that does not necessarily mean that God wants me to abandon my Catholic faith. So, let me think about it and wait for further direction from God." Sister Phoebe rationalized with the fired-up pastor. "Janet must be waiting for me. We are going to Homa Bay together. So I will take your leave." The reverend spent a few more minutes convincing Sister Phoebe that the message was in fact the façade of his church. He made the nun promise that she would forward him the message before he finally let her leave for the matatu stage.

"I will certainly not forward the message to anyone. They want to use it for their own benefit," Sister Phoebe mumbled under her breath as she marched towards the matatu stage to meet Janet. She was shaken up by the sudden and extraordinary energy of the Reverend. The ride to Homa Bay helped Sister Phoebe calm her nerves. She called Okello on the way and was delighted to learn that he would be home by early afternoon. "Janet and I will be at your place as soon as we return from Homa Bay. We really need to talk to you. Yesterday morning..." Sister Phoebe was determined to tell him the entire story but ran out of phone credit. On reaching Homa Bay, they quickly walked over to one of the cellphone shops. The four-feet long storefront had an expensive-looking glass cabinet with over a hundred different phones arranged by brand. The price of each phone was clearly written in black ink on a fluorescent green tag and placed beneath the phone. The shop was busy; it took almost ten minutes for Janet and Sister Phoebe to come face-to-face with the smiling shopkeeper.

"What kind of a phone are you looking for? Dual sim? flashlight? polyphonic ringtone? internet? camera? Nokia? China phone? Samsung? Blackberry?" The shopkeeper rattled off a bunch of options.

"I want a camera phone but not very expensive," Janet requested.

"The China phone is the cheapest one. Nokia and Samsung are a little more."

"Do you have a camera phone with a flashlight?"

"Yes, here's a good one. It is selling like hot cakes. Remember, you cannot take good photos at night." The shopkeeper placed two phones on the counter.

"How much are they?"

"This China phone is 4,500 and the Nokia is 5,000. I have already given you a 200 Shilling discount."

"My friend got this one for 4,000. Why don't you charge me the same amount?"

"Where did she buy it? From my shop?"

"No, in Nairobi."

"This is Homa Bay, not Nairobi. Fuel is very expensive now so rates are up. The best I can do is 4,400. Trust me, it is a very good price. Ask Sister, she has been my customer for a long time."

"OK – give me a fresh piece. Sometimes they have bad batteries."

"Don't worry, I will give you a brand new piece. Check everything perfectly before you leave. Do you live around here?"

"No, we live in Kochia."

"Ringtone, come here," the man shouted. A six-year old boy appeared from under the desk at the back of the shop.

"Go and get a brand new piece of this model from our warehouse. Come back quickly," he instructed the child. "That is my son. He should be back in just ten minutes with your phone."

"Ringtone! Is that his real name?"

"Yes. He was born when I opened this shop. He cried all the time and woke me up. So we named him Ringtone. He has been very lucky for me and my business. Is there anything else I can help you with?"

"Do you know what this message means?" Sister Phoebe presented her phone to the shopkeeper.

Phone Shop in Homa Bay

The shopkeeper turned the phone in his hands, punched a few keys and looked at the message. "I don't know. What do you think it is?"

"It is certainly a message from God," Sister Phoebe said. "But we have very many versions of what it means."

"Yes, yes, it must be a message from God." The man quickly changed the conversation. "Here is your phone. Let me start it for you." He put the battery inside the phone and turned it on. In a few seconds, the LCD screen came to life, went black again, and a few moments later settled on the welcome screen. He demonstrated the camera phone and the flashlight to Janet. Janet tried out the camera and flashlight, and then pleased with the phone, started counting the money.

"Wait a minute, this phone is different than the one you showed us earlier. It is a different color and is much bigger." Sister Phoebe pointed out to Janet.

Before Janet could say a word, the shopkeeper provided an explanation. "Yes, this is actually a newer model. Look – the color is brighter, and the screen on this one is bigger so you can see photos properly. Most customers prefer to have a large screen, just like the blackberry. So the company made the screen bigger but kept the price the same. Would you rather have the old model with the small screen?"

"No, no, I want the new model with the big screen," Janet affirmed. She handed over the money to the shopkeeper and requested a receipt. "Is there any guarantee on the phone?"

"Nowadays, there are no guarantees for people, how can we guarantee a cellphone?" the shopkeeper laughed and turned to the next customer. Janet and Sister Phoebe had a soda at one of the tiny restaurants outside the bus station. Janet put her SIM card in the new phone and made a quick call to Obongo. She was very pleased with the voice quality and the various features. Sister Phoebe was a little unsettled with the experience. Somehow something didn't seem right.

After a 30-minute matatu ride and a brisk walk, they were knocking on Okello's door. Janet's son, Owiti, opened the door and welcomed his mother and Sister Phoebe. Obongo and Odhiambo had arrived a couple of hours back and were animatedly discussing the trade-offs between solar and wind power with Okello. In one corner, the parts that made up the dysfunctional hand-cranked light lay on a white cloth. Owiti, pliers in hand, was fiddling with a couple of the parts.

"Oh - that is Odhiambo's hand light. It was in one-piece yesterday. Did it break or is Okello Junior trying to repair it?" Sister Phoebe's question was met by a grin from the group.

"Our young man is already an expert on operating and repairing audio systems. He has also taken a keen interest in repairing miscellaneous appliances," Okello said with pride. "So, Owiti, can you give us your diagnosis?"

"Sure, Okello and I dismantled the light and found that it is actually a counterfeit piece. The original brand is Super Bright Hand Light but in this one, bright is spelled as B-R-I-T-E. It works just like the original one but there are two problems – the original one has a good quality rechargeable battery whereas this one just has a regular battery. Also, the wires are not soldered properly and one of the connections had broken off. So, when you see it in a shop, it works properly but as soon as the battery is dead, your hand-cranked light is useless."

"But why do we need a battery to begin with? Isn't it hand-powered?" Odhiambo asked.

"When you crank it for 10 minutes, it charges up the battery so that you can use it for the next hour or so. Without a battery, it will give light only when you crank it...which is not as useful."

"So, can you can repair it or will I have to throw it away?"

"I found a rechargeable battery in the workshop and I have connected it. I have also re-soldered the wire. It should be working shortly."

"I don't understand how someone can even benefit from counterfeit products!" Janet asked. "This company that made the light saved only a few Shillings by cheating us on the battery. We are saying that it is fake...but it is still a real light and if they would have put in a rechargeable battery, it would be just like the original one. I am trying to say..."

"I think I understand your confusion," Okello said. "Let me explain. The original company did a lot of work to design this new product. They conducted field testing several times, they arranged permissions from the Kenya Bureau of Standards, and they established the distributor network to make it accessible to customers. They used good quality parts so that people are happy with their product and trust their brand. As soon as the product is successful in the marketplace, another company makes a product that looks extremely similar to the original one. This company did not have to invest their money in developing the product or the market. They also use cheap, poor-quality parts and sell the product at a lower price than the original product. They often give the dealers higher commissions. So, now, the original company starts losing business although they did all the hard work. The customers get a bad quality product and hence form a negative opinion of the brand. This makes it difficult for the original company to launch other products in the market.

They are worried that by the time they start making money on their product, the fake products will take over the market. Some foreign companies now refuse to operate in Kenya for this reason. So these counterfeit products hurt everyone – the honest companies, the customers, and the national economy as well. They threaten economic opportunities for all of us and take away the incentive for companies and their employees to work hard, find innovative solutions to problems and launch products. These companies, many of them foreign, do not pay government taxes either."

"I am thinking about the growing problem of fake drugs. I just read a news article, which estimated that one-third of all drugs, and over half of all anti-malarial drugs, are fake and hence completely ineffective. That is a very big problem – people are dying because of it," Odhiambo added.

"Now I understand," Janet chimed in. "This counterfeiting problem becomes much more serious with food products and medicines. So many times, I have found dirt in bottled water. These people gather discarded water bottles, refill them with tap water, and sell them at the regular rates."

"I think that we should look carefully before buying every single thing," Okello suggested. "Everything is being counterfeited. Look at the number of look-alike brands of water, milk, detergent, margarine, light bulbs, car parts, solar panels, cellphones, radios, TVs...it is a never-ending list. Do you know what the most widely counterfeited item is? You won't believe it!" Okello looked at everyone but but no one seemed to know the answer. "Underwear," he finally said.

"Underwear?" Everyone chorused in surprise.

"Yes, underwear!" Okello said. "I read in the newspaper that the Kenyan economy loses 70 billion Shillings every year to counterfeiters. The government passed the Anti-Counterfeit Act in 2008 but there were many problems and it was struck down in 2012. Right now, the maximum penalty for selling counterfeit products in Kenya is a fine of up to 2 Million Shillings or 5 years imprisonment. But the problem is that..."

"Wait a minute," Obongo exclaimed. He ran to the other room and brought back the two solar panels. "Okello, this one is Odhiambo's solar panel and this is the one we bought yesterday in Kisumu...and I think we have been fooled into buying a counterfeit one." Okello grabbed the solar panels and started comparing them.

"What I have concluded is that if you try to charge a phone that is completely discharged, then the solar panel charges it half-way...but if you connect a phone that is charged more than half, then it actually discharges it," Obongo explained.

"I think you are right Obongo, we have been cheated. Look at the brand name – Odhiambo's panel says 'Mt. Kenya Solar Panels Ltd,' whereas this one says 'Mr. Kenya Solar Panels Ltd.' Look at the workmanship – the fake one is very rough and connectors look particularly poor-quality. I will have to dismantle the panel and do some testing with it tomorrow morning. But there is no doubt that we have been taken for a ride."

"Will you be able to repair it?"

"If your explanation is accurate, then we should be able to repair it. The counterfeiters probably compromised on a few electronic components which ensure that current does not flow from the phone into the solar panel and discharge the battery. I can just add that component and repair it."

"So, who was taken for a ride? Who is Mr. Kenya? Obongo or Okello?" Sister Phoebe teased them. "I am thinking, if two smart people like you can get cheated, what about the rest of the people? Janet, can you show Okello the phone we bought today? I think something is wrong with it too! I didn't like the way the shopkeeper gave us a different model and then the long-drawn explanation."

"Here it is." Janet handed over the phone to Okello, and then drawled, "it has been working perfectly unlike Mr. Kenya's solar panel."

"Oh, this one is definitely a fake phone," Okello affirmed. "You see, the fake ones are generally bigger in size and often times they are available in different sizes and colors. One quick check is to compare the size, colors, location of buttons, and features to original phones."

"Oh my goodness! What should I do now?" Janet asked. "I don't think that the shopkeeper will take the phone back and give me an original phone."

"Another test of originality is the software, as in the phone's operation. Sometimes the phone will freeze and you will have to turn it off and on again. Sometimes you will see a black screen come up during regular operation," Okello continued. "Yaaai, wait a minute! Did you know you have a dual-sim phone? You can use it with two networks simultaneously."

"But I didn't buy a dual-sim phone because it was too expensive," Janet explained.

"The original one is expensive, but the fake one is apparently not! So, you ended up with a fake one but with some extra features not available on the original." Okello disclosed to a delighted Janet.

"An original dual sim phone was 3,000 Shillings more! How can the fake be so much cheaper? I just don't understand," Sister Phoebe said.

"Just the way I explained a few minutes back," Okello repeated. "These fake phones are made from cheap poor-quality components, the counterfeiters don't have to invest in research, design and field-testing. They don't pay government taxes or import duties and there is no regulation of their manufacturing plants. So they can manufacture phones at a fraction of the cost of regular phones."

"I understand that it is not fair. But for me, I am glad I got a counterfeit phone." Janet laughed. "I wanted a dual-sim phone for a long time so I can use both, Safaricom and Airtel. This is surely a gift from God!"

"Talking about God," Odhiambo exclaimed, "Sister Phoebe, did you show Okello the message from God?"

"Not yet! We have just been talking about hand-operated lights and solar panels and fake products." Sister Phoebe said with trepidation in her voice, "And Okello, don't seize this opportunity to tell me that my God is fake, or the message is." She went on to narrate the entire sequence of events to the group, including the various interpretations of the cryptic message.

A brief but passionate group debate on the meaning of the message was finally cut off by Okello. "Why don't you first let me see the message so I can also participate in this debate?" He burst out laughing as soon as Sister Phoebe passed her phone to him.

"Okello, what is it?" Sister Phoebe's voice was trembling and tears were starting to form at the corners of her eyes.

"Oh Sister, I am sorry. I understand that this message means a lot to you. I laughed because I could immediately tell that your phone is counterfeit too. The original brand name is 'Tecno' while your phone says 'HiTecno.'"

"Another one bites the dust," Odhiambo quipped. "I am not showing my phone, or my underwear, to anyone."

"I bought it from the same store as Janet. That man cheated me too," Sister Phoebe admitted. "It has been working perfectly for the last two years. But, let us not digress. What do you think about the message?"

Okello studied the message carefully. "Why don't you give me a little time? I want to do some research on the internet." Everyone's eyes were transfixed on Okello when he returned with a victorious smile on his face 15 minutes later.

"So, Okello, what does the message say? Is it a message from God?" Sister Phoebe asked earnestly.

"We have established that Sister Phoebe's phone is a counterfeit model from China. You might notice that when it starts up, the screen becomes dark and a few Chinese characters show up. First of all, contrary to what Obongo said, there is nothing unusual about Sister Phoebe's phone displaying picture messages like this one. The message that she received is actually a Chinese language character called 'Wei' and it is used to say 'Hello' on a phone. The message is either spam or more likely the result of an error in the phone's software, as in the way it is supposed to operate."

"So, this is not a message from God. All this time…" an embarrassed Sister Phoebe could not control her tears.

"On the contrary, why should this message appear only after two years? Let us choose to believe that it is actually a message from God!"

"A Chinese God!" Odhiambo's timely humor brought a radiant smile on Sister Phoebe's face.

"Amen!" the group chorused. "But what do we do about it?"

"Sister Phoebe's patients, Obongo, Janet, Chief Achieng, Reverend Ndiege, everyone read the message differently. In my opinion, the only plausible interpretation that inspires us to take collective action towards a higher goal is to build a wind power system at Sister Phoebe's home." Okello proposed.

"I agree," Obongo said. "While SUV Foundation helps us with the solar power project, let us work on our own to build a wind power system at Sister Phoebe's home for HIV/AIDS patients."

"I support the project completely but what will Chief Achieng think?" Sister Phoebe wondered.

"That is no problem – he wants Kochia to prosper and will support us too," Odhiambo said with utmost confidence. "But, as far as Reverend Ndiege is concerned, I don't think he will take very kindly to a Chinese God operating in his area and counterfeiting his church."

#6

Mr. Jackson's Secret to Success

"I have been wanting to come here and do something for the orphans…but every single time I make plans, something comes up," Sister Phoebe said as she hugged her friend Elizabeth Atieno. "But here I am for one full week to help you in any way I can."

"Sister Phoebe! Welcome to Clean Hope Orphanage. I am so happy you are here," Elizabeth exclaimed. "Let me show you our home and introduce you to my friends." Elizabeth accompanied the nun to the boys' and girls' dormitories, toilets, kitchen, play room, and the locked storeroom and offices. "Over there, we are building two more dormitories, a computer room, more offices and even a clinic. Clean Hope will be the new headquarters for Hope Orphanages when work is completed next month," Elizabeth proudly informed the nun.

"I cannot believe how clean this place is. The dormitories are spotless. The toilets here are cleaner than the ones at the district hospital. I was planning on conducting a workshop on hygiene and cleanliness. There is no need for it. But, I don't understand, why are there so many waste bins in every room?"

"That is a rule we have to follow. We have very many rules and regulations here," Elizabeth admitted. "Some of them I understand, and some I don't. For example, the cook told me that the director called him and instructed him that there will be no dinner tonight."

"Are you out of food? Why should the children go hungry?" Sister Phoebe was somewhat agitated.

"Yes, the children will go hungry." Elizabeth grinned. "But just wait and see the children's reaction when they find out that there is no dinner tonight!"

Elizabeth was one of two caregivers at the Clean Hope Orphanage at Adiedo Market, a short matatu ride away from Kochia. She had lived in the area for her entire life. Seven years of her marriage did not yield any children but gradually created a rift with her husband. Eventually, he took up a job in Kisumu and left Elizabeth to care for his teenage sister and the homestead. Every month, he would send them a KSh. 2,000 allowance. Elizabeth's experience volunteering at Sister Phoebe's home for HIV/AIDS patients helped her find a small job at an orphanage in Homa Bay. Her first job lasted three months and then the orphanage was shut down by the government for operating without a license. Her second orphanage job ended when the manager tried to rape her and she quit the third one when she did not receive her promised salary for three straight months. Finally, through some contacts, she landed a job at Clean Hope Orphanage. The orphanage also hired her sister-in-law, Apondi, a chirpy teenager and high school dropout, as a Visit Coordinator.

While their home was right next to Obongo's, Elizabeth and Apondi found it convenient to stay at the orphanage with the children. Elizabeth's day revolved around the children – waking them up in the morning, getting them ready for school, caring for the little ones, mending their uniforms, supervising the food preparation, taking the sick ones to the doctor and so on. The orphanage was now her home and she cared for the children just like they were her own. "I prayed for years for a child, and now God gave me 75 of them," she would gladly tell everyone. She slept right next to the door in the girl's dormitory, a Masaai club at hand, just in case there were any intruders. She had a healthy working relationship with Kathy, a middle-aged mother of three, who shared the caregiving duties with her. The cook was a kind old man. He spoke very little but punctually appeared for a couple of hours in the morning to cook the breakfast (porridge) and in the evening to prepare ugali, sukumawiki, maize, beans and the occasional meat. Mr. Jackson made sure that the children and staff were healthy and well-fed.

Mr. Jackson was the owner and director of the orphanage. After Green Hope, New Hope, Bright Hope, High Hope, Good Hope, Great Hope, Energetic Hope, Child Hope, and Living Hope, Clean Hope was his tenth orphanage project. Mr. Jackson completed his Form Four two decades back but fell short by a few points to get admission into a public university. His father could not afford to send him to a private university and so he became a primary school teacher. After a decade of teaching English and Mathematics, he took on a part-time job as an accountant at a local orphanage. The HIV/AIDS epidemic was just starting to spiral out of control, churning out thousands of children left without parents. In Nyanza alone, there were over half a million orphans. Traditionally, in Kenyan society, extended families would take care of children who had lost their parents. However, the prevalence of HIV deeply impacted traditional family relationships. There were over 2.5 million orphans in Kenya, almost half of them due to HIV. The most productive members of society succumbed to AIDS. Unhelpful socio-cultural practices further aggravated the epidemic. Grandparents and extended family were simply unable to take care of the needs of every child. There was a great need for orphanages to fill the void. When the orphanage where Mr. Jackson worked could not take in any more children, he decided to start an orphanage of his own.

Mr. Jackson rented out a small hut close to his residence on the main road. The Safaricom marketing agent painted the outside walls with white and green advertisements. The first month's rent was thus covered and the humble abode came to be known as the Green Hope orphanage. The children's extended families, local Samaritans, and churches donated food. Random tourists and missionaries contributed in their own little way. The children went to the primary school and slept on the floor at the orphanage. Life was difficult but everyone was content. Every week, Mr. Jackson would spend a few hours at the government offices in Homa Bay hoping to receive some funds. His patience and persistence eventually paid off.

One rainy Saturday morning, the local sub-chief accompanied an elderly American gentleman with a big backpack to Green Home. The American missionary spent the day visiting the children and learning about the challenges faced by Mr. Jackson. He was truly impressed with the teacher's leadership in setting up and managing the orphanage. Within a week, he arranged for mattresses to be delivered, had hygienic toilets built, and refurbished the small kitchen. He spent a few hours every day helping the children with their homework and teaching them the importance of keeping their home clean. Mr. Jackson was alarmed at first but soon realized that the old man was truly improving the facilities and operations of their home. The children were very fond of him and his presence enabled Mr. Jackson to do his day job effectively.

When the number of children at Green Hope crossed thirty, they rented out a neighboring hut. Food and necessary supplies of uniforms, shoes, toothbrushes, toys, etc. appeared on time every week. Mr. Jackson often wondered how the old man paid for everything. He refrained from asking for fear that the old man might be offended. The children were happy and he received a little allowance too. There was no reason to spoil

Green Hope Orphanage

the party. Few weeks later, the old man sensed Mr. Jackson's anxiety and explained that he was a retired executive from a large company in America. He had devoted his life to his work. His wife had passed away and the children now had families of their own. When he learned about the HIV crisis in East Africa, he came over to help. He supported several orphanages across the region with his own savings. A few of his old friends helped out too. News of the American benefactor at Green Home spread quickly. Food rations from the children's extended families and the local churches abruptly ended. On the other hand, the orphanage experienced a rapid increase in the enrollment of children. Some children would be brought in by their extended families while others were found on the streets and brought in by the police. A few young children found themselves in the front yard in the morning without any recollection of how they got there. With support from the kind American, Mr. Jackson opened a new orphanage and christened it, New Hope. They hired two caregivers at each of the homes to look after the children.

A few months later, the old man agreed to fund the third orphanage on the condition that Mr. Jackson would quit his school job. Although Mr. Jackson enjoyed teaching at the school, this was an easy decision. He was offered a three-fold salary and an assurance that when the old man would leave, ownership and management of the orphanages would rest on his shoulders. Over the next five years, Mr. Jackson set up ten orphanages around Nyanzaa with plans for ten more over the next two years. Each of them housed 60 to 125 children between the ages of five and twenty. Two full-time female caregivers and one male cook, hired after careful screening, were responsible for day-to-day operations. Mr. Jackson would visit each orphanage once every week and spend a few hours with the staff and children. Each orphanage had at least one resident staff member who lived with the children. If a child was sick, or they were out of groceries, or there was any other pressing situation, she would immediately call Mr. Jackson for advice. The issue would be resolved swiftly and completely. As his health started faltering, the old man returned home. He would visit for a few weeks every year but the promised monthly contributions always arrived on time. Unfortunately, the old man's generous contributions could not keep up with the rising inflation in Kenya. Mr. Jackson was forced to look for supplemental funding to keep the orphanages running.

Two ears and one mouth, Sister Phoebe thought to herself, let me first understand what is happening here before I ask questions or offer help.

Elizabeth led her to a series of small tin shacks behind the girls' dormitory. "Megan, Alexander," she called out, "I would like you to meet my friend, Sister Phoebe. Do you want to join us for some tea?"

"We were just taking a short nap…and are ready to have some chai with everyone." A young white girl and boy emerged from their dark little rooms and cheerfully greeted the nun.

"Where are Chelsey and Apondi?" Elizabeth inquired.

"They have gone to Kisumu and will be back with the visitors tomorrow morning," Megan responded. She stared at the ground, looked up, and peered into Elizabeth's eyes. "I am assuming there is no dinner tonight?"

"You are right. The cook just informed me a few minutes back. Mr. Jackson called him…"

"This has to stop. Mr. Jackson keeps avoiding me every time. I am going to call the police and send that scumbag to prison," Megan yelled and rushed back into her room. "I need some time. I will join you in a little bit."

Kathy, the other caregiver, had gone to the clinic with a sick child. She returned just in time to join the group in the courtyard. Elizabeth prepared hot Kenyan milk tea for everyone.

"So, Alexander, what brings you to Kenya?" Sister Phoebe asked.

"Megan and I are volunteers here. We just finished our Bachelors degrees and decided to take a year off to travel and volunteer before returning to graduate school," Alexander explained.

"So, do you like Kenya? How did you end up here in Nyanza?"

"Yes, we like it here. Everyone is so friendly and accepting. The children are awesome. We went to a placement agency for volunteering opportunities and they brought us here."

"Where is your friend? Is she upset about something," Sister Phoebe asked.

"Megan will be fine. We have had some problems with the placement agency and the director," Alex confided.

"What is a placement agency? What is the problem? If you tell us, we can all try to help you." Sister Phoebe pressed him further.

"We don't want to make a big deal out of it," Alex hesitated, "but I think it is important for people here to know about this too. Megan and I wanted to volunteer in Kenya for two months but did not know where to go. So, we contacted this placement agency and they told us that they could arrange for us to volunteer at Clean Hope orphanage. They charged us eight thousand dollars each - a total of sixteen thousand dollars for our stay here. That is a lot of money for us and we had to borrow money from our parents and take loans to make the payments.

We were promised private transportation from Nairobi, a nice room, all our meals for two months, and a safari to Ruma National Park. We were also told that the agency only charges a small fee and provides money to the orphanage to support their activities. But when we arrived in Kenya, there was no one to pick us up. They told us that their vehicle was under repairs and hence we had to take the bus to Homa Bay. Mr. Jackson brought us here from Homa Bay. The man living in the room next to mine is paying only $30 every month for his rent. Our meals, I estimate, are worth $70 more. So, we should be charged $100 per month. Even with the mzungu tax, it should be $200 per month and not $4,000 per month. We don't know where the rest of the money is going and we feel completely cheated."

The entire group was stunned by Alex's singular narrative.

"Pole sana[1]," Sister Phoebe mumbled. "That is a lot of money. $4,000 is how much an average Kenyan man earns in eight to ten years. Is that why Megan is crying?"

"No, Megan has conceded that we have been cheated by this agency. We don't know how much Mr. Jackson has participated in this scam. We have observed several weird things happening here and Mr. Jackson has not given us any straight answers. There is enough food in the storeroom to last a week. But every time we are going to have visitors, the children don't get dinner the previous day. Megan is really upset about that. She likes children very much. There are new uniforms, toys, books, and lot of other things in the storeroom but we never see the children get them. It is one thing after another. We even saw one of the staff members steal supplies and sell it in the market in Homa Bay..." Alex looked squarely at Kathy. Megan joined the group and parked herself next to Alex.

"Let me clarify something," Kathy said, "The cook and I get paid partially in cash and partially in supplies. My salary is 2,500 Shillings and 50 toothbrushes. Every month, I go to Homa Bay and sell the toothbrushes at 40 Shillings each. That fetches me an additional 2,000 Shillings."

"And what about the cook?" Elizabeth blurted out.

"He is my uncle. He gets 2,000 Shillings and 10 toothpastes every month," Kathy said matter-of-factly.

There was a brief silence followed by laughter from everyone except Kathy.

Kathy, visibly embarrassed, continued talking and defended her employer, "You think that there are unusual things happening here at

---

[1] Pole Sana = I am very sorry (Kiswahili).

Clean Hope. You may be right but compared to other orphanages I have worked at, this place is very good. Also, Mr. Jackson is an honest man."

"He is stealing from the children and giving their toothbrushes to you," Megan accused.

"That was the salary I was offered. I am not doing anything wrong. Why don't you talk to him directly about it?" Kathy retorted. "Let me tell you about my first job. This was when I lived with my husband near the Tanzanian border in Namanga. My husband used to do a small job at a hotel where the busses and shuttles to Arusha took a break. This man and his wife came from England to start an orphanage. They had come for a safari and ran into a social worker in Nairobi who convinced them of the need for an orphanage near Namanga. They paid this so-called social worker a lot of money to organize everything – the land, the construction of the orphanage, supplies, all the permissions. They employed me to help with the children and paid me very well. After six months, one small girl asked the English woman if she could go home. The mzungu lady was confused and asked me to help in translation. As I talked to the girl and some more people, I discovered that this social worker had rented all 25 children at the orphanage from the local communities for a period of six months. Five of the children had been imported from Tanzania. The parents, who had been paid off by the social worker, were quite pleased with how well the English couple were educating and feeding their children. Sometimes they would go to the school to visit their children. The lady had a nervous breakdown when she found out the truth and the man was devastated too. Although several parents urged them to keep the orphanage running, the English people just returned home and never came back. It was a very good job. I wish it had lasted longer."

"You lost your job because of that little girl," Megan sneered. "That is disgusting. How can parents in good conscience rent their children to others? I have never seen such heartless people."

"You will not understand until you have your own child," Kathy smiled. "We love our children and want to take care of them. But we cannot be selfish. A mother wants the best future for her child. In Namanga, life is very hard. Children rarely go to school or get two meals in a day. From the time they are five years old, children have to work in shops, or sell souvenirs to tourists, or herd the cattle. What choice does a mother have? In the orphanages run by mzungus, the child is assured of good food and education. If the child is sick, he or she will be taken to a doctor. Children will play and fight and learn and eat together and grow up slowly like children should...before they have to take on responsibilities like grown-ups. And in this case, the parents could even see their children everyday."

"But Kathy, you don't know for sure that the orphanage will take good care of the children," Alex remarked.

"I was working there and I saw that the English people took excellent care of the children, just like their own kids," Kathy assured.

"OK, but that is just one case. You cannot take it for granted at every orphanage," Alex argued.

"I agree with Alex," Elizabeth chimed in, "I worked at an orphanage where they claimed that the children went to school but that was not the case. The younger children were forced to work at small shops or restaurants while the older children were sent away to Kisumu to work in factories. The manager of that place was a very bad man. I am thankful to God for saving me from him. A few months after I ran away, I read in the newspaper that he was imprisoned for defiling a young girl in his care and the orphanage was shut down."

"I have been working here with Mr. Jackson for four years now. We have never had even one bad incident. Have you ever heard of a single child being abused in any way at any of our orphanages?" Kathy challenged the group. "Mr. Jackson personally screens every single person he hires. Before he hired me, he met with over six people to find out more about me - what kind of person I was, and who I associated with. I have accompanied Mr. Jackson in conducting a background check on some of our other staff members. Before Elizabeth was hired, we met with her neighbors, including Mr. Obongo, and we also visited Sister Phoebe's home and met with some of her patients."

"What about all the foreign volunteers? Are they screened too?" Alex wondered.

"No, they are not screened. Mr. Jackson doesn't know how to screen them. But, the staff members are instructed to be around the mzungus[1] when they are with less than three children," Kathy explained. "In some other orphanages, there is no permanent staff. There are always volunteers coming from abroad to take care of the children. That is not good. Our children are very vulnerable. They get emotionally attached to the volunteers quickly. There is no way to check for bad people who abuse the children."

Elizabeth started shuffling and gesticulating. "Yes, my last job was exactly like that. There were four volunteers – all young boys and girls from America and Australia. They were always arguing how to run the

---

[1] Mzungus = White people (Kiswahili). Also used to describe foreigners, irrespective of race.

place. The director never came. The staff consisted of myself, two middle-aged women, and an elderly cook. We had to follow the volunteers' instructions. Each of the volunteers had one week every month to make all the rules. The rules kept changing and everyone at the orphanage, including the volunteers themselves, were always confused.

"One day, they decided that everyone should run in the morning. Next day onwards, the children were woken up before sunrise and forced to run for an hour. The staff had to run with them. The mamas were on the heavier side and could not run. One of them fainted and had to be taken to the hospital. The second one went home and refused to return until she was exempted from running. The old man was always out of breath and would curse like a sailor while running. It was very inappropriate with all the children around. All the neighbors would gather to see the spectacle of four mzungus running ahead followed by sixty children and then the staff members. Some children from the neighborhood also started running with us. Then the dogs joined us in the mornings too. Three of the children suffered dog-bites and had to take very many injections for rabies. Then the volunteers started running with sticks to chase away the dogs.

"The mzungus concluded that we were running very slowly and needed to eat healthier food. Everyone's food portions were reduced because apparently it was better for our health. Three older boys ran away and never came back. My friend was given food only once a day so she could lose weight and run with the children. We were not allowed to use any cooking oil. Without oil, the chapattis were so hard that children had to team up to break them. Finally, I called the nurse and she advised the volunteers to let people eat enough food. They begrudgingly agreed and let us eat at peace. The morning runs continued without any respite. Some Sundays, the children were not allowed to go to church and were made to clean the entire place. At least one weekend every month was spent planting trees everywhere. As we were planting trees one Sunday, one of the volunteers started talking to a farmer. This man complained about the weeds in his farm and asked if we could help him. He was particularly fed up of the mwangani (spider) plants in his maize and bean fields. Heyyy…and then next weekend, the orphanage almost got burned down and only God saved us from getting lynched!

"Next Saturday morning, the volunteers made us travel down the road and pull out all the mwangani plants. They said that we should help our neighbors by pulling out all the weeds. But you see, mwangani is a weed only on maize and bean fields. Apart from that, it is very nutritious and poor people eat it, just like spinach. The seeds are used as chicken feed and as medicine for pregnant women. They made us carry the plants back to the orphanage to make compost. We had a celebration that evening to commemorate the removal of 500 weeds from the area. When the people found out, they mobbed the orphanage and were ready to burn it down. Finally the director intervened and after hours of negotiation and assurances that we would plant them all back immediately, the villagers agreed to leave the orphanage building intact. It took us three hours to remove the weeds in the morning. But it took us thrice as long to plant the weeds back in. From six in the evening to three at night we replanted the mwangani. We came home hungry and tired in the early hours of the morning. Some children's feet were bleeding. I was relieved that the mob did not burn down the place or break our bones. We took a sigh of relief when the volunteers announced that we had enough exercise that weekend and would not have to wake up in two hours and start running again. The staff and children lodged a complaint with the director and he finally agreed to consult with us and set all the rules himself. I was appointed the coordinator between the director, the volunteers, and the children.

"Then why did you leave?" Alex asked.

"The mzungus were all paying the director to volunteer and run the orphanage. On the other hand, I was expecting to receive a salary from him. He had promised me KSh. 5,000 a month but kept pushing it off to the next month. He always had money for drinking beer with the volunteers, fuel for his car and expensive toys for his children. After three months of working for free, I had no option but to leave. I realized that as long as the volunteers were there, the director could do without my services. I don't understand why you white people come here and take away our jobs? Aren't there any orphanages in your country where you can help out?" Elizabeth pleaded.

"We came here to help the orphanage and the children. We had seen the children's suffering on TV programs and we wanted to help in some little way. We paid a lot of money and were told by the placement agency that the money would go towards the children's food and schooling expenses. What can we do if the people here are corrupt?" Megan defended herself.

"I was feeling guilty about how I had everything I wanted – food, electronics, cars and a good education. I just wanted to give back." Alex admitted.

"That is precisely what the volunteers at the last orphanage told me too. They were all feeling guilty and came here to help. Every time you white people feel guilty, people like me lose their jobs and livelihoods,"

Elizabeth joked. "And every time you feel unhealthy, I have to run until the fat and energy I have stored in my body have vanished. Then, I have to spend my meager savings to buy new clothes."

"Let us not change the subject. Kathy claims that Mr. Jackson is an honest man. Then, why are we skipping dinner tonight and every time we are going to have visitors? He wants the children to look hungry and tired so that the visitors give more money to the orphanage, which he can conveniently keep for himself," Megan alleged.

"Why don't you put yourself in his shoes Megan? It is not a clear black and white situation," Kathy scolded. "I think it is best to ask the children and Mr. Jackson about this issue. The orphanages rely on donations for survival. What are we to do? Send our children to work in shops and restaurants and send the older girls to work in the streets?"

"What I really want to know is how many of the children here are actually orphans," Sister Phoebe finally spoke up, "That, to me, is a very basic question. Is this actually an orphanage, or is Mr. Jackson exploiting the children for personal gain?"

"We don't have to wait long," Elizabeth smiled. "I can already hear the children on their way back from school. Today is my turn to inform them that there is no dinner tonight."

"I cannot believe how you are making an occasion out of it," Megan muttered under her breath.

The group discussed various topics for the next thirty minutes as the children came in and politely greeted the caregivers and volunteers. Sister Phoebe noticed that most of the children's uniforms were tattered and only the older ones were wearing proper shoes. After changing their clothes, the little ones started playing in the front yard. The older boys and girls formed small groups and were engaged in their own conversations. Elizabeth asked all of them to convene quickly.

"Today, we will not have dinner since there is no food," Elizabeth announced. "I want you to finish your homework for Monday and go to sleep before 9 PM. Tomorrow morning you will go to church at 7 AM and be back here at 11 AM." There were a few mock groans followed by high-pitched screams of jubilation.

"Do we have a lot of visitors tomorrow?" a young girl asked.

"Yes, I have been told that there are at least 15 of them. They will be here all day. We will also have a music system!" Kathy informed the excited children. When they went to bed hungry, the next morning always brought mzungu visitors. There would be loud music, singing, dancing and plenty of tasty food – chapattis, beef, French fries and even cakes. Chocolates were guaranteed and sometimes they also received gifts. Neither the cook, nor the caregivers would stop them from getting second or third helpings of the delicious food!

While the younger children liked playing and cuddling with the mzungus, the older ones enjoyed interacting with them and sharing their stories and perspectives. Story telling was the children's favorite activity on Saturday evenings and nights. Kathy gathered about fifteen of the children, boys and girls between 12 and 18 years of age, to talk to Sister Phoebe. The children, caregivers, volunteers and Sister Phoebe occupied one of the long tables in the dining room. Elizabeth introduced Sister Phoebe to the group, who then explained her work with HIV/AIDS patients. "Sister Phoebe came here today and will be with us for the entire week – until next Saturday. She can teach us a lot of things. But first, she wants to learn more about all of you and then we can discuss how she can teach us something new and useful," Elizabeth said.

"I would like all of you to tell me your name, age, where you are from, and how you came to the orphanage," Sister Phoebe requested, "and I would also like to know who your closest relatives are."

The children did not shy away from candidly discussing their past lives. The range of responses surprised Sister Phoebe and shocked the volunteers. Every single one of them had their own unique story. Only three of them were actually orphans, two of them due to AIDS and one due to a highway accident. The rest of them had at least one parent alive and five of them actually had both parents. Many of them had run away from home due to various problems – separated parents, abusive stepparents, beatings at school, not having school fees, or being ridiculed for being born out of wedlock. One eight year-old boy had run away to Nairobi with a friend because he was bored in his village. Some children were from very poor families. Either their parents had left them at an orphanage or they were picked up from the streets and brought to one.

Most of the children had lived at other orphanages before they found themselves at Clean Hope. Seven of the children had lived on the streets of Nairobi, Kisumu or Homa Bay. During those times, other children, police, or security guards had physically and sexually abused them. They were addicted to various drugs like glue, petrol, diesel, nail polish remover and paint thinner. It took them several months or even years to break away from their addictions. While on the street, they would beg, carry luggage, guide people as they parked their vehicles, clean utensils at small restaurants, collect metal objects and plastic bottles for recycling, and engage in other such activities to earn a little money. The younger ones engaged in petty crimes like pickpocketing while the older ones got involved with violent gangs. The older girls often engaged in commercial

A Group of Street Children

sex work. The children's friends still lived on the streets and they were often tempted to leave the rules and regulations of the orphanage and go back to their independent and adventurous lives. The former street-dwelling youth narrated how they liked going to school and wanted to be successful in life but admitted that they missed the free food, clothes, drugs and money that they had access to on the streets. The children credited Mr. Jackson and the caregivers for turning their lives around and giving them another chance at life.

"How often do you meet your families?" Sister Phoebe inquired.

"We have family days once a month and very many of the children's relatives show up," Elizabeth responded. "Especially the younger children's parents. As the children get older, fewer relatives come to meet them."

"My mother does not have money to travel. She is very sick and wants me to go and meet her but I don't have any money," one young girl lamented. "Six months back, Mr. Jackson gave me money to go and visit her. She was so happy. I am going to request Mr. Jackson again for some money."

Several youth commiserated with her and expressed similar desires to visit their families.

"When Elizabeth invited me to Clean Hope, I had planned to conduct workshops on health, hygiene, and HIV/AIDS. I have done that at other orphanages. But there is no need for any such workshops here. So now, why don't you tell me if I can help you with anything?" Sister Phoebe asked. The teenagers broke into animated discussions and nominated a spokesperson.

"We have learned about health, HIV/AIDS and other topics at schools and from the volunteers. I don't know why everyone wants to teach us things we already know. In fact, we have conducted such workshops for the younger children at Clean Hope and also at Mr. Jackson's other orphanages. What we really want to learn is how to find a job. We want to know what we should be doing now so we can find a good job in a few years. We don't want to live in an orphanage and be dependent on others. We want to be self-sufficient and have our own stable families," a young man gave a concise statement.

"I don't know what to tell you. I really don't know," Sister Phoebe admitted. "I will definitely talk to my friends Okello and Obongo to see if they can do something."

"Thank you Sister Phoebe. The exit strategy for young people is the biggest problem faced by all the orphanages and even the government does not know what to do," Kathy affirmed.

The evening winded down abruptly. Elizabeth took the little kids aside and fed them a maize porridge. The tired and hungry children fell asleep as soon as they hit their beds. Megan and Sister Phoebe had a sleepless night, the former's attention on Mr. Jackson and the orphanage's finances while the latter completely consumed by the children's diverse profiles and their emphasis on vocational skills and job opportunities. Sister Phoebe, upset that she could not help the children, decided to leave on Sunday evening. Next morning, Elizabeth and Kathy got the children ready and Alex accompanied them to the church. The women rushed to the kitchen to help the cook prepare lunch for the children and the visitors. Apondi and Chelsey had arrived from Kisumu by the morning bus to review the day's plan with Mr. Jackson and give the children all the last-minute instructions. Apondi, the Visit Coordinator, was responsible for coordinating visits for foreign visitors, government officials and community members to Mr. Jackson's orphanages. Chelsey was another volunteer from the United States, but unlike Megan and Alex, she had lived in East Africa for several years and was familiar with the way of life and doing business.

When the children returned from church at 11 AM, loud music was playing in the frontyard. Apondi and Chelsey swung into action and assembled all the children.

"We have 15 visitors from Europe coming today. They will be here in 30 minutes. I want everyone to be at your best manners when they are here. Yes?" Chelsey cheered up the children.

"Yes!" they shouted in unison.

"And you will all hug the visitors when they arrive and greet them with a big smile."

"Yes!"

"And if they ask you, tell them what you want to become when you grow up - engineers, doctors, lawyers, pastors and teachers?"

"Yes!"

"And always say thank you, please and sorry."

"Thank you, please, sorry."

"And you will not ask anyone to give you anything. Promise?"

"Promise."

"Awesome, then you can go and play for now," Chelsey smiled and disbanded the assembly. She scurried off to do a final inspection of the entire place.

"I have heard so much about you," Mr. Jackson firmly held Sister Phoebe's hand. "It is such a pleasure to meet you in person. I am Mr. Jackson, the director of Hope Orphanages."

"Mr. Jackson, it is nice to meet you too. I came here yesterday and am very impressed with your facilities and the discipline amongst your children."

"I am grateful to you for training Elizabeth before she came here. Full credit for our success goes to the caregivers," Mr. Jackson turned around to face Megan who was rapidly approaching him, "and to the volunteers too."

"Hello Megan, How are you? Kathy told me that you want to talk to me?" Mr. Jackson smiled.

"Yes, I want to talk to you right now. It is very important," Megan insisted.

"Kathy briefed me on the entire conversation that ensued yesterday about the finances at the orphanage, our association with the placement agency, and your consternation about the children going without food last night. I promise to clarify everything on one condition. You will not create a scene this morning. This visit is very important for us and can help us get funding to do vocational training for the older children," Mr. Jackson urged. "Just wait for a few hours and I will set your mind at ease. I want Sister Phoebe to be present at that time too."

After a brief word with Alex and Chelsey, Megan finally relented and went over to her room.

"Is he a hero or a villain?" Sister Phoebe could not make up her mind about Mr. Jackson.

The visitors arrived at the appointed time. They were representatives from various foundations, large non-profits, and aid agencies in Europe. The children were well-behaved and followed Chelsey's instructions perfectly. Mr. Jackson gave everyone a comprehensive tour of the place. Much to the amusement of the visitors, he pointed out every single item in the orphanage, from the 90 dorm beds to the 5 large cooking pots, 12 long tables and 120 plastic chairs. In each room, he indicated the location of the waste bins, with a final count of 25 at the end of the hour-long tour. The exhausted visitors collapsed on the plastic chairs. They played and danced with the children. Lunch was an elaborate affair with beef, ugali, chapattis, salad, French fries and rice. The visitors had brought cakes and chocolates for everyone. They were astounded by the amount of food consumed by the children. After lunch, the dining room was immediately cleaned up for a three-hour long closed-door meeting between the visitors, Mr. Jackson and Chelsey. The caregivers were tasked with keeping the children away from the dining room so that there would be no disturbance. The exhausted visitors finally emerged from the dining room in the early hours of the evening, clicked some more

A Tour of the Clean Hope Orphanage

photos with the children, got into their waiting mini-bus, and sped off towards Kisumu.

"Can we please have some strong tea?" Mr. Jackson requested Elizabeth as he walked back into the orphanage after waving the visitors goodbye. "Chelsey and I are very tired, but, as promised, I would like to meet with the volunteers to answer their questions. Can we please convene in 10 minutes?" It barely took five minutes for all the volunteers, staff and Sister Phoebe to gather in the dining room. Mr. Jackson took a long sip of tea and gave an ear-to-ear smile. "Thank you Megan and everyone for your patience. Today has been a tiring day for all of you. I thank you for your hard work and support for Hope Orphanages. Several questions have been raised about my methods and finances at Clean Hope. I request that you put direct questions to me and I promise to respond to them candidly. At the same time, I beg of you to be discreet and not divulge the details of our conversation beyond the four walls of this room."

"I make no such promises," Megan snapped.

"OK," Mr. Jackson calmly replied. "I hope you realize that I do not need to have this conversation with you. Yesterday, you threatened to go to the police and lodge a complaint. The police, District Commissioner and the sub-chiefs are all my friends. Your aggressive approach will get you nowhere. In any case, we must proceed."

"Why were the children not given food last night?" Megan roared.

"So they would be very hungry today when the visitors were here. I was planning to ask the visitors for funding to cover food expenses and I wanted them to see how much food the children consumed."

"That is just wrong. How can you keep the children hungry?"

"I would rather have them skip one meal than starve for weeks and months. Elizabeth and Kathy have strict orders of looking over the children and making sure that the younger children, the sick ones, and the ones who are HIV positive, are well-fed. The children need to learn to go without a meal once in a while too! We rely on donations for food, school fees, everything! No donations, no food."

"Why don't we start growing vegetables in our front yard like other orphanages do? We have a little land and plenty of children to help with farming?" Alex wondered.

"That is a difficult question. While it is a very good idea to grow our own food, I am against the idea of our children working in the farms. You see, in many parts of Kenya, we have built a culture where we punish children at home and school by sending them to work in the farms. They start associating farming with punishment and certainly don't want to become farmers when they grow up. Chelsey and I are working on a different model where we use greenhouses for year-round farming as an exit strategy for our older youth. The orphanage can then buy the food from the youth at a much lower rate."

"Let us not worry about the youth. They can take care of themselves. Let us focus on the children," Megan suggested. "Last week, I was cleaning the stockroom and saw that there are so many supplies that don't reach the children."

"Please be specific. All the supplies – toothbrushes, toothpaste, toilet paper, books, pencils, erasers – are used by the children. Of course, they are eating all the food in the store room too."

"There is so much cloth in the storeroom but the children are wearing tattered uniforms. There are so many toys but they are not given to the children."

"A merchant in Homa Bay donated the cloth. We need a tailor to make the uniforms," Mr. Jackson explained. "As for the toys, we don't want to encourage private ownership of the toys. Every time the children are given individual toys, they spend more time fighting and less time playing. They leave the toys everywhere and then the children from the neighborhood become jealous and demand toys from their poor parents. So the rule is that they can go and play with the toys in the playroom but the toys don't actually leave the room. The staff can make exceptions when necessary."

"And you are stealing supplies from the children to pay the staff. How can you give the children's toothbrushes to Kathy and toothpaste to the cook?"

"Shouldn't Kathy and the cook also have nice teeth?" Mr. Jackson laughed. "When we got started, very many missionaries and tour groups would visit the orphanage. We needed food, money for rent and staff salaries, mattresses, and many other things. All they brought us were toothbrushes - hundreds of them. I have never quite understood the mzungu fascination for toothbrushes. The Kenyan volunteers were offended and the children were amused when the tourists used this gigantic model of teeth and a toothbrush to teach all of us how to brush our teeth. I begged the staff to sit through the humiliating workshops and collect the free toothbrushes at the end of it. God sent us toothbrushes and we started using them to pay for everything – food, staff salaries, even toilet paper. In those days, one toothbrush fetched us three rolls of toilet paper. You see, a toothbrush cannot replace toilet paper – they have their own unique and important jobs. No one donated us toilet paper but the toothbrushes kept coming. Sister Megan, think about it in a simple manner. People donate toothbrushes that we spend as needed. The toothbrushes and toothpastes are a form of currency. Also, the people in this area have benefitted greatly from the cheap toothbrushes, which I hope will please the mzungus."

"But now you get so much money from the founder, all these donors, and placement agencies," Megan said. "Do you keep accounts for everything?"

"Yes, we keep accounts for everything, even the toothbrushes," Mr. Jackson grinned. "We have an eleven-person board of directors and they can audit the accounts any time they wish. The District Commissioner is on the board, Chelsey is on the board, there is the MP, Reverend Ndiege is on the board too."

"I want to see the accounts. Why don't you make them public?" Megan demanded.

"I can let you see them in my office but they are not public records and you cannot take a copy with you," Mr. Jackson explained. "There are many reasons for that. You cannot walk up to any company or non-profit in your country and ask for their detailed financial statements that lists all their income and everybody's salaries!"

"Let me shed some light on the finances," Chelsey offered. "My primary role here is to help Mr. Jackson manage the finances and I have done the accounts for the last year and a half. Just to give you my background, I have an MBA from a reputed university in the United States and have worked as a management consultant for several years. I came here to work with Mr. Jackson three years back. My grandfather helped Mr. Jackson start these orphanages and he requested me to use my consulting experience to help Hope Orphanages. With advancing age, my grandfather's health bills increased and the recession decreased his earnings from investments. Consequently, the money he could send Mr. Jackson gradually reduced. Last year, my family contributed less than half of the total expenses for the ten orphanages."

"We were, and still are, struggling to raise more funds," Mr. Jackson admitted. "We started reaching out to other potential donors – large non-profits, aid agencies, tourist groups, anyone. Here is the problem – the big fish are difficult to work with. They need formal proposals and we don't have the resources to develop them. The tourist groups are good but they don't understand our problems. Everyone wants to come, play with, and sponsor, the younger and cuter children. They want to send the most intelligent children to secondary schools. What about the children who don't meet their definition of being cute? What about the ones who were abused so much that they are now afraid to come out of their rooms and interact with tourists? What about the children who don't enjoy school but have other talents?

"Megan said earlier that she was not concerned about the older youth because they would take care of themselves. I disagree. If you give the small children food, love, and a structured educational environment they will grow up just fine. The challenges really start as they grow up. They need more specific training and mentoring. They need money to visit their families. They need money to go to the cities to see what the world outside looks like. They need special clothes and shoes. The young women have their own set of needs. When we ask donors if they want to sponsor a six year-old child or a sixteen year-old child, their response is very predictable! They always support the younger children! So what are we to do? Abandon the ugly, unintelligent, and older children when they need us most?"

Chelsey took over the conversation, "Mr. Jackson and I thought about this problem and decided that we will present our sponsorship opportunities such that the donors cannot select a particular child. We point donors to the profiles and needs of about six to eight children, as representatives of the larger group. Some donors insist on sponsoring a particular child and we have to bow down to their wishes. In that case, multiple donors end up sponsoring the same child. We use these funds to support all the children. We are legally protected through the language in the contract and we feel like we are ethically doing the right thing that benefits the most number of people. I can assure you that our board of directors has taken a very practical stance on this matter and given us their vote of confidence."

"But you also make so much money from volunteers like us. Alex and I are each paying 1,000 dollars a week for staying here while it costs you less that 25 dollars a week," Megan ranted.

"I understand your situation. You are paying a lot of money. The volunteers cost us about 100 dollars a month while we get twice as much from the placement agency. The 100-dollar profit pays for staff salaries. Again, it is the same problem. Most donors fail to understand the importance of full-time staff members. They assume that the children will take care of themselves."

"Where does the rest of the money go?" Megan drawled, not really wanting to know the answer.

"It is clear, isn't it?" Mr. Jackson said. "That is the placement agency's profit. I am sure they have their own marketing and organizational costs, and commissions paid to those who bring them the volunteers. It is a business, just like ours."

"How can you refer to the orphanage as a business?"

"Put yourself in my shoes. We deliver a high-quality product — children in our care never miss a day at school. We try our very best to make sure they are healthy and happy. We manage facilities effectively, pay the staff on time, and raise funds to sustain operations. We are always seeking new opportunities to improve our children's wellbeing and help them find jobs when they have to leave. It is just like a business."

"So how much money do you personally keep from the profits of your business?" Megan asked.

"I don't mind telling you." Mr. Jackson smiled. "Until last year, I used to make between 300 and 1,200 dollars every month. However, this year, for the past six months, I have not paid myself a single Shilling."

"That is substantially more than what you pay your staff. That is so unfair."

"The money ebbs and flows. Sometimes I make 1,000 dollars and when things are tough, I forgo my salary. What makes you think that I should not be reimbursed for my abilities? I could make much more money in other businesses. I chose to improve the quality of life for our children. I did not choose to be perpetually poor. My job and Kathy's job are very different. I work many more hours than her and while Kathy is assured of her monthly salary, I am not."

"Megan — do you mean to say that Bill Gates and President Obama should draw the same salaries as their janitorial staff?" Chelsey asked.

"Why don't you get more volunteers to help out? That way you can cut costs further and even make some money?" Alex asked.

"Actually, I would prefer not to have volunteers unless they are going to stay for at least six months. And even then, I don't want them to interact with the younger children. I believe that the little ones need stability and maternal relationships which only long-term local caregivers like Kathy and Elizabeth can provide. Children get emotionally attached with short-term volunteers who give them so much love and attention. When the volunteers leave, the children are left lonely and traumatized. It becomes very difficult for our staff to bring these children back into the real world."

"Did you just get us here for the monthly 100 dollar profit?" Megan asked.

"The 100 dollars keep the staff employed — which is critical for our mission. But, frankly, short-term volunteers are too much of a headache for just 100 dollars. My staff and I end up spending too much time on your logistics and little projects with the children. I think volunteers like you can be very helpful in interacting with the youth and teaching them useful skills – using computers, photography, how to become a safari guide, tailoring, and making uniforms. Heyyy…there are so many useful things they can learn. And in the process, our young people will teach you a few things too," Mr. Jackson suggested.

"I think you are right Mr. Jackson," Alex agreed. "Megan and I will try to focus our energy on the youth and try to share some skills with them. I wish we had this conversation earlier."

"Mr. Jackson, I was very surprised that most of the children are not actually orphans. I am sure you know that?" Sister Phoebe inquired.

"Yes, Sister. We know that very well and it mirrors the reality at orphanages across the country. When I opened my second orphanage, I observed that the profiles and circumstances of the new entrants were vastly different than the HIV/AIDS orphans in the first orphanage. The children at Green Hope, my first orphanage, were in extremely delicate conditions and had nowhere to go. Over time, it seemed to me that children were being sent to the orphanage by their parents or extended relatives. I personally reached out to the parents and pleaded with them to take back their children and raise them. But, they were convinced that I could give them a better education and life than they ever could. Very many children end up on the streets due to various reasons and we bring them here. It is very difficult to reconnect the children with their families. Someday I would like to have a few dedicated social workers just to reconcile the children with their parents and families. My thinking on this issue has evolved over the years. I don't like the word "orphanage," I would rather call them Children's Homes. But that concept does not work as well with donors because they just don't understand our problems. My job is to create the best environment for the children that are entrusted to my care, irrespective of who they are or what circumstances brought them here."

"You said that you were going to discuss exit programs for the youth with the visitors," Sister Phoebe asked, "did you have any luck? That is something I am very interested in too."

"Indeed, they understand the importance of effective exit programs. They have agreed to fund a pilot project to build greenhouses so that our youth can engage in year-round horticulture for the local markets. We will be building three greenhouses over the next six months. Chelsey will be leading the project and will keep you informed about progress."

"Are there any more questions for me?" Mr. Jackson took a deep breath and looked around the room. "I hope I have answered your questions sufficiently and you won't have to talk to the District

Commissioner now." He looked at Megan and smiled. She smiled back.

Sister Phoebe broke the silence. "One more question, Mr. Jackson. I don't understand. Why do you have so many waste bins in every room and along every corridor? Isn't one in every room sufficient? Everywhere I look, sure enough, there is a waste bin! They are everywhere! Heyyyy!" Sister Phoebe's earnest tone caused the room to erupt in laughter.

Mr. Jackson waited for a few minutes to get everyone attention. "I have learned that mzungus are as fascinated with waste bins as they are with toothbrushes. Once a donor cut off our funding for one full year because there were only three waste bins in the boy's dormitory. They insisted that there must be one waste bin for every three children. From that unfortunate day till this moment, I have always maintained the golden three-to-one waste bin ratio in my orphanages. It is the single most important factor in our success."

#7

The Headmaster's Harambee MBA

Mr. Masinde's footsteps echoed along the empty corridors of the Strong Bamboo Primary and Secondary School. He gently pushed the creaking door and entered the classroom at the very end of the hallway. He looked around the classroom until his gaze rested on the blackboard. It was a section of the wall painted with three coats of black oil paint. Over the last twenty years, the paint had peeled off in several places and the plaster had come off at a few spots. Students had professed their love by etching their sweetheart's name into the wall with a geometry compass. Mr. Masinde smiled when he recognized one of the names. Small pieces of chalk and a dirty washcloth lay on the windowsill at the corner of the wall. The last period must have been a botany class, he thought to himself as he observed the crude sketch of a leaf with notes on both sides, it is so difficult to read from the board. Maybe that is why our scores are dropping – students never understand what the teacher is writing on the board.

Mr. Masinde sat on one of the benches and rested his forehead on the desk. Thirty years ago he was one of the pupils in that classroom. After finishing Form four, he went to college in Kisumu and came back to his alma mater as a secondary school teacher. He worked his way up to become the headmaster of the school. He had walked to the school and back, every day since he learned how to walk. This journey was going to end, or at least change forever in two months. The secondary school was going to be shut down due to financial problems.

While eight years of primary education in Kenya were free, the four years of secondary education were not. Government-built primary schools were in place since the colonial period. Although students were required to pay school fees during the Moi years, President Kibaki had made primary education free for everyone in 2003. While primary schooling was accessible to the masses, the government had built very few secondary schools. The elite private secondary schools, many of them run by foreign organizations, were expensive and beyond the reach of the masses. The government schools were affordable and of moderate quality. Students in Kochia, like their counterparts countrywide, strived to score enough points in the primary school exams to gain admission to government secondary schools. For the thousands of children who were not accepted to the government schools, Harambee schools offered the only alternative. Harambee literally means, 'let's all pull together' and captures the Kenyan spirit of working together to overcome problems. Kenyans have a deep faith in education and quickly embraced the concept of Harambee schools. Local communities raised funds and built secondary schools to meet the rapidly increasing demand created by free primary education. The emphasis on community-level initiatives to expand education helped overcome the state's limited resources and foster a sense of communal and national unity among Kenyans.

While the capital costs of harambee schools were covered by community funding drives, the operational costs were a different challenge altogether. A few of the harambee schools received marginal funding from the government but most of them were solely reliant on student fees and charitable donations to meet their operational expenses. As community demographics and values evolved, and HIV/AIDS tightened its grip, the charitable donations gradually reduced and the schools essentially became private schools that provided a service for a fee. In the absence of any discretionary funds for capital expenses and maintenance, the Harambee schools fell behind government schools in terms of class size, teacher training, and educational facilities. The low quality of most Harambee schools was reflected in the poor exam scores of the students and their low rates of advancement to post-secondary education. While the harambee schools of Nyanza were considered model schools for a long time, they were badly hurt by the HIV crisis and the gradual migration to the cities. The epidemic kicked off a vicious cycle with higher school fees leading to a decline in enrollment, which in turn compelled school officials to increase the fees further. The Strong Bamboo secondary school was one of many such schools facing this crisis. Mr. Masinde would have to shut down the secondary school unless he was able to solve the massive fiscal challenges in the next two months.

Mr. Masinde was a linguist and not an economist. Before he became the headmaster, he taught English, Kiswahili, and History. He was a stereotypical teacher and was popular in Kochia for his kindness, jolly nature, and organizational skills. He was known as an honest man who often poked fun at himself to convey his point. His public speaking skills were excellent, rivaled only by the likes of Reverend Ndiege. He was always willing to engage in community events and encouraged his students to do the same. But managing the monthly school accounts pushed him to the limits of his arithmetic capabilities. His lack of business acumen was manifested in poor fiscal planning and absolutely no fundraising to supplement the school fees. He was aware that the financial situation of the school was worsening. He had expressed his concerns to his friend, Mr. Jackson, the Director of Hope Orphanages. Mr. Masinde ignored Mr. Jackson's suggestions to develop yearly plans for the school.

Our headmaster is perpetually singing about the importance of science and mathematics but he cannot even manage the school finances himself, the students would laugh. He turned down Mr. Jackson's offers to help for fear of being ridiculed by his staff and students. While he did not mind poking fun at himself for everything else, the thought of people making fun of his math skills terrified him. Mr. Masinde was a broken man. If he had to down the shutters of the secondary school, he resolved to commit suicide, or at least go away to some far-flung corner of the country where no one would know him.

It wasn't until he heard his panicked wife shouting his name in the hallway that Mr. Masinde recovered from his reverie. He realized that he had been sitting in the classroom for over two hours deliberating his options. He quickly ran out and pacified his wife as they went home and settled down for supper.

"If you don't speak to Mr. Jackson, then I will," she threatened the headmaster. "And if he cannot do anything, I will also speak to Janet and Obongo."

"Yaai yai yaai! Why don't you understand? You know how much everyone likes to gossip. Please don't tell anyone," Mr. Masinde begged.

"Don't worry, they are trusted friends and will not gossip. I am sure Mr. Jackson and Obongo can find a way to avert this crisis. Do you have any other option? It is either asking for help or closing down the school."

"But what will they say? I will become the laughing stock of Kochia and no one will send their children to Strong Bamboo."

"Didn't you once tell me that a bamboo is strong and survives because it bends with the wind," his wife smiled. "Just trust me and I am sure everything will be okay."

The next day, during the short break in the morning, Mr. Masinde called Mr. Jackson and requested him to come over to the school in the evening.

"Sure, I can come over right now, or in the evening. Is there a problem with one of our children? Did they play any mischief?" Mr. Jackson asked.

"Oh, your students are all doing very well. In fact, they are my very best students. There is another important matter for which I need your advice. Can we please meet in the evening?" Mr. Masinde's request was accepted by Mr. Jackson.

Almost one-third of the children in the secondary school came from Mr. Jackson's orphanages. These children followed strict regimens for studying and often received help from volunteers to complete their homework. Consequently, they regularly outperformed the regular children in academics as well as sports. Mr. Jackson always paid the fees for his children on time and never complained about the fee increases. In contrast, many of the other students had not paid fees for years. The kind headmaster did not have the heart to throw them out.

I wish more of our children came from Mr. Jackson's orphanages, Mr. Masinde thought to himself, then this situation would never have come about. Strong Bamboo would have been in a very stable financial state…and we would likely have the highest test scores in Nyanzaa.

Mr. Masinde knew that his wife would not be able to refrain from mentioning his problem to Janet and Obongo at the merry-go-round[1] meeting in the afternoon.

She will tell them half the story and then they will fill in the blanks and make more assumptions. I should rather just speak to Obongo myself. There is no point waiting, Mr. Masinde conceded, and as soon as I tell Obongo, he will suggest that I talk to Okello and Sister Phoebe too. The headmaster took a deep breath and picked up his phone. He called the three of them and invited them to the school in the evening. Promptly, at the appointed time, Sister Phoebe, Mr. Jackson, Okello, and Obongo arrived at the school. After greeting them individually, Mr. Masinde led them to the corner classroom. For any other meeting, a staff member would have been present to provide the tea. This time around, the headmaster sent the staff home, prepared the tea himself, and carried it over to the classroom.

"Is everything okay? Where are your staff members?" Sister Phoebe wondered.

"I need some personal advice from all of you and so I thought that I

---

[1] A merry-go-round is an informal system used by groups of people to save money. They are formally known as Rotating Savings and Credit Associations (ROSCAs).

should prepare the tea myself," the headmaster said.

Each of them introduced themselves to Mr. Jackson and then gave him an opportunity to discuss Hope Orphanages with the group.

"Friends, thank you for coming here this evening," Mr. Masinde called the meeting to order. "The reason I called you is very grave. The problem is that we barely have adequate funds to keep the secondary school running beyond the next two months. Let me be clear – at the end of this academic year, we will have to shut down the secondary school. Also, I have just received a notice that the education ministry people will be conducting an inspection of the school facilities. We don't have any money to upgrade the facilities and with the current state of affairs, we will never pass the inspection."

"But what about the primary school?"

"Remember, primary education is free. All the teacher salaries come from the government and they give us some money for managing the facilities too. There are no major problems with the primary school. So it will remain operational."

"But when the new school year starts, you will receive the students' fees. I don't understand the problem."

"The problem is that not all the students actually pay their fees. Some pay partial fees and some of them don't pay fees at all. They come from poor families. Surely, inability to pay must not be a barrier to education for the hardworking students."

"Then how did the school survive so far?"

"We received some government aid, an annual donation, and we had three primary teachers who were volunteering their time teaching in the secondary school. This month brought some bad news. The aid was stopped, the donor died, two of the kind teachers are retiring at the end of the year and one of them is moving to Kisumu with her husband."

"Besides the teacher moving to Kisumu, the rest of the issues could have been predicted in advance. Then we could have taken action earlier," Mr. Jackson chided. "Why did you wait for so long?"

"Indeed, you are right. The problem is that fiscal planning is not my expertise and we don't have the money to hire an accountant. I take full responsibility for the situation. This is where we are. I would like you to advise me on what to do next. I don't want to see the school shut down." The humble headmaster pleaded.

"So, how much money do you actually have in the account?" Obongo asked.

"All we have left in the account are teacher salaries for the rest of the year and provisions for the final examinations."

Obongo broke the long silence, "I suggest that before we advise the headmaster on potential solutions, we should study the school operations and understand all the problems."

"Yes, and we cannot separate the financial problems from the teachers' and students' concerns," Okello added.

"Mr. Jackson and Okello can study the school accounts. Sister Phoebe and I can review the facilities and talk to the teachers and students and report back," Obongo proposed.

"I don't want the teachers or students to get suspicious about your presence and start gossiping," Mr. Masinde stuttered. "That would disrupt classes and bring our school to a standstill immediately."

"We shall engage with the school under the guise of doing an independent assessment to determine how the local community can play a larger role in the school's operations," Okello suggested.

"Amen," the delighted headmaster said. "Let us meet here the Sunday after next. Please don't be afraid to ask me any questions that can help you in your work. I appreciate your help very much."

Obongo and Sister Phoebe decided to meet at the school the next morning and start their reviews and interviews. Mr. Jackson and Okello walked over to the headmaster's office.

"Here's the account book," the headmaster said as he handed over a dog-eared coverless notebook that listed the income and expenditures of the school. "And here are the fee receipt books with counterfoils for fees collected by the school over the last so many years."

"Heyyyy! This notebook has all the accounts of the entire school!" An astonished Mr. Jackson held the notebook in his hand and burst out laughing.

"Yes, but I can assure you that it contains every single transaction with dates and amounts very clearly written. And it is very accurate. Not a single transaction has been missed for any reason," the embarrassed headmaster reassured.

Okello took the account book with him while Mr. Jackson picked up the fee receipt books. They decided to meet every evening until the next scheduled group meeting on Sunday afternoon, about two weeks later.

"I have informed the teachers and students about your presence at the school. They have indicated their interest in talking to you." Mr. Masinde welcomed Obongo and Sister Phoebe next morning.

Mr. Masinde returned to his duties while the duo took a leisurely walk around the school facilities. The teachers were in the staff room sipping their tea, reading the newspaper and chatting with their colleagues. They were eager to share their stories of life at the school with Obongo and

Sister Phoebe. While they were grateful to have a job, they expressed their dissatisfaction with their salaries, lack of resources, and the quality of students. As the teachers came in and went out of the staff room, the stories, opinions and guffaws of laughter flowed freely.

"Most students have no motivation to learn. They are just sitting there like bags of potatoes. If they are not motivated to learn, how can I teach them? I have no motivation to teach either."

"I think my students are very motivated to learn English and history. I think they really enjoy listening to stories. There are plenty of stories in English and history textbooks but none whatsoever in mathematics. What can you do?"

"I am trying to get a transfer to Kisumu or to Eldoret but I don't have any good connections in the ministry. I am just here teaching and counting days until the transfer is approved."

"I don't want to go to Kisumu, it is the same salary and more expenses. I am looking for a driver's job in Dubai or Saudi. I have a large family to feed and they are really struggling."

"I am the only science teacher here. At my previous school, we had a science lab. Students loved chemistry practicals because they were exciting and engaged multiple senses – they could see the colors change; they could smell the results of their experiment. Alas, there is no lab here. Students just memorize the experiments for the exams."

"Yes, I agree. We have to tailor our science teaching towards answering national examination questions. At the end of the day, that is all that matters – exam performance."

"I am just waiting for Raila to become the President. I am sure that he will give us a very big pay raise and make sure we get our pension. Then I will retire."

"I am a mathematics teacher but I teach Kiswahili. Whether I teach Kiswahili or mathematics, I get the same salary. With mathematics, there are always students that will come to you afterwards and ask more questions. Yaai yaai yai! It is too much work. Teaching Kiswahili is very easy – I just dictate the lessons. Don't tell everyone but I also have my own trading business to run."

"I am retiring this year. But I am worried that I will not get my pension on time. I want to keep working at the school but I am told I have to retire and create space for the young teachers."

"There are very few ladies on the teaching staff. We need more role models for the girls."

"We have a very big problem with the girls. They are vanishing from secondary school faster than the fish from Lake Victoria."

As lunchtime came about, the staff room got busier and louder. Heated arguments about salaries, duties, and politics punctuated the chaos in the staff room. Sister Phoebe and Obongo excused themselves and proceeded to the playground. They settled down on a bench to compare notes.

"That was some discussion!" Sister Phoebe exhaled. "I was very uncomfortable towards the end. The teachers became so agitated."

"They almost came to blows," Obongo grinned. "But we learned so much. I have 25 pages of notes. The teacher's lack of motivation was troubling but I understand their problems. After all, my father was a teacher all his life."

"I want to know why girls are dropping out. That is not good for the school or our society."

"Indeed. The lack of science labs and the teachers being forced to retire are also big problems."

"Obongo…" Sister Phoebe pushed her glasses up her nose. "Both of us must not forget our immediate goal. There are obviously a lot of problems but we are here to find ways to keep the secondary school running past this year."

Obongo nodded in agreement. His attention was captivated by the frolicking children, tightly packed into their pants, sweaters, and monkey caps, running around and playing with their tires.

Sister Phoebe and Obongo parted ways after a quick lunch of boiled eggs and bread. Obongo proceeded to inspect the classrooms, defunct laboratories, and other facilities. Sister Phoebe headed to a meeting with senior girls from the secondary school.

"I would like to know why girls are dropping out of school," Sister Phoebe asked the girls. "I am not a teacher and I am not connected to the school. So, please don't be afraid to tell me about the real problems. I will not share your identity with anyone." Sister Phoebe's assurance seemed to allay the girls' anxiety. They gradually started opening up and sharing their experiences.

"Sister, I think there are many different problems. My parents are teachers and they have always encouraged me to study. My best friend did not have such a supportive environment at home. She was fed up of the daily arguments at home and just stopped coming. She is getting married next month."

"I am planning on leaving school at the end of this year. I am just wasting my time and my mother's money. Even if I finish secondary school, I cannot afford to go to college. So what is the use of going to school? I will just join my mother's vegetable shop in Homa Bay."

Schoolchildren Playing with Tires

"One teacher after another – they just come and start writing on the board or they start dictating. We just have to sit there all day and write in our books. Then we go home and memorize everything we wrote that day. It is so boring."

"I want to become a scientist or an engineer. But I don't understand how memorizing all these details will help me become a scientist."

"I really want to study but I have a six-month old baby. He is often sick and I have to take care of him. So, I cannot come to school regularly or complete the homework on time."

"Yeah, I have a similar problem. I have to work in my father's restaurant after school. I cannot study at night and then I fall behind. Some of the teachers beat us if we have not done the homework."

"Sister, no one talks about this but…" the head girl shyly confided, "at the school, there are no separate toilets for the girls. The common toilets are very dirty and their doors don't close properly."

"Yes sister, that is a real problem. We are afraid of going to the toilet. We don't have any privacy. A few of the boys trouble us by pushing the door open and running away."

"My goodness," Sister Phoebe bellowed. "That is unacceptable. Why hasn't the school management taken any action?"

"The bathrooms are all the way over there so teachers don't even know about this problem. No one has ever asked us and we don't know whom to complain to," the head girl admitted. "So we just run home to use the bathroom. If we are late for class, the teachers think that we were out gossiping with friends. They scold us and ask us to go home."

"And what about the boys troubling you? Does that happen everyday?"

"Only sometimes. There are a few bad boys. We know who they are and stay away from them. It is not like other parts of the country. I have stayed in many different places and have seen worse things. I think our school is much better compared to those places. Our teachers never trouble us here."

"Besides the toilet situation, there is also another problem," one student insisted. "When girls have their period, they have to stay home for a few days. They miss school again and again and fall behind. Once they build up absences, it is difficult to catch up and then they just drop out of school."

"I am fortunate because my aunt from Nairobi brings me the necessary supplies. My other friends cannot afford to buy sanitary napkins and resort to using pieces of cloth, used blankets, or even tissue paper. Sometimes the girls are in pain but don't have the necessary medicines. They just stay home."

"The teachers are mostly men – they don't understand and we can't tell them the problem. They think that we are lazy and don't want to study. They punish us for missing school and not doing the homework. They send us back home and again we fall behind."

"Sister, can you help us in any way? If you can find a solution to this problem, I think that we can keep a lot of girls in school."

"I am not sure what I can do but let me think about it." Sister Phoebe was taken by surprise at the students' plea for help. The discussion continued for a little longer and then the group dispersed since the students had to attend a class.

For two hours, Obongo took detailed notes in every classroom. Missing lights, broken windows, blackboards with paint peeled off, walls with broken plaster, broken chairs and desks, were all recorded. He patiently observed teachers and students in the classroom. Some classes were exciting and the students were engaged while students in other classes seemed bored and dozed off. Teachers were missing in a few classes with the students whiling away their time playing in class or on the playground. He took that opportunity to speak with the students about their studies and future plans. The boys echoed sentiments similar to the girls' frustration with the chalk and talk pedagogy and their musings on the purpose of their education. A few other issues related to paying fees and dropping out of school emerged during these conversations.

"I need to start earning and saving money to pay the dowry for my bride. If I study for six years more, my parent's savings will be wiped off and it will be 15 years more until I can get married. I am a romantic man and cannot wait so long. I will just start working after this year and start saving for the dowry." A young man's candid confession was met with guffaws of laughter.

"I don't understand the relationship between what I learn in school and the world we live in. For example, when I go home, my illiterate family members ask me all kinds of questions. How to repair bicycles? How to store potatoes for a longer time? How to get bank loans to expand our dairy business? What does a particular verse from the Bible mean? I don't know the answers to most of their questions. Then I ask my father for money for the school fees. When he asks me what I study in school, again I don't have a good answer for him. I am just told by my teachers that some day I will be able to apply my knowledge to get a job. So, I have decided to take their advice, stay in school and ultimately get a Bachelor of Arts degree."

"Your BA degree will certainly help you win over a beautiful girl," the romantic young man lamented.

"Today was a very productive day for both of us," Obongo remarked to Mr. Masinde when they convened at the end of the day.

"Your teachers are very cooperative and the students are very smart," Sister Phoebe concurred. "I am particularly impressed with the head girl and her friends. They educated me about several challenges to retaining girls in secondary school."

"Wonderful! What did you find? What should we do next?" the excited schoolmaster asked.

"It is too early to discuss our results. We need to triangulate the data. We need to confirm the accuracy of everything we have been told. For the next few days, we will be back here to talk to teachers and students and study the facilities. We might even talk to a few parents. You will have to be patient with us." Sister Phoebe gave a reassuring smile.

"I have a question for you, Mr. Masinde," Obongo said. "I came across a large classroom with over twenty computers in it. The room was locked up and I was told that is has been so for a long time. Can you please shed some light on it?"

"Yes, we received those computers as a donation from a NGO last year. We had 25 of them. Two were stolen, two were destroyed by an angry cow, and one of them is in my office. The remaining 20 computers are in the lab."

"Why aren't you using them?" Obongo was puzzled.

"It is a long story. The computers are not needed for regular schoolwork. We had a part-time science teacher who wanted to start a computer student club. He arranged for the computers from this NGO. They just appeared on our doorstep one afternoon. We were completely surprised. I was convinced we were being scammed. But how, I could not tell. This man was unstoppable. Very smart fellow. He started the club and enrolled the interested senior students. He taught me Windows and Microsoft Office. The attendance at school increased drastically, but so did our electricity bill. Finally, I had to ask him if the NGO would pay for the power. That was not to be. He suggested that we charge the students an extra fee for the power and also give him an extra salary. He held a meeting with parents and they were actually willing to pay. So we followed-through on the plan and the club started growing."

"That is a very good idea. It is a win-win situation for everyone," Obongo's eyes lit up.

"So it seemed to me. I was as excited then as you are right now," Mr. Masinde affirmed. "The attendance increased, we started getting inquiries from new students, the teacher was very motivated, the children started studying hard to get into the computer club. It was picture perfect."

"Then what was the problem? Why did such a good idea fail?" Obongo implored.

"Jealousy. We had over a hundred students in the club, each paying 300 Shillings every month. Our young man made 20,000 Shillings extra – much more than his regular salary. As soon as the other part-time teachers found out about it, they came to me with all sorts of proposals for other clubs. The English teacher wanted to start a book club, the science teacher wanted to start an astronomy club, the geography teacher wanted a wildlife club. Our gardener came to me one morning to express his desire to start a vegetable growing club. If that was not enough, a local restaurant proposed that we must also have a teacher's club to discuss management of the student clubs. I grew an aversion to the word 'club'. It was such a headache. The teachers would not take 'no' for an answer. They started rallying and bribing their students to demand all these clubs. They met with parents, most of whom were clearly not interested in all these clubs. The parents complained to me about the teachers' unannounced home visits and intimidation. The problem spiraled out of control when the teachers started threatening the computer teacher and his students. Finally, I had to intervene and close down the computer club. The young man and his students were all very sad, and so was I. But what else could I do?"

"That is definitely very unprofessional of the teachers. Why didn't you get rid of the teachers or report them to the police?"

"At that time, and even now, we relied heavily on part-time teachers. They are willing to work for less salary. If I would have gotten rid of them, who would teach all the students? I didn't want to involve the police because it would attract media attention." Mr. Masinde lowered his voice to a whisper. "And besides, we even had a powerful local policeman who insisted on starting a police club at the school!"

Mr. Masinde's narrative left Obongo baffled and excited at the same time.

Over the course of the day, Mr. Jackson had meticulously reviewed the receipt books for the past five years and tabulated student payments over that period. Meanwhile, Okello had studied the school's expenses. Several questions had emerged from this exercise and a meeting with Mr. Masinde had been arranged for the evening. Obongo and Sister Phoebe had long left when Okello and Mr. Jackson arrived at the school.

"Sorry Headmaster to keep you waiting. The expense book was complicated but I must say that it was well-organized," Okello complimented the delighted Mr. Masinde.

"I told you. I am not a mathematician but I know how to keep accounts," the proud headmaster said.

"Just like you suggested, the income by way of fees, is less than expected because several students have not been paying their dues. I intend to conduct my own inquiries into the financial capability of these students. All I need for the moment are details about government aid, financial donations and in-kind services received by the school over the last five years," Mr. Jackson requested, "And also the complete roster of students attending secondary school irrespective of whether they are paying the fees or not."

"That is easy." The headmaster pulled out his personal diaries over the past five years and provided the details. He went over to the staff room and returned with the attendance books for all the classes.

"Wonderful," Mr. Jackson exclaimed, and then turned to Okello. "My friend has several questions about the school's expenses."

"Mr. Masinde, I noticed several payments to Mount Homa Computer Services. Can you please tell me what these are for?" Okello requested.

"For the exam papers. We give Mount Homa Computer Services the question papers written by the teachers. They prepare them on the computer and give us the nicely organized printouts for the exam," the headmaster explained.

"Heyyyy! That is a lot of money. You are paying them KSh. 40,000 every few months for setting up the exam papers and then 30,000 more for all the printing. Why do you need to spend so much money?" Okello was puzzled.

"In the past, we used to write the exam questions on the blackboard. But there were too many problems. The blackboards get old and difficult to read. The students had to sit close together to read from the board. Then they would copy from one another. No matter how careful we were, they always had questions about the exam paper and the teachers would have to explain it again and again. The entire operation was very inefficient and stressful. Several times we had fights amongst the students when the exam was going on. They wanted to sit close to the board so that they can read the questions clearly. The computerized exam papers solve all these problems and hence the teachers like them very much. There is much more clarity. Teachers can space out the students in multiple classrooms. Students find it difficult to cheat and the cheaters can be caught easily."

"I can see the benefits. But this company is charging too much money."

Exams in Progress at the Strong Bamboo Secondary School

"I am aware of that. We tried two other companies in the past but somehow the exams leaked out each time. Mount Homa is expensive but very trustworthy." The headmaster shrugged.

"I think I might have a solution for that," Okello said. "Changing topics, can you tell me how many full-time and how many part-time teachers you have at the secondary school?"

"We have five full-time teachers and four part-time contract teachers. There are also three primary school teachers who are volunteering at the secondary level."

"Why are the teacher salaries so different. The full-time teachers make up to KSh. 60,000 a month while the part-time ones make as low as KSh. 15,000. That is a big difference!"

"Yes, the salary depends on very many factors – educational qualifications, years of service, and others which I would rather not discuss."

"You said that some of them are retiring this year?"

"Yes, the three primary teachers are leaving – two of them retire and one is leaving for Kisumu. Also one of our full-time secondary teachers is retiring."

"Do you conduct any evaluations of the teachers? Which teachers are good and which ones are not?"

"We don't have any formal evaluations. But I can give you my opinion. You must remember that the full-time teachers are unionized so we are married to them."

"Yes, I understand. We will contact you again if there are additional questions. Otherwise we will see you at the meeting next week," Okello promised. "I spoke to Obongo earlier today and we are coordinating our actions."

"So, do you think we will be able to keep the secondary school running?" the headmaster asked earnestly.

Okello and Mr. Jackson looked at each other, gave a slight smile, shrugged, and walked out of the headmaster's office.

For the next five days, Sister Phoebe and Obongo spent most of their day at the school. They interviewed all the teachers and many of the secondary school students. Obongo brought in a construction worker and a painter to get a cost estimate for the classroom repairs. Sister Phoebe went a step beyond and personally paid a fundi[1] to get the bathroom door fixed. Mr. Jackson met with the parents of students who were behind on their fee payments. He discovered that many of the

---

[1] Fundi = handyman (Kiswahili)

defaulters were guardians of orphaned or abandoned children. These good samaritans were already stressed beyond their means. Most of them worked daily jobs and were caring for 3-5 orphaned children with their meager earnings. They valued education and sent their children to primary school. Primary school was free and the books, uniforms and miscellaneous items could be cobbled together from neighbors, extended family and savings. Hand-me-downs of uniforms and shoes were very common. Secondary school, however, was a completely different challenge. The fees at Strong Bamboo were about KSh. 15,000 a year and the ancillary expenditures such as books, uniforms, mattresses added up to KSh. 15,000 more. For families with mean monthly incomes of KSh. 5,000 per month, KSh. 30,000 was half their yearly income!

When families struggled to pay for their own children, paying for their relatives' children was even more difficult. Some families succumbed to the necessity of putting their children to work so that they contribute to the family income. Other families pulled off amazing feats of endurance and selflessness to send their children to secondary school. When the students' performance in school started flagging, the families often caved in, and pulled the children out of school. Mr. Jackson, with his decades of experience with thousands of children, understood the deep roots of these tough choices. Mr. Jackson was heavily invested in the Secondary School. Over one-third of the 300 children at the school came from Hope Orphanages. The next closest school was 12 kms away and it could not accommodate the overflow from Strong Bamboo, if it were to shut down. Mr. Jackson spent the week running from pillar to post – meeting with the education ministry, health ministry, and youth services. Most meetings ended with enthusiastic handshakes but honest apologies or empty promises. Realizing the futility of seeking help from governmental authorities stretched to their limits, he changed course. He started speaking to headmasters, teachers, students and university graduates from prominent national and private schools. On the team's request, he scoured the marketplace to find talented young teachers who might be looking for their first break in the teaching profession.

Sister Phoebe and Obongo's presence at the school during the first week boosted the headmaster's confidence and instilled faith in triumphing over this monumental challenge. However, as the second week marched on, the headmaster's stress levels and anxiety increased manifold. By Friday, he was a complete wreck. He called in sick and spent most of his day in bed. Obongo's courtesy call to give him hope was met with an apathetic grunt. The headmaster was convinced that the school's fate was sealed and nothing could be done to reverse it. He skipped church on Sunday morning and got out of bed just to prepare for the meeting in the afternoon.

The entire team convened in the afternoon at the school premises. Sister Phoebe had invited Odhiambo, the CEO of Moneymaker Toilets, to the meeting. Obongo's son Owiti had also been requested to attend the meeting. Mr. Masinde brewed some fresh Kericho tea for everyone while his wife served fresh beef samosas and egg sandwiches.

"Welcome again to Strong Bamboo." Mr. Masinde bowed. His eyes welled with tears as he thanked his friends "I am very grateful to you for your hard work over the last two weeks. Mr. Obongo called me on Friday afternoon and informed me about the breakneck speed with which everyone has been working to save the school. I was told that Mr. Jackson traveled all the way to Nairobi for this purpose. I applaud everyone's dedication. Whether we succeed or fail, I will forever be indebted to you. I pray to God to give every person such wonderful friends and every community such committed champions. Now it is time for this old teacher to sit down and the businessman, Mr. Jackson to take over."

"Let us get started," Mr. Jackson commanded. "We have about sixteen issues to discuss and as many decisions to make. All the issues are interconnected but we have to start somewhere. I will start by reporting on the problem of collecting fees. The young man here, Owiti, will be keeping the minutes. We can vote on the solutions at the end of the meeting. Ofcourse, the headmaster will have the privilege of vetoing any of these proposals. Are we ready?"

Mr. Jackson looked around the room for a vote of confidence. Owiti braced himself for the whirldwind of facts, observations and proposals from the fast-talking entrepreneur.

"We have 310 students in the secondary school – 180 boys and 130 girls. 105 of these students are from Hope Orphanages. Their fees are paid in full. It must be noted that Hope Orphanages has not defaulted on fees even once over the last ten years. Off the 205 other students, 75 students' fees are completely paid up. Then there are 80 students who have paid between 20% and 90% of the fees. We might be able to recover some of these funds and we can talk about ways to do that later. A handful of these students' families can certainly pay their fees – we need to be stern with them. That leaves us with 50 students who have not paid a single Shilling. My staff visited their homes and found that 45 of these students are orphaned or abandoned children in the care of their extended families. The other five students come from extremely poor and broken-down families. I think that all these families must be applauded for encouraging their children to go to school. These 50 students will now be on the roster of Hope Orphanages and Hope will pay their fees for the upcoming year. The students will stay with their families, who will still be responsible for the ancillary educational expenses."

"Oh my goodness," Mr. Masinde exclaimed. "That is 750,000 Shillings. I think that in one stroke, you solved all our problems. Where will you get all that money from?"

"That is my problem." Mr. Jackson assured the shocked headmaster. "I have been promised some emergency funds from the government and a private donor. We also have our own savings that we will be investing in these children. These funds will not be available at once but you will receive them in a timely fashion. My friend Obongo has put together a detailed report and cost estimate for the classroom repairs. The first KSh. 250,000 will be spent on these repairs. Work will commence at the earliest so that it is complete before the school inspection. I must warn you that these funds will come with strings attached."

"What kind of strings? What are your conditions?" Mr. Masinde asked.

"First of all, you will hire a certified accountant. I will personally audit the accounts. Secondly, we will have to shuffle the teachers and tie their salaries to performance. Finally, there will be a nine-member oversight committee that will meet on a monthly basis to review the school's operations and take corrective action as needed. The headmaster will be accountable to this committee."

"Those are all good things for the school but…." The headmaster's voice showed some concern. "So now you will take over as the headmaster of the school?"

"No! Rest assured that you will remain the headmaster and administer the school. Strong Bamboo is a harambee school and this committee will help you address problems as they arise. If this committee had been set up earlier, we would not have been on the verge of shutting down. The school needs the community, just as much as the community needs the school. This oversight committee is the formal interface between the two. Practically, you can think of the committee members as your unpaid staff that will help you solve problems and improve the school."

"That would be good for the school but—" Mr. Masinde mildly protested.

Mr. Jackson continued, "While the non-payment of fees is an immediate problem, the larger issue is retaining the students. A school cannot work without students. Last year, we had a total of 390 students. We lost 80 students in a single year – 59 girls and 21 boys. Let me repeat – if we keep losing students, we will not be able to raise the necessary revenues to pay the salaries and other expenses. Our team found several causes for this high dropout rate. Let us start with the teachers. Okello has looked into their salaries while Obongo and Sister Phoebe have actually met with all of them. We have five full-time teachers and four contract teachers. The highest-paid full-time teacher is retiring at the end of this year. Thank God! We will recover 60,000 Shillings every month and that can be used to hire three part-time teachers."

"Mr. Masinde, are you aware that the physics teacher's attendance at the school is very poor?" Okello jumped into the conversation. "Students as well as other teachers reported that this man has his own fishing business and rarely shows up for his scheduled classes."

"Yes Okello," Mr. Masinde admitted. "I have received many complaints. I have spoken to the teacher several times but it does not help. He is a friend of the District Commissioner and..."

"He must be removed from the payroll immediately," Mr. Jackson bellowed. "The District Commissioner is on my advisory board and has been consulted about this matter. He is supportive of my proposal. Further, I have also spoken to the education ministry about this issue as well as the teacher's union. The union has made it clear that they do not stand behind teachers who are cheating. Here is a draft letter to relieve the physics teacher from his job. You need to sign it and send it to the teacher by registered mail." Mr. Jackson handed the draft letter to the headmaster.

"Heyyyy! You people are very very fast," the headmaster stuttered. "You even came prepared with the letter to relieve this man of his job! I wonder how many more such letters you have in your pocket."

"There is also one contract teacher whose attendance is very poor. No letter is needed for him since his contract expires in six weeks anyways," Mr. Jackson added. "And before I forget, the District Commissioner has instructed me to warn you, and everyone here, that no favors should be accorded to anyone claiming to be his friend or relative."

"Once the Physics teacher is relieved of his duties, we will save 40,000 Shillings every month. These funds can be used to hire two more contract teachers," Okello proposed.

"That is a good plan. But there is one problem. Where will we find all these contract teachers?"

"In the best schools and universities of Kenya," Mr. Jackson proclaimed. "I have already lined up ten candidates for these five teaching jobs. All of them have Bachelors degrees in different fields and are looking to enter the teaching profession. Five men and five women – all of them very excited about this opportunity. I have met a few of them in-person and they will be here next week for interviews. We need to select five or even seven of them – the best ones!"

"But are they willing to work for KSh. 20,000 a month?" Mr. Masinde wondered.

"KSh. 20,000 will bring them here for their first job but it is not enough to keep them satisfied. They are very smart people and we need to identify additional opportunities for them to make money. At the end of the day, that is what will keep them at Strong Bamboo and in Kochia."

"I don't understand," Mr. Masinde exclaimed. "We have seen time and time again the problems that arise when teachers start working elsewhere and stop paying attention to their duties here."

"The problem, my friend," Mr. Jackson insisted, "is not the teachers working elsewhere. The problem is that they are not working at the school and no disciplinary action is being taken against them. There is no accountability mechanism whatsoever. Henceforth, the teachers will have to inform the headmaster and fill up a simple form before they engage in additional income generation. You will have to check for conflict of interest. If their school attendance or teaching suffer, they will face disciplinary action. Mr. Masinde, we are proposing a fundamentally different contract. The teacher's salaries will be directly tied to student performance in the exams. I will work out the formulae and the contracts. In essence, when the students don't perform well in the exams, the teacher's salary is cut. When the students do well, the teacher receives a bonus."

"That is surely very harsh."

"So is life. We evolve or we perish."

"Our teachers are not accustomed to such contracts," Mr. Masinde insisted. "And there are so many factors that influence student performance in the exams."

Mr. Jackson smiled. "I assure you that my magic formula will look at class performance and not individual performance."

"I agree with your approach Mr. Jackson," Sister Phoebe said. "But the basic problem with the educational system is the exam-centric approach. And now, through the contracts, we are incentivizing teachers to prepare students to excel in exams. Shouldn't we give more importance to their actual actionable knowledge?"

"I understand your concern," Mr. Jackson said, "but we cannot fight the entire educational system. The only way our students will get admission to college and get jobs, and the only way our school will stay afloat will be by boosting the student's exam scores. Unfortunately, it is the only widely-accepted metric of student success. Hence, I feel that it must be our primary focus. Alongside, we will work to develop their practical knowledge and create pathways to decent livelihoods. However, that cannot take precedence. We are married to the exam-centric educational system., at least for the time being."

"This is very radical. We must consult the contract teachers and see if they will agree with this," Mr. Masinde suggested.

"No, Mr. Headmaster," Mr. Jackson roared. "You will not consult with them, you will inform them. You are the headmaster and you have the authority to propose the terms of the contract to the part-time teachers. The teachers have the right to reject the offer. If you don't feel comfortable, I can do it on your behalf. This school will work only if you become strict, and hold the teachers accountable."

"And you will hold me accountable?" the perplexed headmaster's grin triggered a wave of laughter.

"Indeed," Mr. Jackson confirmed, "and collectively, we are accountable to the students, their parents, and to the community. If there is one thing this country needs, it is accountability and discipline."

Sister Phoebe segued the conversation back to retention. "While poor teaching is a major contributor to lower exam scores and students dropping out of school, there are other issues as well. The best way to retain the students is to create a welcoming and liberating environment where they want to learn from teachers and from each other. In our interviews, we found that students are fearful of teachers, the girls are scared of boys, the contract teachers are scared of the full-time teachers and every single person is scared of exams. This culture of fear is not conducive to learning."

"Sister Phoebe," Mr. Masinde interrupted, "these are all philosophical issues."

"I think some are philosophical, others psychological, but most of them are very practical," Sister Phoebe said. "Some teachers, like the English teacher, are beating the students on a regular basis. This is illegal and must stop immediately. Also, in the past two weeks, several students were sent home and asked to return with the fees. There are three teachers who are appointing themselves as the bursars. This needs to stop as well. We must do everything within our power to keep the students in the classroom."

"I agree with Sister Phoebe," Obongo added. "Many students are dropping out because they fall behind and then find it very difficult to catch up again. Remember, falling behind starts with just one missed class."

Sister Phoebe continued, "This year alone, 59 secondary school girls dropped out. That is a tragic loss to the entire community. Some fell behind due to household chores, or because they had babies to look after, or they did not see the value of their education. Maybe some of them are just lazy. But there are two bigger problems. First, there are no separate toilets for the girls. Infact, even the door of the common toilet was broken and the girls had to run home to use the toilet. They missed classes and fell behind. They did not know whom to complain to. I got the doors repaired for now. Separate clean toilets for the girls must be built at the earliest."

"I was not aware of the broken door," Mr. Masinde admitted. "I will ask the gardener to manage the toilets and report problems. But, we don't have funds to build additional toilets."

"The second challenge is that the girls don't have access to sanitary supplies or medicines for their periods and hence they miss class for several days every month," Sister Phoebe continued.

"Sister," Mr. Masinde exclaimed, "that is a woman's problem. What are we men supposed to do about it? We are digressing from our mission."

"My friend," Mr. Jackson said, "every woman's problem is also a man's problem. We need to keep our young women in school and it is our duty to remove any obstacles in that path."

"The least you can do is acknowledge the problem, sensitize the male teachers, and when girls miss school, design ways for them to catch up again," Sister Phoebe suggested.

"I think that we are really straying from our mission," Mr. Masinde insisted. "What does it have to do with the school's financial problems?"

"Headmaster, let me repeat again," Obongo offered. "When girls miss school, they fall behind in studies. This triggers a vicious cycle. As the arrears build up, their exam scores suffer and they lose confidence and hope, which affects their studies further. Their poor parents get frustrated and pressure them to stay at home. Eventually, they leave school and there is one less fee-paying student. In the past year, we lost 59 girls – that is 885,000 Shillings in lost fees."

"My goodness, Masinde, do we now need to discuss the importance of educating girls?" Mr. Jackson asked sarcastically.

"No, friends," the headmaster apologized. "You know I am a firm believer in women's empowerment through education. But I did not understand the relationship between the women's issues and education. We don't talk about these things very much because it is a taboo in our culture. But now, I understand."

"Now it is my turn Gentlemen," Odhiambo proclaimed with an ear-to-ear grin. "Sister Phoebe, Okello and I have already worked out plans to address these problems. I have inspected the current toilets and I am sorry to report that they are very unhygienic and falling apart. I propose to build two separate toilet blocks – one for boys and one for the girls. There will be four toilets in each block."

"My friend, I could have done that long time back but there is no money," Mr. Masinde explained.

"That is my job!" The story-teller of Kochia stood up and rubbed his hands. "Here is how it will work. My company, Moneymaker Toilets, will pay for the construction of these toilets. We will complete the construction in the next four weeks. The students and the teachers can use the toilets free of cost. But any outsiders will have to pay a small fee, only 10 bob, to use the toilet."

"That won't work," Mr. Masinde declared. "Outsiders are not allowed at the school. No one will pay to use the bathroom. Who will collect the money? Surely you don't want teachers to now become money collectors outside toilets. We will become the laughing stock of Kenya."

"Odhiambo's company now has 20 toilets and they are all making money," Okello said. "The school is not liable in any way. So, let us please let the man talk."

"When Obongo was explaining the vicious cycle about students, I realized that the toilet is just like the school. The toilets need proper cleaning and maintenance. When the toilet cleaning falls behind, it becomes difficult to clean, and then it falls behind further. It gets worse and worse over time and spreads disease. People quickly get diseases, especially we Luos, and then we die. That's one less fee-paying customer for the toilet."

The headmaster was not particularly pleased about the analogy but chose to remain silent. The rest of the team struggled to suppress a smile.

"We need a person to actively manage and clean the toilets. This person will be our employee and we will pay her. She will be responsible for collecting the payments from customers."

"So, you are using my school to make money! What will people say?" the headmaster argued. "How does this address the problem of the women's periods?"

"The people will say that the headmaster is ingenious! You provide land. We build the toilet. Your students use it free of cost and we provide a paid service to outsiders. The income generated is used to keep the toilets hygienic for your children and the customers. Every girl in the secondary school will get up to six sanitary pads from the toilet-keeper every month completely free. We just need the list of female students from you every year. The toilets will be built on the edge of the playground near the vacant building. That is very close to the main road and we will attract very many customers."

"Mr. Masinde," Okello asked, "there is one vacant building towards the edge of the playground. What do you plan to do with it?"

"Nothing. That little building has been vacant for very many years. Now that you have asked, I am very sure you have made some plans for it!"

"Indeed!" Okello smiled. "We want to move the computers there. We will conduct lessons for secondary school students in the morning and use it as an internet café for outsiders in the afternoon and evening."

"Who will pay the electricity bill?"

"I will pay the electricity bill, the internet charges, the salary of the caretaker and the computer teacher. Owiti will manage the internet café and teach the students for the first six months."

"What if a computer breaks?"

"We will repair it."

"What if it gets stolen?"

"First, Owiti will break the man's head. Then, we will replace the stolen equipment."

"The internet café is a very good plan. That will boost our business as well." Odhiambo was delighted. "If you can sell soda at the internet café, I will really appreciate."

"Let me give you another reason to support our plan," Okello offered. "Right now, you are paying 70,000 Shillings on exam papers every few months. Owiti will do it for only 50,000 Shillings."

"How is that even possible?"

"He will take the money in advance and buy an integrated printer and photocopier. Owiti will do the layout for the exams on his computer and get the printouts. We will do it in a way that there is absolute secrecy. After the first exam, subsequent exams will cost under 20,000 Shillings!"

"All this talk of business is difficult for me to digest. I will need to sleep over it."

"Sure headmaster, we understand that these are a lot of new ideas. But, we have spent hours debating the proposals before we came to you. We think that this is the only way we can provide clean toilets and computer education to all the students and the necessary supplies to the girls. We are taking the risk, not you. We are promising you these services for two years. Also, all our business records will be available to the oversight committee for review."

"…and surely, Mr. Jackson will be auditing them." Mr. Masinde smiled. "So I am not worried about that. But I still need time to understand everything. It seems to me that we have solved all the problems. I congratulate…"

"Not so soon," Sister Phoebe interjected. "We have a few more issues to discuss. I will go back to my favorite subject – the challenge of retaining the students. It is essential that we implement some health education program for the students. Particularly, we need to conduct de-worming drives and educational workshops on HIV/AIDS, adolescence, hygiene and related topics. The girls, in particular, need to be counseled on healthy relationships and sexual activity. We must act to prevent them from engaging in transactional sex and relationships with older men. As most of you know, I do a lot of HIV/AIDS work and also conduct workshops. If the headmaster is willing, I would be glad to conduct these workshops at Strong Bamboo after school hours."

"Very good. That would be very kind of you. I would further request you to also conduct workshops for the teachers and sensitize them to these issues," Mr. Masinde urged. "I will attend it myself. I think I am now starting to understand the connection between student's health, educational achievement, school economics and socio-economic progress of our community and country."

"Since we are nearing the final exams, we will start the workshops in the new academic year. I will identify the topics and start developing the content," Sister Phoebe promised.

Mr. Jackson, who was sitting back in his chair and staring out of the window for the past 30 minutes spoke up, "We have discussed methods to incentivize and motivate the teachers, the toilet keeper, the internet café manager, and everyone else…except the children. The question in my mind is: how do we motivate the students to study?"

"We must also recognize that for teachers and everyone else, financial incentive is not necessarily adequate," Sister Phoebe remarked. "I did not become a nun to make more money."

"And neither did I start Moneymaker Toilets to get rich overnight," Odhiambo added.

"When I was a child, the one thing I never learned," Obongo lamented, "was to push a tire with a stick. I tried every day. I never succeeded. Never understood why. It caused me a lot of emotional distress and my confidence level dropped. I would cry every time I saw other children playing with tires. Last week, at Strong Bamboo primary, I found the answer. I always played with my tire alone. At the school, there were twelve children playing with it. They took turns without fighting even once. One boy would push the tire and run with it. The rest of the boys, all ran behind him. My friend, Mr. Jackson, will say that it is very inefficient. But, the older boys taught the little ones how to run with the tire. When a boy failed, the others would encourage him and build his confidence to try again, that very moment. THAT VERY MOMENT – that is important. They tried and tried and eventually they succeeded. The secret was the unconditional non-stop motivation from their friends."

Yes, you are very right," Mr. Masinde's wife jumped with excitement. "I have been married to a school teacher, and hence a school, for the last 27 years. Every day, I spend an hour or two talking to students struggling with their studies. Especially the ones who have been thrown out of class by teachers. When I talk to the children, I just motivate them and tell them inspirational stories and try to build their confidence. Now I am so popular, that when students are punished, they come straight to me for some motivation and support. It is my unpaid job. It actually works very well. It also works with my husband. Just today morning, he was so upset and..."

"That is enough I think," the embarrassed headmaster urged.

"I have an idea," Okello offered. "Sister Phoebe, remember you told me how the elderly residents at your center get bored and want to venture out and talk to people? I am thinking, can we bring them here once every week to cheer and motivate the students...and the teachers? There is a Professor Mitra in England who has successfully implemented a similar concept before. I saw his TED talk on the internet."

"Yes, we can try that," Sister Phoebe laughed, "but most of my people are uneducated. They will not understand anything that is going on in the classroom."

"I have only studied up to fourth grade, the headmaster's wife confided. "Education does not matter...we just need to hug them, talk to them, praise them a little, pat their back, and encourage them."

"I think we should certainly try this," Mr. Jackson concurred. "But in parallel, we also need to have monthly meetings with the school teachers, students, their parents, and our committee. This will serve many purposes. We can formally recognize and motivate students, engage the parents in their children's education, and exert some social pressure on parents defaulting on fees. The teachers can also learn about the children's background and living conditions and teach them better. It doesn't cost the school anything at all and strengthens the community."

"I am very pleased. This will generate a lot of business for the toilets," Odhiambo grinned.

"I support the idea because it is perfectly aligned with the philosophy of a harambee school," the headmaster concurred, "and I think that it might even be an appropriate venue for our students to become teachers…and tell us about their problems and provide suggestions. They can also rally behind Obongo as he fulfills his life-long ambition of learning to push a tire."

"There are a few complicated problems in the world which have simple solutions," Sister Phoebe mused. "I learned that some of the teachers don't use the blackboards because the chalk is not provided to them and they are unwilling to spend 5 bob from their pocket to buy chalk. We can have computers and cellphones and all these other things, but as far as learning is concerned, we must not underestimate the power and influence a teacher has with chalk in her hands and curious minds in front of her. That's where we separated paths from other animals millions of years ago, and I think, the teacher with the chalk will wield just as much power thousands of years forth."

Sister Phoebe's narrative was met by claps, shouts and tears. Mr. Masinde was too overcome with emotion to give another long-winded thank you speech. With folded hands, he peered into each of his friends' eyes to convey his gratitude. It took him a few days to understand the business side of things and the necessity of money changing hands to sustain the toilets, the computer training, and the school. Strong Bamboo Secondary School was thus re-envisioned, re-vitalized, and re-organized.

Mr. Jackson delivered on his promise of funding the 50 extremely impoverished students. At a modest ceremony at the end of the academic year, these children and their families were commended for their perseverance and given educational scholarships. During the second year, the school had sufficient funds to provide their own scholarships to those in need. Mr. Jackson helped the skeptical headmaster negotiate the new contracts with the teachers. The teachers were actually quite receptive to the idea of linking their salaries to student performance. They preferred it over the tyranny of being indentured to the school at a low salary and not being allowed to officially and proudly engage in additional income-generating activities. Obongo personally supervised the repairs at the school. He never learned how to push a tire. The Moneymaker Toilets were commissioned within a month and the customary Bible was placed on top of each building. Odhiambo's net profit from these toilets exceeded 30,000 Shillings every month. He happily spent half the amount (~100 Shillings/student/month) on

Annual Awards and Motivation Ceremony at Strong Bamboo

sanitary napkins for the secondary school girls. Painkillers were also made available free of cost to girls who needed them. The great story-teller reveled in talking about his exploits with sanitary napkins at every school function, community gathering, wedding or funeral. It caused the headmaster, the teachers, the students, and their parents, very many uncomfortable moments. However, thanks to his efforts, it was not a taboo topic in Kochia anymore.

Owiti helped jumpstart the internet café and computer classes at the school. He saved the school boatloads of money that was previously spent on printing exam papers. Inquiries for new admissions at Strong Bamboo skyrocketed when news about the free computer classes and well-educated teachers spread. Many of the girls who had dropped out re-enrolled at the school. Sister Phoebe's workshops on relationships and adolescence were well-received by the students and teachers alike. Sister Phoebe was a tad bit irritated by the numerous requests from students for Odhiambo to conduct the workshops in her place. She encountered several problems with having elders from her center visit the Strong Bamboo school once a week to praise and motivate the children and teachers. Parents were concerned because most of the residents were HIV positive. After a series of educational workshops and promises that the residents would never actually touch the students, the parents agreed to the plan. The program was so successful that several neighboring schools also requested the motivational service. The residents quickly instituted a daily "praising fee" of 50 Shillings for children and 100 Shillings for adults. Sister Phoebe was disappointed by the blatant commercialization of motivation. Okello suggested celebrating the entrepreneurial spirit of the terminally-ill patients rather than despairing over the inevitable evolution of community values. The headmaster eventually agreed that the oversight committee was very beneficial to himself and the school. A year later, work had commenced to build science laboratories at the Strong Bamboo Secondary School. Since that day, Mr. Masinde fondly referred to the four-hour meeting on Sunday afternoon as his "Harambee MBA."

#8

The Fisherman's Sweet Fate

"I have not heard from my brother Phillip since the last fourteen months," Paul Otieno agonized. "Peter and I have searched for him everywhere."

"We have asked all his neighbors, all the fishermen in Ngegu, and even the fish mongers." Peter Omondi's voice trembled as tears welled up in his eyes. "We have checked with the police and inquired with the morgues, all the way up to Kisii and Kisumu."

"Mr. Obongo," Paul pleaded, "we have come to you for assistance because my brother Phillip spoke very highly of you. He told me that you knew everyone in Nyanza and could help us."

"Pole sana," Obongo commiserated, "I have not heard from Phillip in a very long time either. He used to be very active in our Empower Kochia Group. Everyone liked him. Then he just stopped paying the monthly dues and coming to the meetings. I tried to reach him several times but he was nowhere to be found. You might remember I visited you in Homa Bay once when I was trying to locate him."

"Yes. That was just a few weeks after he disappeared. I thought he would come back in due time. He has disappeared for a few weeks in the past but he always come back. I thought he might have gone to Nairobi to spend some time with our elder brother, Paul. People said that he had been seen often with a Kikuyu woman. So I thought he must have gone with her to central Kenya. But now, it is over a year and we cannot hold back any longer. Please do whatever you can to help us find Phillip."

"I am happy to help you," Obongo offered, "but I am not sure what I can do. You have already asked everyone about Phillip and…"

"Just come with us," Peter cut in. "Your presence will help us get more information. My brother has a car. Twende[1]. Twende."

"Right now?" Obongo was a little surprised.

"Yes, we cannot wait any further." Peter pressed Obongo's hand. "Paul has to go back to Nairobi tomorrow evening to resume his duties."

"You waited fourteen months to come here and now you can't even wait for some tea?" Janet walked in from the kitchen with three cups of hot chai on a white plastic tray." Have some chai and then you can proceed."

"Yes, we should have come here earlier. Days became weeks and weeks became months. You know how it is." Peter smiled politely as he picked up the tea. "Erokamano[2]."

"Phillip is the youngest in our family and has always been very impulsive and unpredictable," Paul remarked. "What is most surprising to me is that on one hand, he loves Ngegu and fishing so much, and then he just disappears like this. In my heart, I am very sure that Phillip is alive and well."

"Amen," the group chorused.

Everyone stood up for a brief prayer led by Janet. The brothers and Obongo then jumped into Paul's tiny car and started off on their quest.

"I think we must go to Ngegu first," Obongo proposed. "That is where Phillip lived and all the fishermen knew him well. We can follow his trail from there."

"I talked to them last week," Peter said. "They insisted that they did not know where he was."

"Instead of asking whether they have seen Phillip, we should delve into the circumstances around his disappearance," Obongo suggested. "Let us assume that he is fine and has left Kochia by his own free will. We need to find out what compelled him to leave and where he might have gone. Like Paul said, Phillip really enjoyed fishing. So, he is likely to be somewhere along the shores of the lake."

A twenty-minute ride on the bumpy roads of Kochia followed by a very brief and smooth drive on the newly-completed highway brought the trio to the small fishing village of Ngegu. Peter and Paul looked over the placid waters of the majestic lake, the second-largest freshwater lake in the world. A few fishermen were sitting by the shore sorting their morning catch of Tilapia and Rockfish. They recognized Obongo immediately and struck up a conversation. A quick round of introductions followed.

"Phillip was a good man. He lived right here," a fisherman said,

---

[1] Twende = Let's go (Kiswahili)
[2] Erokamano = Thank you (Dholuo)

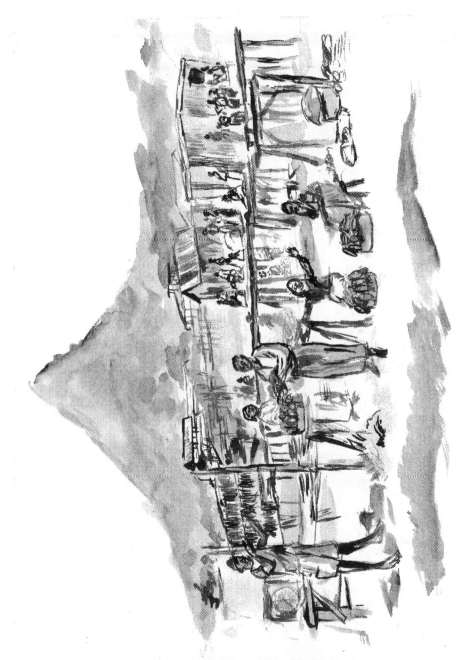

Fishmongers in Homa Bay

pointing to a tiny shack overlooking the beach. "His home has been empty ever since he left last year."

"The door is open. Where are all his belongings?" Peter asked.

"I think he left with some of his personal belongings. There is a bed, some clothes, cooking utensils, and other miscellaneous things still lying inside. Just the way he left it. We are very proud people here. No one will take something that does not belong to him," the fisherman assured.

"Phillip liked fishing and was very good at it. Could he have gone to a different place where there are more fish?" Obongo asked.

"Actually, he did not come fishing with us. His fishing friends were all in Homa Bay and he sold his fish there because it fetched more money," a fisherman explained. "What I find very surprising is that his boat is right here. The green one named 'Nam Lolwe Queen' is his. It is actually a very good boat – worth more than 30,000 Shillings."

"That is odd. Why did he not take his boat or sell it?" Paul wondered, "Do you think he left on his own free will or was there foul play?"

"We don't know. We have heard rumors that he got into trouble with the fisheries officers in Homa Bay. Also, he was often seen with a Kikuyu woman. She even came here and lived with him. They seemed happy together. But she was still a Kikuyu who stole a Luo man's heart. You can call it foul play if you like." The fisherman chuckled.

"Was he making good money fishing?" Paul's simple question seemed to fire up the fishermen.

"We don't know about him. Right now, all fishermen are unhappy. The water hyacinth has come back again. It grows very very fast and chokes our boats and also the fish. It takes us at least 45 minutes of hard work chopping the vegetation to reach the open waters. By the time we get there we are already so tired."

"The Nile Perch are also becoming very difficult to catch. We barely get one or two big ones in a week. Until six months back, we would go out and come back with 2-3 big Nile Perch every trip. But now, they are all gone."

"The fisheries people are making things very difficult for us. There are always new rules on the nets we can use and what fish we can catch. Yaai yai yaai!"

"Several of our colleagues have abandoned their work and now they are doing small jobs in Homa Bay and other towns. Maybe Phillip took up an office job somewhere too?"

"We should go to Homa Bay and speak to Phillip's friends right away," Obongo suggested. They thanked the fishermen and rushed out to the car. Thirty minutes later, they were talking to a small crowd of

A Fisherman Mending his Nets

fishmongers at the market in Homa Bay. These women, young and old, purchased fish from the fishermen, cleaned it, deboned, gutted or filleted it as necessary, and sold it on the makeshift tables at the marketplace. All the women recognized Phillip immediately, either by name, as the owner of the Nam Lolwe Queen, or from the photo that Paul was carrying with him.

"We haven't seen him here for some time. He was such an honest man. He would always sell us fish at a good price and not expect anything in return but the agreed sum of money."

"Some of the other fishermen know that we depend on them for our livelihoods and survival. They make us sleep with them before they will sell us their fish. But Phillip was a good man. If the Kikuyu woman would not have won his heart, I would have surely taken him as husband."

"Phillip helped us all by lodging a police complaint against the corrupt traffic police. This policeman would arrest us when we were transporting the fish to the market by claiming the fish were immature. We had to give him 200 – 300 Shillings every day as a bribe. There was little profit left for us then. We are poor people. Now there is not much Nile Perch either. Once Phillip lodged a complaint with the police, this corrupt man was transferred."

"He had some problem with the fisheries people. I think you should talk to other fishermen or just go to the fisheries office. It is very close – just five minutes on the road to Kisumu."

Paul spotted a young fisherman mending his nets by the lakeside. He was eager to talk and expressed that he would himself like to know what became of Phillip.

"He is my friend. We often went out on the lake together," the fisherman informed. "Then last year, the fisheries people came and took away his nets. They said that the nets were smaller than the prescribed size. Phillip went to the fisheries office and spoke to everyone but they would not listen to him."

"Tch, Phillip was very honest since he was a child." Paul protested. "I cannot believe that he was breaking the rules. I grew up here and I know the fisheries people are very unfair. They can even impound your boat. Phillip is not the kind of person who would do something so stupid."

"Aye," the young man raised his chin and affirmed. "The fisheries people decide what to do. Sometimes they will let you go with a warning and sometimes they will take your nets or even take away your boat. They take you to the judge. You have to pay a lot of money in bribes or fines to get your nets back. Every few months, they burn the nets and everything else they have confiscated from the fishermen. Some people even end up in prison. Have you…err checked in the prison, just in case?"

"My brother cannot be in prison," Paul growled. "Phillip owned a good boat. If indeed he was in error, he could have paid the fines and extricated himself from the problem."

"Indeed," the young man agreed. "Most of us here actually just work on someone else's boat and get a small portion of the catch in return. Phillip's boat was very good. After his nets were taken away, he was trying to get a loan to buy a new net. I could not help him because I did not have enough money."

"How much does a net cost? What amount was he looking for?" Paul inquired.

"He never said. The regular net costs 720 bob and lasts five years. The Chinese one costs 400 bob but lasts only two years. Even if he selected the Chinese nets, it would cost 8,000 Shillings. We need to go deeper into the lake nowadays and need to tie at least 20 nets together."

"He would certainly have to go to a bank or a fishing cooperative for that amount," Obongo remarked. "We can go and inquire there."

"I think you must first go and talk to the fisheries people," the fisherman suggested. "After his nets were taken away, I saw him 3-4 times. He went to the fisheries office many times. Then he just disappeared. No one knows where he went."

The trio thanked the young man and headed to the fisheries offices. They felt energized and much more confident in their search now.

"Yes, I remember Phillip." The elderly gentleman at the Fisheries office leaned back in his chair. "Our officers conduct regular inspections of the fishing boats and the nets. The net size must be larger than 5 inches for Tilapia and 8 inches for Nile Perch. Phillip and his friends were using a 4 inch net for Tilapia. We warned them about it twice and then the third time, we had to impound his nets."

"What difference does it make whether the net is four inches or five inches?" Paul asked angrily.

"A very big difference! We don't want to catch the small fish. We want them to get bigger, spawn a lot of eggs and then get caught once they are mature. This is important to ensure a sustainable supply of fish from the lake."

"All the fishermen we talked to insist that it is getting difficult to catch fish," Paul retorted. "So what are they supposed to do?"

"Follow the rules." The officer smiled. "We are here to help them in the longer-term. Our fishermen don't understand the harm they are causing by using finer nets and catching the fingerlings. Some of them use chemicals like methylene and propylene to intoxicate and kill the fish. The poor fish go blind and float on the water. Then they collect them and take them to the market. Then people eat these fish and fall sick. Some fishermen use monofilament nets. These result in a higher catch but they are very cruel to the fish. If only they follow all the rules—"

"How much is the fine? Did Phillip try to pay the fine and get the nets back?" Paul interrupted the officer's lecture.

"The fine is about 30,000 Shillings or six months to two years in jail," the officer said. "Phillip tried to aggregate the funds for the fine but he did not succeed. I told him that—"

"Does it mean that you sent him to prison?" Paul asked.

"No, we don't put people in prison unless it is a very extreme situation. The fishermen with the monofilament nets – we have sent some of them to prison. Every month we get about 20 such cases and we just confiscate their nets and burn them in a big bonfire."

"Why do you burn them? That does not help anyone!"

"If the nets are here, then the fishermen try to bribe our people and that creates more problems for us. So, we just burn them. It works very well. We have very few repeat offenders."

"Surely – if you take away their nets and boats and burn them, the poor fishermen will never be able to fish again or offend again," Peter protested.

"So, when did you see Phillip last?" Obongo asked.

"He came the day we burned the nets and pleaded to me. He said that he had these nets for a long time and when the rules changed, he did not have the money to buy new nets as per the new rules. He was very sad but he talked to me very nicely and apologized several times. I felt sorry for him but I was helpless. After that, I did not see him again."

"This seems like a dead end," Peter sighed. "I don't know where to go next, Mr. Obongo. There is no point talking to banks since Phillip was not successful in getting the funds to regain ownership of his nets. Even if he talked to the banks, they would not know where he is now."

"We are grateful for your time, Sir," Paul addressed the officer, "and we apologize on our brother's behalf. We understand that what he did was wrong and hurts everyone."

"There is no need to apologize. The fishermen are suffering due to various problems and we are here to help them now and in the longer term. Sometimes we have to be harsh but…" The officer started rambling again and then got up with a start as his eyes fell on his watch. "I am already late for a meeting at the lakeside. The entire beach management unit will be there. Some of them, I believe, are good friends with Phillip. They were all caught together with the small nets. You are welcome to come with me if you want to talk to them."

"Let us go," Obongo said. "We can all fit inside this humble car."

Ten minutes later, the four of them alighted from the car at the end of the drivable road and started a fifteen-minute walk to the beach.

"Do you see the water hyacinth?" The officer pointed to the dark green vegetation enveloping the lake. "The fishermen are troubled because it blocks the beaches and makes it difficult for the boats to go into the water. It grows very fast. Even after all that hard work of pushing the boats through the thick growth to get to the water, the fishermen come back almost empty-handed."

"Why is that?" Obongo was intrigued. "Surely the hyacinth is not eating up the fish!"

"Actually it is," the officer explained. "The fish need the oxygen dissolved in the water. The hyacinth saps oxygen from the water, making it difficult for the fish to survive. The other big problem is that the nets get entangled in the vegetation and are destroyed. The poor fishermen then have to buy new ones or borrow nets from friends. But now, you see, so many nets have been lost that fishermen have started migrating to the cities in search of jobs."

"Yaai yai yaai! I remember we had a similar crisis several years back. How was the problem resolved at that time?" Obongo asked.

"No one is completely sure but we think that the biological solution worked the best. A certain kind of weevil was set free into the hyacinth and this weevil population gradually consumed the weed."

"That seems like a very cost-effective solution. But what if the weevil starts eating regular crops?"

"That is something we are always worried about with biological solutions. It is the better of the bad options. Earlier, we used chemical solutions like pesticides to eliminate the weeds but they pollute the water and cause various diseases in the long-term. The weevils also pose a small risk but they are much better than pesticides."

"Can the weevils also propagate any illnesses?"

"Not the weevils…but the water itself is a problem. The hyacinth impedes the flow of water and the stagnant water then becomes a breeding ground for mosquitos, snakes, and other marine organisms. In some other parts along the lake shore, there has been a rise in the incidence of malaria, filaria, bilharzia, and even typhoid because of the water hyacinth."

"I was aware of the problem but did not realize how it deeply impacts the people's livelihoods as well as their health," Obongo remarked. "We only have a small portion of the lake. It must impact Uganda and Tanzania even more than us. Are you coordinating with them?"

"The only Ugandan I am coordinating with, is my wife." The officer laughed. "And, believe me, it is very difficult at times. I hope that the ministries are coordinating but it is a very complicated problem. It impacts many different ministries and departments – agriculture, fisheries, trade and commerce, water resources, transportation, rural employment, health, environment and even the military."

"That is good. So now all these ministries are trying to solve the problem and putting their resources to good use."

"On the contrary, now no one is sure what problem they need to handle and what the correct communication channels are. When internal communication is so difficult, international coordination, I am sure, will be even more so."

"Maybe, they need to form another ministry for water hyacinth," Obongo joked.

"Surely. The ministries are like our matatus. They have a common motto – there is always room for one more," the officer retorted.

"How do you plan to solve the problem this time?" Obongo asked. "Will you be releasing the weevils again?"

"We have been notified by the central administration that American scientists have found a particular weevil in South America which is perfect for our purpose. American and Kenyan scientists will be coming here in two weeks to make the final decision and take action."

"So you are meeting with the fishermen to inform them about how you will solve the problem?" Paul joined the conversation.

"Not exactly. We have a small problem here. All the fishermen want to have this hyacinth removed immediately. They see it as a threat to their survival. But these two people insist that the weevils should not be used and they have lodged an official request with the beach management unit. It is beyond my understanding why they are taking such a foolish stance," the officer grumbled. "They are just wasting everyone's time."

"What is a beach management unit?" Obongo asked.

"It is a community-based system for resource management of the lake. Every beach has its own BMU consisting of representative fishermen, boat owners, fish traders, boat builders, net menders, net sellers, fish processors, etc. and it is coordinated by the fisheries ministry. The BMU is responsible for educating all the relevant stakeholders about their interaction with the lake. They also make all the rules and enforce them. If someone has a problem, they report it to the BMU. There is a discussion about the problem and then the entire unit makes a decision. My job is to make sure that the decisions align with the relevant laws. I am also responsible for coordinating between the ministry and the BMUs."

"That is certainly a very different approach. Does it work?"

"Earlier, the fishermen did not like us too much. In fact, during the post-election violence, they completely burned down our offices and all our records. But community-based management works much better than traditional policing models. Now the BMUs understand the realities that drive our decisions and they educate the rest of the people about the importance of following the rules. This approach has been very successful for all of us."

A few minutes later, the officer and his newly-formed friends were greeted by the BMU at the beach. Twelve members of the BMU had come over for the discussion on the hyacinth issue. After a round of warm handshakes, they settled under the shade of a small tree. Sensing Paul and Peter's anxiety about finding their brother, the fisheries officer started the meeting with a query about Phillip's whereabouts. Everyone indicated that they knew Phillip well but had not heard from him since he disappeared a year back.

"I am very sorry that there is no good news for you," the officer turned to Paul and sympathized. "Why don't you give me your phone number and if I get any new information, I will contact you immediately." Peter dictated his phone number to the officer. The officer entered it into his phone and gave Peter a missed call. Meanwhile the head of the BMU had called the meeting to order, welcomed the group and urged a young man to put forth his grievances without further delay. The scorching sun, the high humidity, and the series of disappointing news had taken their toll on Peter, Paul and Obongo. They turned around and scanned the tiny huts on the shore for a soda shop. Finding none, they looked at each other and slowly started their walk towards Peter's car.

"My name is Benson. I have been sent here by my boss, Mr. Phillip. He spoke to the chairperson of the BMU last week and requested..." the young man's words trailed off as Peter ran towards him with extraordinary energy.

"Hey!!!" Peter shrieked, "you just said that you don't know Phillip's whereabouts. And now you are talking about him."

The young man, visibly shaken up by Peter's sudden rush towards him and angry demeanor, blurted out, "I know five different Phillips.

There are very many of them in Rongo. If you come there with me, I will surely introduce you to all of them."

"So, you are from Rongo?" Peter asked.

"Yes, I grew up in Kericho but now I work in Rongo."

"Where is Mr. Phillip from?"

"He is from Rongo. Everyone knows him there."

"OK" Peter sheepishly stepped back. "We are just trying to find my brother. Sorry."

"Phillip is a very common name around here." Obongo agreed and then looked at Peter and Paul. "If you gentlemen don't mind, I would like to stay here for a few minutes to learn about this issue."

"Sure," Peter shrugged, "Paul and I will wait over there in the shade. It is very hot here."

"We must proceed," the chairperson of the BMU suggested. "Some of us have to go back to work in the afternoon. Please, Mr. Benson."

"So, I was saying that...," Benson drawled, "my boss, Mr. Phillip spoke to the chairperson yesterday and requested that your BMU be kind enough not to deprive us of the vegetation..."

"Hey!" an old fisherman roared, "Did you say deprive? Is that what you said? This vegetation is depriving us of our food and our livelihoods. If we don't find a solution, we will perish. Our children, our women, will all die. We are the ones being deprived because of this hyacinth."

"Please calm down, baba," the chairperson intervened. "Mr. Benson, you must appreciate the time and opportunity we are giving you. Can you please get straight to the point?"

"I want your permission to remove the vegetation and take it away from the lake," Benson requested.

"Who are you? What are you saying? This is a lot of vegetation. All the way up to there." The chairperson stretched out his hand towards the horizon. "How will you take it and what will you do with it?"

"Our fisheries officer will confirm that pesticides will harm the fish and pollute the water. It will also harm your sukuma crops when you use lake water for irrigation. Your families will fall sick when you drink the water. The biological solution with weevils is better than pesticides but it also has its own problems. Instead, we will bring our trucks over here with eight to ten people to physically remove the vegetation and take it away. And we will do it without any cost to you. Totally free."

"But, what will you do with it?"

"Don't worry about that. We are solving your problem."

"It will take you months or even years to remove it physically. We cannot wait so long."

"Actually, we will carve out a way for you to reach the lake in just two days. We have a boat that can go out in the water and start chopping off the hyacinth. In one month, over half of the hyacinth will be gone. If you don't believe me, I can put you through to the chairperson of a BMU near Kendu Bay. Our trucks are there right now."

"When will you start?" the puzzled chairperson inquired.

"It is 12:30pm right now. We will have one truck here at 2 PM to start the work. From tomorrow onwards, there will be two trucks and about fifteen people working all day."

"By the time you remove it, more hyacinth would have grown."

"No problem. We will keep clearing it quickly and only keep the minimum as suggested by the fisheries people."

"We don't want any of it. Not a single plant," the old man declared.

"Actually, Benson is right," the fisheries officer jumped in. "The water hyacinth is also helping us in a few ways. If the hyacinth were not there, the lake would be covered with algae, which would consume all the oxygen and destroy the fish. Also, the hyacinth helps various species of cichlids grow and it protects the small fish from the Nile Perch. So we must actually preserve some of the hyacinth."

"And the marshy areas where the hyacinth grows is also where a lot of Tilapia are born. We don't want to disrupt their lifecycles or that will be the end of our Tilapia supply," Benson chimed in.

The chairperson turned to his group. "This is certainly a very unusual situation. I am not sure what to think about it."

The old fisherman turned to Benson again. "Even for a moment if we believe you, that you will take the vegetation away, why don't you tell us what you will do with it?"

"Why do you worry about that, baba? You will be able to go to the lake again. That is all you should care about. Just trust me," Benson reassured.

"Officer, what do you think? Do we have the mandate to let this gentleman take the hyacinth?" the chairperson turned to the fisheries officer.

"Indeed! It is your lake. I don't have any objection whether you give him the permission or not."

"But, what is your personal opinion?"

"I think there is no harm in letting Benson do as he says. As of now, we must be realistic. We really don't have a solution in the short-term. Benson has promised to start work very fast. Our scientists will come here in two weeks. But they have said that twice in the past. I have been told that they have a very effective biological solution. When they come, if the vegetation is still here, we can let them implement their solution."

"OK, then," the chairperson proposed, "before we proceed to vote, does anyone have any questions?"

For the next thirty minutes, another round of questioning on what Benson would do with the hyacinth followed. Benson repeated his stance three times while Peter and Paul came back and settled down next to Obongo. They found the discussion fairly entertaining.

Finally, the frustrated chairperson forced a vote on the topic. The BMU voted 7-5 to let Benson commence his work. Five individuals voted in the negative because Benson refused to clarify what he would do with the vegetation. The meeting thus ended around 1:30 PM and the BMU members went their separate ways.

"I hope you find your brother soon. If I hear anything, I will certainly call you." The officer promised Paul. He shook hands with everyone and started walking towards the main road.

I must inform Okello about this hyacinth issue. But, first I need to find out more, Obongo thought to himself. He stayed back to talk to Benson. "Hello, Mr. Benson, Obongo is my name. I am the head of the Empower Kochia Group. I want to talk to you more about your hyacinth project."

"It is nice to meet you Mr. Obongo. However, let me tell you – there is nothing more I can share."

"Whom can I speak to about it?"

"The only person who can provide you more information is Mr. Phillip himself."

"Why don't you give me his phone number and I will call him right now. That way I can also find out if he knows anything about the Phillip we are looking for."

"Mr. Phillip is in an important meeting with the engineer until 3 PM. If you give me your phone number, I will pass it on."

"What if we come with you to Rongo in the afternoon?" Obongo proposed.

"You are very curious people here in Homa Bay," Benson smiled. "Let me assure you that it is of no use. I will take the truck there in the evening and empty all the vegetation into one big field. Then, there are three workers who take it inside the workshop. Even I don't have permission to go inside there. I don't know what happens there and neither will you. Wambui supervises the operations herself."

"Who is Wambui?"

"She is Mr. Phillip's wife. And please don't tell me that you want to go talk to her today because she is also in the meeting with the engineer.

Anyways, now I must go." Benson took Obongo's number and scurried off towards Homa Bay town with his ear pressed against the phone, barking out orders.

Obongo was too excited to wait for two hours for Mr. Phillip to call back. The next steps were very clear in his mind. He turned to Peter and Paul, who were now getting ready to abandon their search and head home.

"Gentlemen, I propose that we immediately go over to my friend Okello's house. He can give us the best advice on what to do next."

"I think we are just wasting time and petrol," Peter sighed. "I think that we must search for Phillip in Central Kenya now. We must try to find out more about the Kikuyu woman."

"On the contrary, I think we are back on his trail and should be able to find him soon. Didn't you hear Mr. Phillip's wife's name? Wambui is a very common name amongst Kikuyus."

"I like your optimism Mr. Obongo," Peter said, "but why would Phillip go to Rongo and never come back. Rongo is barely an hour away. Also, I don't think he will get involved with this hyacinth business. That cannot be. But if you insist, we can talk to your friend."

"I insist. Okello is the best problem solver in Kochia, maybe even Nyanza or Kenya. Also, I would not be surprised if...if..." Obongo's eyes lit up. "Let us please proceed to Kochia immediately."

The three of them packed themselves into Peter's tiny car and headed to Okello's residence.

"We have been expecting you." Okello burst into laughter as he opened the door. He stepped aside so that Paul, Peter, and Obongo could be face to face with Phillip.

"My God! Phillip!" Peter screamed as he ran to his brother and held him by the shoulders. "Thank God, you are alive! Where have you been all this time?" Paul incoherently mumbled before he was overcome with emotion. The brothers spent the next ten minutes coming to terms with the fact that Phillip had been found and was in good health. As a bonus, they even got to meet his girlfriend, Wambui, for the first time. Wambui's greetings in fragmented Dholuo were adequate to impress Peter and Paul. They warmly welcomed her to the family.

"Mr. Obongo, you are a genius," Peter stammered in disbelief. "Not only did you find out where Phillip was, but you even brought us here immediately. How is that possible?"

"Peter and I were with you the entire time, but we completely failed to follow your chain of thought," Paul joined Peter in thanking Obongo.

"To be honest, I am a little surprised to see Phillip too," Obongo admitted. "I was expecting to see only Okello here. But when Benson said that his boss had a meeting with an engineer, there was a glimmer of hope that he might be referring to Okello. We don't have very many engineers around here. But Okello, you said that you were expecting us?"

"Benson, in his characteristic style, sent me a long text message about his meeting with all of you," Phillip informed the group. He passed on Obongo's phone number to me. Okello and I were just talking about the message when you knocked on the door."

"So Benson was lying to us all along!" Paul fumed.

"No, Benson is a very honest chap. He does not know that I come from this area. In fact, only two or three people know about it."

"Okello, surely you knew. You did not bring this to my attention either," Obongo complained.

"Infact, I was shocked, just like you, when I met Phillip a few hours ago," Okello said. "I was supposed to meet a Mr. Phillip from Rongo about some machinery and when I opened the door, it was none other than our own Phillip."

"And you did not even tell your brothers about your whereabouts. We were so worried. Imagine how difficult it was for us to make inquiries at hospitals and morgues. This is most unfair," Paul reprimanded his younger brother.

"I apologize," Phillip replied earnestly. "I am clearly at fault and I am very sorry for causing all of you this heartache. It is a long chain of events and if you give me some time, I can tell you how things unfolded."

"Please tell us right now," Peter urged. "We have been dying to know where you have been."

The three brothers, Obongo and Okello settled around the dinner table while Wambui prepared tea for everyone.

"My problems started when I was caught by the fisheries people for using the wrong size net to catch Tilapia. It was my fault. I was aware that the rules had changed but I did not have the money to buy new nets. I wish the authorities would provide loans, or at least give us some time, to switch over to the new size nets. They just come up with new rules and expect us to follow them with very short notice. The fine amount was about the same as the cost of the net itself. I went and pleaded to the fisheries officer but despite his sympathies, he could not help me."

"We actually met him just this morning and he was very supportive."

"Yes, he is a good man," Phillip concurred, "but he was bound by his duties. Six of us were caught. Three got their nets back by hook or crook and went back to fishing. One went to Nairobi in search of a job and one ended up doing petty work in Homa Bay. I did not know what to do. Wambui had some savings and that supported us for a few days. Then we decided to go to Wambui's brother's home in Karatina."

"Why did you not mortgage your boat or use one of your friends' boats?" Paul asked.

"If I mortgaged my boat to buy new nets and if the nets got stuck in the vegetation, I would be completely doomed. If I would sell my boat and buy new nets, I would still have the same problem. It takes 45 minutes just to go out to the lake. I would have to borrow a boat for many hours a day to catch some fish. That was not practical either because the boats are all busy at peak times. So, I just decided to keep my boat in Ngegu, go out and earn some money to buy new nets, and come back when I had the money."

"Why did you not contact us?" Peter chided his brother. "We could have helped you. Did you not have enough faith in your own brothers?"

"I am sure you would have helped me but my pride got in the way. How would I admit to you that the fisheries officials confiscated my nets because I broke the rules? Didn't father always advise us to take responsibility for our actions? Everyone in Homa Bay had found out about the issue. I was ashamed to stay here and answer people's questions and stand their jokes and subtle taunts."

"What kind of job could you do in Karatina?"

"Actually, none," Phillip admitted. "With help from Wambui's brothers, I could have become a matatu driver or a tomato farmer. But, how could a fisherman, all of a sudden, become a farmer or a driver? I could have learned over time but I could not bear to spend my life away from my people, my lake and my fish."

"So, you moved again from Karatina to Rongo?"

"I barely lived in Karatina for a week. Then one day, we were having tea at the Starbucks hotel with Wambui's brother, talking about my options when Professor Onyango tapped on my shoulders. He was visiting Karatina for some research project and stopped for tea before heading back to Nairobi. We ordered another tea and started talking. We talked about his project in Karatina, and about the elections, and how things were in Homa Bay and Kochia. Then he asked me if I knew anyone who could help him with a project in Rongo. Before I could say anything, Wambui declared that I was looking for a job close to home. She even told him about the problems with the hyacinth and the fisheries people. I stared at the floor in shame but the Professor was very understanding. The two of them then convinced me to take up the job in Rongo."

"So, what kind of job are you doing? What does it have to do with hyacinth?" Paul was getting a little restless.

"The hyacinth came much later. My first job was coordinating with sugarcane farmers, truck drivers, and Professor Onyango," Phillip explained.

"Coordinating is what I do as well, but I rarely get paid for it," Obongo remarked. "Who pays your salary?"

"The Professor. He is a very smart man and he is very well-connected, just like our friend Obongo here," Phillip continued his narrative. "Through his contacts, he had discovered that there was a large market for brown sugar in Nairobi. Several times, he would come to Rongo to collect the brown sugar."

"What is brown sugar?" Paul asked.

"If you take sugarcane juice and boil it, the water content evaporates. What is left behind is this brown viscous substance. Then you pour it in vats and it solidifies into brown sugar. The sugar mills purify it further to produce white sugar. The brown sugar is used for cattle feeds, pharmaceuticals, and other industries.

"They grow a lot of sugarcane in Rongo. The farmers can either sell their sugarcane or convert it into brown sugar and sell it at a higher price. The problem is that the price of sugarcane varies significantly in the local markets, as much as 300%. The farmers make a lot of phone calls to determine the prices in the different markets and then decide where to take their sugarcane. They end up spending a lot of money in communication and transportation. They prefer to just stay on their farm and produce brown sugar, which saves them the effort and cost of trying to sell their sugarcane. But the brown sugar has no value in the local market. In Nairobi, brown sugar sells very fast – you get cash-on-delivery. Transportation is very expensive and the farmers are not coordinated well-enough to make the trip to Nairobi themselves. They are farmers and while they are happy to do the value addition by making brown sugar, they generally don't want to get involved in trading it. They want to sell it as soon as they can and collect their money.

"Professor Onyango had some sickness in the family and as the hospital bills went on accumulating, he was looking for ways to make some extra money over weekends. He discovered the market demand for brown sugar in Nairobi and established connections with traders willing to buy it from him. He knew a few sugarcane farmers in Rongo and he traveled there a few times, met with the farmers, and offered to buy brown sugar from them at attractive rates. Every few weeks, the Professor would go to Rongo and pick up the brown sugar. But the problem was that the farmers would promise certain quantities, and then when the Professor would reach there, they would not have it ready. In a single trip, the small truck could carry about 2,000 kgs but the Professor was barely able to collect 700 to 1,500 kgs from the farmers. He was collecting small quantities from several farmers and hence he spent a lot of money on phone calls – to arrange for the brown sugar, make confirmation calls, and then last-minute coordination. So, my job was to stay in Rongo, coordinate with all the farmers and the Professor and make sure that the entire stock of 2,000 kgs was ready when the Professor came for pick-up."

"That seems like a very simple job," Paul remarked.

"It is actually a very difficult job. Working with farmers is very complicated – there is always some problem. Sometimes, the cooperative's sugarcane crushing machine is not working and sometimes it is raining and hence the boiling process becomes very slow. Sometimes the vats are not cleaned properly and sometimes they forget to guard the vats and cows end up eating them. The most important part of my job was quality control of the brown sugar. The farmers don't care much about the product. They just throw the brown sugar clusters on the ground. The traders in Nairobi then refuse to buy it. So, I was responsible for educating the farmers about the need for a high-quality product and helping them standardize their operations so as to make their process more sanitary. There are over 60 farmers that I am working with and it takes away a lot of my time."

"I see that it is a difficult job," Paul agreed, "but I am sure the Professor's phone bill is now lower too."

"Indeed. The professor told me last time that he used to spend about 2,000 Shillings for every trip and now he only spends 200!" Phillip beamed, "So now he has increased my commission."

"Do you get a monthly salary or just the commission?"

"I get a place to stay and a commission for every truckload of brown sugar I put together. It is actually very good money."

"But, what happens if the crop fails or something else happens and you are not able to assemble the necessary quantity?"

"Then I don't get paid! I could not have argued with the Professor anyways, but he explained to me his way of thinking and doing business. He said that I will be paid only if I do a good job with everything and deliver goods that he can deliver to his customers. The first time, he reduced my commission because the quality of some of the brown sugar was not good. Now, I am very careful and I make sure that all the brown sugar I buy from the farmers is of good quality. If they have a problem, I work with them to solve it. Even the farmers are more careful now because if their sugar is not good, I just reject it. They work harder but they also make more money."

"I think this is a very good system," Okello added, "because now you are a partner in the business rather than an employee. You have an incentive to work smarter and harder and the Professor is not taking an unnecessary risk."

"There are a lot of business opportunities here but our people don't pursue them because they are afraid to take the risk," Obongo affirmed. "We need to find ways of reducing the risk and then our people will engage in new business opportunities and really prosper."

"But, how did you jump from sugarcane to hyacinth?" Paul asked.

"So, life continued very well for two months. We saved up enough money to buy new nets. I ached to come back home to Ngegu and start fishing again."

"Wait a minute," Okello said. "If you saved enough money for full-size nets in just two months, it must be a very lucrative job?"

"Indeed, I was saving more than three times the money in Rongo than I would save catching and selling fish in Ngegu. But I did not like it there. It is cold all the time and the food is different...and I am far from the lake and the fish. Hey – I just wanted to be home." Phillip laughed. "But then Wambui found out that the hyacinth problem was getting worse and the fishermen were really struggling to make ends meet. Once again, she convinced me to stay back in Rongo. She also preferred it because she was helping me with the brown sugar work and she really enjoyed that. In Ngegu, she would just have to sit around all day."

"It is all my fault," Wambui agreed. "I am not used to sitting at home and cooking and cleaning. I wanted to work and earn some money too. Also, the Professor had done so much for us, how could we just leave him and come here? So, I told Phillip that if we cannot live near the lake, let us bring the lake to Rongo. We thought we would start a business selling fish from Homa Bay in Rongo. I went to Homa Bay twice to find out the current rates of fish. But the fish supply had reduced substantially because of the hyacinth problem and as a result, the prices had increased very much. We could not sell the fish in Rongo and make it a worthwhile endeavor."

"I am glad you are doing well in Rongo but I still don't understand your reasoning for staying away from Homa Bay and all of us," Peter remarked.

"It was just my pride. I had lost face in Homa Bay when my nets were taken away and I was ashamed of coming back and facing my friends until I had the money to buy new nets," Phillips explained.

"I don't think anyone cares about such issues anymore," Obongo said. "You cannot ruin your life just to uphold your pride. You were not the only one whose nets were taken away. All the fishermen have had some problem with the authorities at some time. You just live with it."

"So, did you start the fish business?" Paul asked.

"No, as I said, it was not worthwhile. We were so frustrated with the hyacinth problem. Finally, we came to the conclusion that instead of giving us fish, God was giving us hyacinth and we must make the most of it. The next time the Professor came to Rongo to take the brown sugar, I asked him if there was anything we could do with the hyacinth. He was not sure, but he promised to find out and advise me during his next visit."

"I spoke to several people in Rongo and even went to Kisumu to talk to fisheries and agriculture officials, but no one knew what could be done with the hyacinth. It was three weeks until the Professor came back to Rongo. Meanwhile, Wambui had brought a few plants back from the lake and we had left them outside our home. Most of the plants rotted while a few of them had been crushed during the trip and they started drying up very slowly. The Professor said that we could actually convert the rotting plants into a fertilizer. There was only one problem – most of the plant is actually water and it had to be removed first. I had an idea. There was an old manual sugarcane crusher lying around in the workshop. The farmers used it before they got the diesel crusher from India. So, I tried to crush the plants in the machine and it actually worked. It is very easy. You just put the plant in it and rotate the wheel. The water falls to the floor and you get the crushed plant out. The machine removes over three-fourths of the water. To cut a long story short, the rotten hyacinth makes very good fertilizer for banana trees and other local crops. We can actually sell a bag of rotten hyacinth, I mean the fertilizer, for 100 Shillings."

"So you are making money from the useless vegetation?" Paul was shocked. "Why hasn't anyone else figured that out?"

"Because most of us just look at the vegetation and keep complaining about how it is depriving us of our fish," Obongo exclaimed. "And there are others like Phillip who see it as an opportunity for making compost and fertilizer!"

"At my family farm, we have been composting organic matter and using it as a fertilizer for generations," Wambui added. "But there is not much farming happening here on the lake. People just grow sukumawiki and maybe some bananas or beans or maize. It is only for themselves and not for the market. When I came here, I was shocked that just ten minutes from the lakeshore people were starving but did not engage in farming."

"Indeed," Obongo concurred, "we consider ourselves fishermen and not farmers. When children misbehave, they are sent to the farm as a punishment. So, when they grow up, our young people don't want anything to do with farming. You ask them where the vegetables come from, they will tell you that they come from the market. But they don't know and don't care about how they get to the market."

"I was one of them," Phillip admitted. "But I have realized that instead of being fixated on fish, I need to see what all is around me and how I can make the most of what God has given me."

"Bravo Phillip," Obongo roared. "Okello, our friend here is following your and Odhiambo's footsteps!"

"Well friends, let us give Phillip an opportunity to complete his story. He still has very many plans up his sleeve. So, Phillip, tell us about what you are doing with the dried hyacinth."

"Surely. So, the hyacinth takes some time to dry – between one to four weeks depending on the weather and how much we turn it with a rake. But after it has dried, we cut it into small pieces, mix it with a binding agent, and compact it to make fuel briquettes. These briquettes look like a stack of 20 small chapattis. They are a very good replacement for charcoal. The Professor actually analyzed the briquettes in his lab and found out that they provide more heat and produce less toxic fumes than charcoal. They are more environment-friendly and less expensive than charcoal. We are now trying to understand how we can manufacture the briquettes from the hyacinth on a larger scale. If we are successful, we can make a higher profit compared to the fertilizer."

"I have heard about briquettes but have never seen them," Peter remarked. "Are people willing to use them?"

"Maybe they will be a little hesitant at first because they are not familiar with them...but after using it a few times, they will realize that it is very cost-effective. They can actually reduce their cooking fuel costs by half. Also, there are health benefits that they might appreciate in the longer term," Phillip explained.

"Why were you meeting with Okello then? Is he going to join your business?" Obongo asked.

"We would love to have Okello join our business," Phillip said. "But he is a very busy man. We need about ten machines for compressing the raw materials into briquettes. Our second and more immediate need is for portable machines for crushing the hyacinth. Okello has agreed to start designing both machines for us."

"Why do you need a portable machine?"

"The problem is that the hyacinth plant is 95% water. The transport to Rongo is very expensive and laborious. Instead of taking the plant as is, if we can crush it and then load it on our truck, we can take about ten times more material in a single trip. So we want a portable machine that can be used by the laborers at the lakeshore."

"Won't you need many of these crushers?"

"We need ten of them at the earliest but I suspect that very soon, we will need many more."

"I did not realize how big of a business this is! You have trucks and boats and so many employees!"

"Actually, we don't own any of the assets and we are not even making much money right now," Phillip confided. "We started with just a 30,000 Shilling loan from the Professor. We hire trucks and people on a daily basis. They are not paid for the number of hours or days worked. We just pay them when the material reaches our workshop in Rongo. Similarly, several youth are out of work and we hire them to go into the lake and fetch us the hyacinth. They are also paid for the amount of material they bring in. Benson's job is to organize the entire hyacinth acquisition operation. He is an honest man and we pay him every day. Wambui personally supervises and pays the truck driver and all the laborers."

"Don't all laborers expect to be paid on a daily basis for the period of time worked?"

"Yes, they do. We tried it that way but it does not work for us. They work when they like, take many toilet breaks, keep making phone calls. We cannot run a business like that. So, we changed our model. Now, we pay them when they bring the plants to the workshop, or rake the chopped plants and provide us the dried material, or do some other task that will directly help us make money. This model works very well."

"I don't understand. How do you actually quantify their work?"

"Most of the times, by weight and quality check," Phillip explained. "For example, the laborers rake and turn the chopped plants so they dry quickly. When they are ready, we weigh the material and pay them 10 Shillings for every 5 kgs dried. If it is not dry enough, Wambui will send them back to dry the material further."

"I don't think the people around here will agree to work like that. The daily workers prefer to work for four hours or eight hours and be paid at the end of the time."

"That has not been a problem for us. The unemployment rate in most parts of our country is over 40%. While the lazy ones refuse to work for us, the hardworking ones end up making much more money than they would in a regular daily job."

"Don't you need a special boat for removing the hyacinth?"

"Yes, you need a special boat to cut the vegetation completely and remove it. Our laborers just go into the water and pull out the plants. It is not the most efficient way to do the job but we cannot afford a big boat. The manual approach is very cost-effective and it keeps many people employed. Also, it simplifies our business model. After including all our expenses – the boat, trucks, laborers, Benson, etc. it costs us 75 Shillings for a 5 kg bag while we sell it for 100 Shillings."

"And what about the fuel briquettes?"

"We are not selling them yet – just using them for making brown sugar. It saves us a lot of money. Once we get the machines from Okello, we will start manufacturing and selling them in the market."

"So Phillip," Paul asked, "Won't the BMU people be upset when they find out that you are making money from the hyacinth? Why not share some profit with the BMU and keep them happy?"

"That is our biggest problem," Phillip grimaced. "In fact, in one community, they have refused to let us take the hyacinth. It is not like they planted the hyacinth or own it! We are solving their problem by taking it away and clearing their path to the water. Our margins are very low. The profit of 25 Shillings does not include Wambui's and my salary or the cost of the machines or any other incidental expenses. They wanted 25 Shillings for every bag of compost we were selling. How can we do that? It will completely ruin our business."

"But you know our people," Paul insisted. "They will find out that you are making money and they will stop you from taking the hyacinth. Why don't you charge your customers a little more and then pay the community some money?"

"That is not possible. We have considered it but our customers are unlikely to pay a higher amount."

"Paul is right," Obongo concurred. "You need to find a way to keep the communities happy or your business will come to an abrupt end."

"But we are solving their problem," Phillip protested. "How can they expect money from us? We are actually saving them a lot of time and money."

"No, my friend," Okello chimed in. "Saving money is not valued as much as making money for someone. And, at least in this case, saving time does not even count. If you ask the fishermen what they value more – two hours or 50 Shillings, most of them will tell you 50 Shillings. They have all the time in the world, or at least, that is what they think."

"Have you seen all the advertisements for water pumps or fertilizers or fishing nets?" Obongo added, "They always advertise how the customer can make more money with the product."

"I get your point," Phillip conceded. "We have done some calculations. We can pay the community 5 Shillings per bag for letting us take the hyacinth and not interfering with our business."

"There are two problems with that," Obongo pointed out. "First of all, 5 Shillings is a very small amount and more importantly, whom does the money actually go to?"

"It should go to the community," Phillip said confidently. "Don't you agree that it should benefit everyone and not just one person?"

"I agree that it should benefit everyone," Obongo said, "But whom will you physically give the money to, and how will you know that it goes towards a cause that helps everyone? Can you give the money to the sub-Chief?...the head of the BMU?...the headmaster of the local school? ...the doctor at the clinic? Most importantly, how do you demarcate the community? Which homesteads are a part of the community and which are not? Who will make that decision?"

Obongo's agitated voice and critical questioning surprised the three brothers and Wambui. The long silence was finally broken by Okello. "I think I understand what my brother is trying to say. The problem he is describing is that we tend to use the word community very freely. In the olden days, it had a specific meaning. People did not travel as much and lived in close proximity like one big family. Surely, they had their arguments and fights, but they knew that they had to survive together. They were all accountable towards one another. But in today's world, that accountability cannot be taken for granted. We need explicit accountability mechanisms – just the way the Professor pays you only when you do your job correctly. He is holding you accountable and you are holding the farmers accountable."

"Wait a minute," Phillip interjected. "I am completely confused. First you said that we must give the community some money and now you are saying that there is no such thing as community anymore."

"Let me explain," Okello clarified. "I am not saying that there is no community. We are very much a part of one or more communities and we are interdependent on each other. At the same time, we make more individual decisions than collective decisions. Any collective action, just like individual actions, needs accountability."

"So, Okello, what do you propose?" Phillip asked in exasperation.

"I propose...I propose..." Okello stuttered. "Why don't you give me some time to think about it?"

"No problem," Phillip smiled. "After all, I am a simple fisherman and very new to this business of doing business."

"So, Phillip, will you now come back to Ngegu?" Peter changed the subject.

"Right now, Wambui and I are coordinating the brown sugar business for Professor Onyango and we are also working very hard on this hyacinth business. Things are slowly starting to come together and if Okello designs the machines for us, then I am very sure we will be successful. As such, it does not help to move back to Ngegu right now."

"But, isn't it better for your hyacinth business to be located in Homa Bay or Ngegu?"

"Not really. While the hyacinth comes from here, it is a lot easier to dry it in Rongo because there is less humidity there. Also there is a ready market for fertilizer and briquettes in that area," Phillip explained.

"Besides, we really enjoy working with Professor Onyango," Wambui chimed in. "He has been very kind to us. When we suggested that we wanted to work on this second business, he was extremely supportive. He went out of his way to do the necessary research and help us get started. We cannot leave the Professor's work and go elsewhere."

"I wish that everyone would be just as supportive as the Professor," Phillip said. "I am so frustrated with the BMU people in the other place. We are solving their problem and on top of that, they want money from us. They don't want to profit from the hyacinth themselves but they will not let us profit from it either, just like the dog in the manger who will not eat the grass and neither let the horse eat it. Obongo, you said that we need to find ways to reduce risk for our people who want to start new businesses. I think that even before that, we need to make people understand how this crab in the bucket mentality is hurting everyone and impeding progress."

"Phillip, I understand your frustration," Okello jumped in. "However, I suggest that you don't make this situation an 'us' versus 'them' issue. Sometimes, we are just as guilty of being on the other side of the fence. The biggest enemy of the crab is the crab itself. We just need to find smart ways to rise above, and help the other crabs rise up too so that collectively, we can all get out of this bucket of poverty and hopelessness."

"Anyways, I am not here to preach," Okello winked. "I have a potential solution for you. Instead of making the hyacinth crushing machines portable, why don't we strategically install them at maybe two or three locations along the shore. The fixed machines will be more durable and cost us less than the portable machines. Then, whoever is interested in doing some work and earning a little money can bring the hyacinth from the lake, squeeze the water out of it and sell it to you! You just sit there with your weighing scale and let the people do the rest of the work."

"That is an interesting idea," Phillip agreed. "But what if they crush the hyacinth and take it away without selling it to us?"

"Let them take some of it home," Okello chuckled. "Their neighbors will nag them until they bring it back to you in a few days. You know it has a foul smell. Most of the fishermen don't have a good application for it. They don't need the compost and making the briquettes is not easy. Besides, as you pointed out, there is hardly a local market for either of them."

"That is true, and they can take some and crush it manually even now if they want to!"

"Unless they are serious about starting a business, you have nothing to worry about," Okello advised. "If they indeed start a business and compete with you, it will force you to make your business more efficient. Competition is good for all of us. Either ways, everyone wins."

"But I don't understand how it solves the problem of community expectations," Wambui asked.

"I understand it," Phillip's eyes lit up. "In the previous case, we are benefitting from the hyacinth and people are expecting a share from the proceeds. But now, everyone in the community has an opportunity to benefit from it. The benefit is very tangible and immediate – they do some work, they walk away with some money!"

"Actually, that is a good thing for us too," Wambui concurred. "Instead of having 15 laborers, we will have many more. Some of them will tire away in a few days, but others will stay. But what if..."

"No more what ifs," Okello interjected. "Just do a trial with three machines at one location and see how it works. We can speculate forever but doing a trial is the only way to know."

"Okello, I like this idea very much," Phillip said. "I have always wanted to help my friends here in Ngegu and Homa Bay in some way. Now, I can help them in two ways – by making it easy for them to reach the water and also giving them an opportunity to earn a little money while cleaning up the lake."

"This last year has been very enlightening for me," Wambui mused. "In my church, my pastor always used to say that instead of giving a man a fish, you teach him how to fish. However, now I have learned that even if a man knows how to fish, has very good nets and a sturdy boat, lives next to a very large lake with millions of fish in it, he could still starve.

There are laws to be followed, norms to be respected, big fish that eat up the smaller ones, hyacinth that colonizes the lake shore – just so many things that separate the hungry man from his fish."

"Yes, and I have learned that you cannot keep blaming the fisherman or the fish or the nets or the laws either," Phillip laughed. "Remember I used to joke that the Maasai people think that all the cows in the world belong to them, the Meru people have their miraa[1], and the Kikuyus have their matatus...just like that, all the fish in the world belong to us, the Luos."

"Do you mean you don't believe that anymore?" Wambui teased.

"I still love my fish. But I also think that God has given us much more than fish and cows and miraa and matatus, and we must make the most out of everything that we have. If God gives us hyacinth, we must endeavor to make the most out of it."

"And since God has given us cell phones..." Paul pulled his younger brother's ear. "We must make the most out of them and keep our near and dear ones informed of our whereabouts."

It was almost sunset when Wambui and the three brothers finally jumped into Paul's car and headed to Homa Bay for a family dinner. They were extremely grateful to Obongo and Okello for bringing them all together. They decided to visit Rongo next morning to tour the brown sugar manufacturing facilities and review the hyacinth operations. Benson was shocked to see all of them together. He really liked Okello's plan of crowdsourcing the crushed hyacinth and making the machines available to anyone that wanted to use them. Over the next week, Okello traveled to Kisumu and bought manual sugarcane crushing machines and re-engineered them to work with water hyacinth. Twelve of these machines were delivered to Phillip in just two weeks. They were installed in groups of three at four different locations and proved to be very successful. The local people would cut or pull out hyacinth from the lake, crush it with the machine, and sell it by weight to one of Phillip's staff persons. Phillip ended up reducing his overhead costs significantly and further boosting his profits.

The briquette making machines took longer than a month to design and prototype. Phillip ran into problems while establishing a reliable supply chain for the binding agent for the hyacinth briquettes. When this chronicle was being written, Phillip was still experimenting with the machine and the composition of the briquettes. Phillip put the briquettes on the back burner because the brown sugar and composting businesses

---

[1] Miraa = A flowering plant whose stems and leaves are chewed as a social custom. Miraa is a stimulant and is illegal in some countries. It is also known as Khat or Qat.

The Fishing Village of Ngegu

were booming. As word about the hyacinth presses and the composting business got around, Phillip decided to visit his friends in Ngegu and Homa Bay. They were delighted to see him and were surprised and very proud when they learned that he had originated the water hyacinth business that was now providing income to over 100 individuals along the shore.

However, the person who was happiest to see Phillip and learn about his exploits was the fisheries officer. "We took away your nets and see what all you accomplished," he said to Phillip and embraced him tightly. "You are a role model for all of us. I will surely nominate you to the East African Task force for Water Hyacinth that has been constituted and will be meeting in Kampala next month."

The fishmongers in Homa Bay were jealous of Wambui and congratulated her on winning over Phillip's heart. The members of the Empower Kochia Group warmly welcomed Phillip and Wambui back to their community. The elders insisted that Wambui must learn Dholuo so she could converse with everyone, and more importantly, participate in all the celebrations. "We will teach you Luo every evening," the old women promised, "but you must teach our young people how to run and grow a business." Wambui happily accepted the invitation.

Everyone was particularly pleased to learn that Phillip was planning an official church wedding the following month. Wambui was also pleased with all the love and attention she received from Phillip's friends, family and neighbors. Although she had to return to Rongo to resume her work, she promised to come back to Ngegu and meet with everyone at least once a month.

"Now you have a successful brown sugar business and a beautiful wife," Janet teased Phillip. "Surely, a big party is in order to celebrate your sweet fate."

#9

Mzungu Memories: A Conversation over Busaa

"This is one of our most unique cultural contributions to the entire world," Odhiambo pulled out the reed straw from his mouth and proclaimed. "Where else can you find a food that is also a drink? It fills your stomach, gives you energy and makes you feel very happy!"

"No! No! No! Odhiambo," Reverend Ndiege scolded, "Busaa is surely a unique drink, but don't confuse the stimulation you get from it with real happiness. There is only one path to true happiness and that is through Jesus Christ."

"Come on Mzee," Odhiambo challenged the man of God. "Tell me, don't you feel good when you drink soda? You are on your third big bottle and I can see the fourth one has its cap removed and is patiently waiting for you."

"I love soda." The Reverend smiled. "But it does not have alcohol in it. Your drink, on the other hand, contains alcohol and is known to transform saintly men into sinners."

"Let me tell you Reverend," Odhiambo drawled, "when we were teenagers, we would drink milk with a special vegetation, three four, five, big glasses and then we would have so much fun. Please don't tell me that milk and grass are also alcoholic substances!"

"I am not arguing with you, at least not when you are in an inebriated state," the Reverend nodded his head and shrugged in mock anger.

The entire group chuckled as Odhiambo continued his stories about getting high and doing silly things when he was younger.

Phillip's friends and neighbors had gathered at the Lake View Hotel in Homa Bay to celebrate the success of his brown sugar and fertilizer businesses and his engagement to Wambui. The attendees were very happy to have him back in their midst in Homa Bay. Phillip's brothers, Paul and Peter, had sponsored the party. The Lake View Hotel stood right on the shore of Lake Victoria, a short walk from the Homa Bay market and matatu stage. The owner, John Ouma, was from Kochia and very supportive of activities that would benefit his home area. While the cost of tea was 60 Shillings for everyone else, Empower Kochia Group members enjoyed a discounted rate of 30 Shillings. More importantly, unlike other restaurants, bars, and cafés, John would let them sit in his restaurant and discuss their business for as long as they wanted. Over time, Lake View had become the default meeting place for the group members, whether it was to discuss projects or just socialize with their friends. John Ouma had closed his shutters to the general public for the day so as to devote his full attention to the party.

Paul and Peter had earlier considered hosting a traditional party at Peter's homestead. Okello had agreed to provide his music system and the big loudspeakers. The plan was to slaughter two goats and arrange soda, beer, and chang'aa for the guests. Chang'aa is a popular spirit made by distilling corn or bananas. It was banned by the government for a long time because of the frequent deaths and blindness it caused due to methanol poisoning. Such accidents had increased in frequency because unscrupulous bootleggers adulterated it by adding stolen jet fuel, embalming fluid, or even battery acid. The reason for increasing its potency was to meet the market demand for low-cost drinks that provide a good 'kick'. The Kenyan government legalized chang'aa in 2010 in a mostly unsuccessful effort to take business away from such bootleggers and attract formal companies with better quality control to explore the market. The big companies could not compete with the informal players in providing a potent drink at a very low price. Women in various parts of the country held demonstrations against the legalization and wide availability of chang'aa claiming that their husbands, brothers and sons were addicted to the vicious drink. While most of the chang'aa addicts were men, there was a gradual increase in the number of women too. The protestors pointed out the subsidiary impact of the drink, in terms of lost livelihoods, frayed relationships, and risky sexual activities that exacerbated the spread of HIV and other sexually transmitted diseases.

Sister Phoebe had led several such demonstrations in Kochia. Eventually, she realized that most of the chang'aa producers were poor women trying to eke out a living. Making the spirit illegal would just drive

The Lake View Hotel

the production and sale underground and actually make it more dangerous. The consumers, mostly men, would take more money from their wives or mothers to buy the illegal brew. At the same time, the police and local mafia would end up with a substantial portion of the chang'aa producer's meager earnings. While Sister Phoebe abandoned her campaign to shut down chang'aa dens, she maintained her tough stance against such places operating near schools. After just three weeks of protests and meetings, chang'aa dens near schools were shut down, or rather, moved to farther locations. Sister Phoebe expected her friends to set a good example for the relatively uneducated citizens of Kochia, Ngegu and nearby areas. When she heard about Peter's plans of serving chang'aa at the party, she immediately marched to his place and scolded him until he backed down from the plan.

Once the chang'aa was off the menu, the loud music seemed rather pointless to Peter. Also, Phillip liked fish much more so than goat. Thus the goat, chang'aa and loud music plans were cancelled in favor of a more sophisticated get-together at the Lake View Hotel. John Ouma took it upon himself to source the freshest Tilapia fish and cook it into a stew as well as fry it. It would be served with salad, potato fries, and sukumawiki. While chang'aa was struck off the menu, the attendees could still enjoy soda, beer and the traditional alcoholic drink, busaa. While negotiating with Sister Phoebe, Peter had struck a compromise by replacing chang'aa with this milder, safer, and more nutritious drink. Busaa is a fermented porridge made from sorghum, maize, or millet flour. It is as much of a nutritious food as an alcoholic drink and is served during social and religious ceremonies. Busaa is heated in an earthen pot over a small fire. The drinkers dip their reed straws into this common pot. Typically, a group would consume a few of these pots during a drinking and chatting session. Peter's aunt was specially invited from Siaya to prepare the busaa and Obongo's deceased father's ancient brewing pot was used to grace the occasion. Paul, Peter, Odhiambo, Phillip, Obongo, Okello, Reverend Ndiege, Chief Achieng, the fisheries officer, Benson and a few others pulled up chairs outside the hotel to sip their busaa and exchange stories.

"I like beer and I love whisky, but nothing beats the taste of busaa," the fisheries officer remarked. "Especially when you are sitting with friends and talking about life – the good times and the bad times."

"You are absolutely right," Chief Achieng from the SUV Foundation nodded in agreement. "Whisky and vodka is served in all our parties and we have beer for every official dinner. While I don't mind partaking in some of it, busaa is the best drink. Busaa makes me feel very relaxed. I feel at home."

A Conversation over Busaa

"You have beer with every dinner!" Peter exclaimed. "That is a lot of beer and a lot of money!"

"No. Not every dinner," Chief Achieng clarified. "We have very many meetings, seminars and training events that culminate in a group dinner. It is customary to serve beer during these events. Besides, I don't have to pay for them, the foundation pays for it."

"Isn't that a waste of money? Shouldn't the foundation money be spent on projects that help the people instead?" Obongo asked pointedly.

"Yes, that is a valid argument," Chief Achieng beamed. "But you see, if we invite people to training events, we have to feed them and keep them happy. Moreover, the cost of soda, tea, and beer is about the same at the hotels where we host these events."

"Why do you host your training workshops at such expensive places then?" Obongo argued.

"I don't make those decisions. My boss's boss decides that," Chief Achieng explained. "These mzungus have their own way of doing things. After having worked with the foundation for over ten years, I can follow their thinking most of the times. But sometimes, hey, they do things that leave me completely confused."

"There is a reason they are called mzungus," Odhiambo quipped. "They just go round and round in circles. Nothing has changed since our forefathers' times – they were mzungus then and are mzungus now – confused people wandering aimlessly."

""Is that true?" Peter asked, "I never realized that the word 'mzungu' is derived from 'zungu'!"

"Yes," Obongo said, "the first mzungus were actually explorers and they went round and round trying to find and climb tall mountains and locate the sources of our rivers. Our ancestors never quite understood the purpose of all these harsh journeys and called them mzungus, or the confused people who wander aimlessly."

"Our foundation is working on many projects related to renewable energy, water purification and other things," Chief Achieng continued. "The mzungus all have their heart in the right place. They want to reduce poverty and improve the life of our people. But....but, I don't understand some of the funding decisions they make. For example, three years back, we received a proposal for a solar power project in Kericho. This community was very well-organized. Twenty of them pooled their money together, rented some land, grew tomatoes and other vegetables and sold them in the local market. In two years, they had saved enough money to purchase large solar panels for domestic lighting. Through some contacts, they found a reliable agency in Nairobi to come to Kericho and install the solar panels. They used their own money to buy the solar lanterns. However, these people did not know that they also needed a charge controller and batteries. Now, they were short of KSh. 40,000 and came to us for assistance. I was very impressed with all the work they had done. I made the mistake of assuring them that the foundation will help them bridge the gap.

"So, I went to my boss and he made me write a ten-page proposal. I prepared it by the next day and expected the KSh. 40,000 check to be written in a day more. My boss forwarded the proposal to our head office in Washington. They were very impressed and dispatched two people from Washington to Kericho to visit the community and study the project. Three weeks later, I escorted two mzungu ladies to Kericho. They stayed there for five days and interviewed all the group members. They went on a two-day safari and even learned how to make ugali. They were very excited about the group's leadership and congratulated them many times. Every day, some group members were invited to have dinner with us. Surely, I thought, on the last day they would provide the funding to the group and inaugurate the project. Then, on the last day, they told the community members that they will report back to their boss on how pro-active and advanced this group was. They expressed their confidence that the project would certainly get funded, and maybe they would initiate more projects with the group. The group members were not sure whether to be happy or sad. They looked at me and I just looked at the heavens above. All the group members brought some gifts – packets of local tea or coffee or maize flour for the visitors. They were hoping that the funds will soon be released and they will have light at home.

"I got a missed call from the group members every day but did not hear from the headquarters for two full months. Finally, they sent me a 264-page report about the Kericho project. It took me a week to read it. The report again congratulated the group and recognized it as an exemplar of grassroots activism, entrepreneurial passion and excellent organization. The report concluded that the unique work and needs of the Kericho group called for a special grant category. They further recommended that this new funding vehicle must be designed and implemented within one year and the Kericho group must be invited to apply for it soon thereafter. I was very upset when I read this report. I did not know what to tell my friends in Kericho. My credibility was at stake here and so was the foundation's – if only the mzungus would realize that!

"The next morning, there was great jubilation in the office. Apparently, the two mzungu ladies had indicated to their boss that our furniture was a little shabby and computers were getting old. The head office had released KSh. 2 million to purchase new furniture and computers for our eight-person staff. A second email informed us that the two of them were returning to Kenya in a week's time to interact more with the Kericho community and develop the new grant program. Surely, I thought, if the mzungu ladies and I go back to Kericho, we will all get lynched – if not physically, definitely in spirit. I ran to my boss and explained the whole situation. He insisted that he had no discretionary funds whatsoever. As per the new rules, every single expense had to be approved by Washington. He assured me that providing KSh. 40,000 to the Kericho group would never get approved since it was in the pipeline already. I argued with him for an hour. I requested him to discuss this problem with headquarters but he refused. I lost my appetite and my sleep over this issue. The Kericho group had now moved on from missed calls to phone calls on a daily basis. I kept falsely assuring them that the funds would be released soon.

"Then on the fourth day, as I was slouched in my chair pondering my upcoming trip to Kericho, I got an idea. I ran to my boss and requested KSh. 42,000 from him for a therapeutic rattan cane chair with a straight back. I insisted that my doctor had advised me to use only this particular chair that applies pressure at certain points and dissuades people from slouching. My boss was a little shocked by the extremely high cost. He pointed out that my colleagues had selected trendy leather-backed and well-cushioned chairs from Nakumatt at lower costs. I stood firm on my demand and rationalized that a traditional bonesetter designed these exclusive chairs with precise pressure points, and hence they were very expensive. Finally, he relented and agreed to release the funds. It took three more days to get the advance in hand. I took the next matatu to Kericho and went straight to the group leader's home. I handed him KSh 40,000 and made him promise me that this must be kept a secret. I said, 'This is a special kind of grant. Just say that the group came up with the funds to complete the project. Once the foundation is convinced that you are independent problem-solvers, they will initiate a much bigger project here in Kericho. Then we will benefit much more. If they find out that I gave you the money, the project is over.' The group leader promised to do as I said.

"Then I took the overnight bus back home from Kericho. As soon as the market opened, I purchased a cane chair and tied three small cane baskets to its back to make it look authentic and therapeutic. I paid KSh. 1,500 for the chair and the three little baskets and an additional KSh. 500 to the amused man to make a receipt for KSh 42,000. My colleagues hooted when I carried the chair to my office. They joked about it for the next few months. It was actually a very uncomfortable experience sitting on that chair for eight to ten hours every day. While I was able to remove those silly baskets after two weeks by claiming that those pressure points had been fixed, I had to use the chair itself for two years more. However, I would rather sit on an uncomfortable chair for ten years than lose my honor and credibility amongst my people! After that experience, I swore not to make any promises or even give the faintest assurances or hope to any community groups. Till this day, I have not understood why the mzungus spent KSh. 4 million to gather data and 2 million more to buy new furniture and computers but refused to release a paltry sum of KSh. 40,000 for the Kericho group. Were my actions justifiable? I have thought about it many times and concluded that I did the right thing for the Kericho group, the foundation, the mzungus, and for me."

"Achieng, you came up with a very practical solution for the problem," Reverend Ndiege said. "Alas, I was not as successful as you. I ran into a similar situation before I came to Kochia. I was first on attachment, and then the assistant Pastor, at a church in Kericho. Most of the congregation was involved in tea and coffee farming. Every summer, we had a group of 18-20 people come visit us from the state of Minnesota in the US. They had been coming for many years, even before I was affiliated with the church. They preached the Bible, taught at our primary school, and built one or two homes. Some years, they came with doctors and conducted medical or dental camps. They were very good people and our community looked forward to receiving them every year. Two months before they would arrive, everyone in the community would start asking me when the mzungus were coming. The children would be talking about eating chocolates and playing all day. All of us liked it so much.

"One year, I took some of them on a morning walk through the tea and coffee plantations. One excited coffee farmer gave them a big bag of coffee beans. We came back to the guesthouse and the mzungus informed the rest of their friends about the fresh coffee beans. Now they insisted on roasting the beans and making coffee! I explained that while we grow so much coffee, we don't actually drink it. We are a tea-drinking country. Sometimes, we drink Nescafé or Africafe or just go to the restaurant and drink whatever they serve us. But, they were very determined about making fresh coffee, the right way. So, I brought a big pan from the church kitchen and we roasted the beans, one batch after another, on a small fire. The next task of crushing the coffee beans was more challenging. While I went home to home inquiring about a pestle and mortar, the mzungus put the roasted beans in the pan and started crushing them with a hammer. The rest of them completed whatever they were doing and now the entire group of twenty mzungus was working on the coffee project. By the time they completed grinding the coffee two hours later, a big group had gathered to witness the coffee hammering ceremony.

"Even the head pastor came out to see what the commotion was about. I tried to hide in the crowd because I was afraid he was going to berate me for the unfortunate fate of the pan. It was very severely dented after all that hammering. But the pastor was so pleased at the sight of over a hundred people carefully observing the mzungus prepare coffee that he extemporaneously started preaching on the importance of dedication, perseverance, and teamwork. The mzungus considered it most appropriate to serve coffee to the crowd. Consequently, another small fire had been started and the pastor himself fetched the biggest pot in the church kitchen and placed it on the fire. The mzungus emptied their bottled water into this great pot and when it started boiling they added all the ground coffee. Some mzungus had scurried off to purchase sugar from the market while the dentist ran back to his room and emerged with stacks of little paper cups. Finally, we tasted the fruits of their hard work. While our pastor always preached about sweet fruits that follow hard work, these fruits were very very bitter. Apparently, the beans had been roasted more than necessary. No matter how much sugar one added, it did not seem to help.

"A few people tasted the coffee and ran into the bushes to spit it out. As word about the bitterness of the coffee got around, the crowd quickly dispersed. A young man confided to me a few days later that they were as scared of refusing the coffee as they were of consuming it. The children started crying after tasting the coffee and quieted down only when the mzungus retreated to their rooms and came back with chocolates for each one of them. The mzungus were naturally disheartened by this turn of events but consumed the coffee stoically. They put out the fire under the giant cauldron, had their dinner, and went to sleep. The next day, we toiled until noon to dispose off the coffee in the field, clean up the giant pot and pan, and find the little paper cups that were strewn all over the place during our people's desperate flight the previous evening. I had to rest for two full days to regain my health. After this misadventure, I was convinced that the mzungus would not mention coffee again. I was completely wrong.

"Next year, they came back with a new group of 20 people. The coffee leader from the previous year was back and on the first day itself

Children Gather Around the Mzungus

he informed me that the coffee from our area was the best there could be. He had taken some home and succeeded in having the coffee roasted, ground and prepared by a professional. He had specifically come back to take enough coffee home because everyone in their church wanted to buy it. He had even contacted other churches in the region and they had all agreed to purchase our coffee. He insisted that this would be better for our farmers because they would earn more money than selling it to the local agents. I was very hesitant in getting involved in this business – my duties were religious in nature after all and I did not want to get stuck in any business. I eventually agreed to arrange a meeting with the coffee cooperative for the following week.

"The mzungus offered to buy 1,000 kgs of coffee immediately and then import 5,000 kgs every harvest. They offered the coffee farmers three times as much as the local agents on the condition that they would grow a specific kind of Arabica coffee. The coffee farmers were still hesitant but when the mzungus put the hard cash on the table, some of the farmers picked it up. Now, you see, the coffee farmers have their own network of middlemen and agents that they sell to. It is actually a very complex business but they have been doing this for very many years. While the coffee farmers might not get the best rate from these middlemen, they are assured that the coffee will be purchased and they will earn at least some money. As promised, the mzungus took the 1,000 kgs of coffee and split it into 20 bags – one for each of them, and carried it home. They also arranged for a man in Nairobi who picked up the coffee and shipped it to them after every harvest. This system worked very well for two years. The farmers were happy and so were the mzungus. With every coffee payment, there was also a small allowance for the church. So we were also very happy. The mzungus actually increased the quantity to be shipped to them by about 1,000 kgs every harvest cycle. Several farmers now grew the specific coffee and sold it exclusively to the mzungus.

"The mzungus requested me every few months to coordinate with the farmers and communicate to them the amount for the next harvest season. Then one day, I was informed that the coffee leader had passed away and there was no one to coordinate the coffee distribution on their side. Thus, the coffee imports would be stopped with immediate effect. As soon as I received the message, I ran over to the cooperative office. The head of the cooperative advised me to be very careful how the news were shared with the farmers. We called a meeting with the farmers and explained the situation. They were very angry because now they did not have a market for their coffee beans. They expressed that they should have been given atleast six months notice to make alternate arrangements for their harvest. Now, I said, surely the mzee was not aware of his impending death. They started questioning me. 'Why can't the mzungus find someone else to take over the coordination? Last year, when we shipped 100 kgs less, they were unhappy and told us how we need to improve our organization. This year, they are completely ending our deal. Where do we take our coffee now? Who will buy it? How do we feed our families?' These were all valid questions but I had no answer for them. I called the head of the American church but I was told by his assistant that he is a man of God and does not concern himself with such business endeavors.

"I tried the same defense with the coffee farmers but it did not work. The farmers insisted that I was to blame since I was the one who introduced the mzungus to them and served as the liaison thereafter. The meeting got louder and angrier. A few well-wishers informed me that I was needed outside the room. When I stepped out they caught my hand and made me run across the mountain. I was in hiding for two days while the elders reasoned with the farmers. After that day, things were never the same for me. Whenever I was in the community, everyone stopped talking or whatever they were doing and stared at me. I was constantly living in fear. Finally, on the pastor's advice, I transferred to another branch of the church in Busia. I swore to never ever get involved in any business transaction, whether it was with our people or with the mzungus. I never quite understood why the farmers were so upset about the issue. Surely they could sell the coffee to someone else.

"A few months later, I ran into the pastor of the Kericho church at a seminar and we started talking. He informed me that the incident had very grave consequences for the farmers. The farmers who sold part of their crop to the local agents survived because they were paid for some of their coffee. But the others were forced to sell their specific type of coffee to agents at throwaway rates. First, the agents refused to buy the coffee altogether as retribution for not selling to them for all these years. After a lot of pleading and intervention from the cooperative leaders and the pastor himself, they agreed to purchase it at a throwaway rate. The agents insisted that there was no market for it and they were just doing the famers a favor. The farmers went from making three times as much money to making a quarter of the regular coffee price. Some had to pull their children out of school and others had to migrate to the city and work as laborers to save enough money to engage in coffee farming again. I don't necessarily blame the mzungus but I felt very bad for the farmers. The mzungus lost their morning coffee while the farmers had their lives disarranged.

"Now I understand." Sister Phoebe joined the conversation. "Why we don't see you with mzungu groups like some of the other churches that seem to be hosting mzungus year-round."

"Please join us Sister." The Reverend moved aside to make space for her. "Actually, I like having mzungus at the church and they have been very supportive in building the church and the congregation. But I am always nervous about digressing from our religious mission into any kind of business activities. I welcome mzungus to the church and host them in our humble guesthouse. As a matter of principle, I never step out of the church premises with them."

"I see your point," Sister Phoebe said. "I have had some mzungus volunteer at my home for HIV patients too and they have been very helpful. However, none of them have expressed interest in doing any business."

"What I don't understand," Peter said, "is that what happened with the Kericho farmers could happen anywhere. Instead of the mzungus, it could have been a Kenyan company that cancelled the contract."

"Yes, but if it was a Kenyan company, there would be a formal contract with six months notice. If the company broke the contract and refused to buy the coffee, the farmers could take them to court and seek damages."

"What you also need to remember," the Reverend added, "is that many such contracts are not committed to written documents. They are done on a trust basis and there is a social contract that either parties will look out for the other side and not imperil their business and personal lives. In this case, the mzungus were expected to honor the unwritten contract and purchase the upcoming coffee harvest. That would give the farmers a fair opportunity to realign their market linkages for the next harvest and beyond."

"Why did the agents refuse to buy the coffee?" Phillip wondered.

"Many reasons," the Reverend explained. "First of all, it was a different kind of coffee and the agents did not have a buyer ready for it. It was very last-minute and so the agents did not have time to find buyers in their network. The bigger issue here was that the agents were known to the farmers for many years and there was a trusted relationship. When the coffee farmers started selling their coffee to the mzungus, that trust was betrayed a little bit. While the agents empathized with the farmers' self-interest in making a little more money, they wanted to punish the farmers for not selling to them. In many ways it is good, and in some ways bad, but the truth is that all our interactions with others are based on trust."

"Very well-said Reverend," Sister Phoebe remarked. "I have found that people from other places often don't appreciate the importance of trust in our culture. Let me tell you about one unusual and uncomfortable situation I had with mzungus. I have not been able to decide whether it actually helped us or hurt us. You can tell me what you think."

"Sure Sister," Peter said, "but give me two minutes..." He ran off, only to return with a bottle of soda for Sister Phoebe and a fresh pot of busaa for the rest of the group.

"So, I was saying..." Sister Phoebe started her story. "Every year, we have a few mzungu volunteers from Germany come to our home for HIV patients. They talk to the residents and help them with their daily activities, work in the shambaa[1], and help in any other way they can. All our residents are terminally-ill. They are very lonely and many are in pain. They enjoy having someone to communicate with. It is very refreshing to see how well they communicate with mzungus although they don't even speak the same language. Our people keep talking in Luo or Kiswahili and the mzungus speak in their language. But, I can see that they are enjoying each other's company – just holding hands and talking away for hours.

"Most of our volunteers are middle-aged women, and a few men from time to time. Last year, we hosted these two young people from Germany. One of them was the son of a mama who visits every July. The other young man was his friend. They were barely 20 years old. The mama had suggested that they should come to our home and help us since she, herself, could not travel that year. Unfortunately, these young people could not relate to our home and the residents, most of whom were one or two generations older than them. They came to me and asked me why we were not taking more residents even though there were many more HIV patients in the communities around us. I told them that we did not have the resources, in terms of staff, food, and space, to take more residents. They immediately started interviewing everyone they could find – the residents, their relatives, our staff, all the idlers around our shambaa, people in the communities, ministry officials. They somehow found out who was donating money to our home and started talking to them as well. It was very peculiar. Every day, a few people would come and ask me who these boys were, and I had to explain. It started taking up a lot of my time but I kept encouraging and supporting

---

[1] Shambaa = farm (Kiswahili)

them. I thought their report might be beneficial and they would learn something valuable during their time in Kenya.

"Then, one morning, I was woken up by a phone call from the German mama. She demanded an explanation for misappropriation of funds and poor facilities at our home. I was completely taken by surprise and in my sleep I gave her some incoherent answer. I think she was crying and shouting at me but she was speaking so fast that I could not understand everything she said. I tried to sleep after that but I could not. An hour later, I went down to the residents' ward. Then the phone calls started, one after another, from our donors, the health ministry officials, even the district commissioner. Yaai Yai Yaai! They had received a report from the German boys the previous evening alleging corruption and misappropriation of funds. The report claimed that the staff was not being paid their salary as promised and the residents did not have proper beds or sanitation facilities. I was so saddened and upset about the report. All of Kochia knows that the accounts and operations of our home are completely transparent. We have a big notice board where I put up the detailed budget and expenses every three months.

"I was on the phone non-stop until noon, and then received many more phone calls until sunset. I denied the allegations as being completely untrue and invited everyone to come to our home and talk to me and review our account books. That day was the worst day of my life. I tried calling the mzungu boys but they had turned off their cellphone. Finally, in the evening, I was able to reach them. They agreed that they had written a report and sent it to everyone by email. I told them that their allegations were completely untrue and I wanted to read the report myself. They told me that they were in Homa Bay lodging official complaints with the District Commissioner and the police. When I heard the word 'police,' my body just froze and mind went numb. I thought, after spending all these years serving the people, I was being called a criminal. I just disconnected the phone and ran to my room.

"I remember crying uncontrollably on my bed. The next morning, the matron came to my room to wake me up. It was past 10 AM. The matron suggested that I get ready and have breakfast soon because the District Commissioner had called and indicated that he was going to stop by. I asked her if he had mentioned anything about the police or arresting me. She insisted that the DC was in his usual serious mood. He asked how many residents we had, said that he will visit us later in the morning, and hung up. Sometimes, even if you have done everything right and there is nothing to fear, so many bad thoughts run through your mind. I started praying incessantly. I quickly got ready and even put on my sweater just in case I have to spend the night in prison. I started gathering my medicines and some clothes to take with me to the prison. The matron was quite amused with my behavior. By the time she prepared tea for me, the DC was knocking on the door. The two German boys were behind him. I welcomed them inside and offered them tea. There were no policemen with them – my prayers had already been answered. I felt more confident now.

"The DC had a big box covered with newspapers. He put it aside and got straight to the point. He confirmed that the young men had filed a police complaint about corruption at our home. He had come to meet me and discuss the allegations. The DC handed me a copy of the spiral-bound forty-page report. I told them that I was very surprised and disappointed that such serious allegations had been made without even asking for clarifications. The DC agreed with me and said that he had already spoken to the mzungus about it. While the DC enjoyed his tea and the mzungus played with their phones and spoke to each other in German, I read the report from end to end. It took me barely 15 minutes to read it. There was atleast one photo on every page. It was like one of those children's books. The childishness of the report was reflected in the obvious observations and absurd allegations. Everything that we did at our center was deemed corrupt and inappropriate! When I finally looked up with a puzzled look, the DC gave me a very uncharacteristic smile that melted my worries away.

"'So, there are two issues we need to talk about,' the DC said very seriously. 'First, we have these allegations that need to be addressed. And secondly, there is the damage control that needs to be done as soon as possible.' Apparently, the mzungus had sent the report to everyone that had interacted with our center in some way over the last seven years. They said that over 200 people had received the report and meetings had been held with over ten different offices around Kochia and Homa Bay. They expressed that they did not want to risk having the allegations swept under the carpet because it was a serious matter and people's lives were at stake. I was completely shocked at the damage that had been done to my reputation and the future of our home. 'Sister Phoebe,' the DC said, 'now that you have read the report, can you provide an explanation.' It took me a few minutes to gather the strength to speak. I told them that, 'The first 20 pages of photos showing the poor facilities are very real. The first allegation about poor facilities is very true. Some chairs and beds are broken, the bed sheets have holes in them, the pit latrine door does not lock very well, and two rooms don't have lights. Everything is true – but what can we do if we don't have the money to

213

fix it?'

"'The second allegation is that we received a grant from an NGO to upgrade the facilities but the money has been misappropriated by me. This allegation is completely false because while we have been told that we have been awarded a grant, we have not actually received the funds. You can call the NGO and confirm it with them. When we receive the funds, we will immediately commence the repairs. The third allegation is that many of our staff members have not been paid their salary. I was amused that the report also has photos of our staff members. We have only four staff members here and, as has been determined in the report, they have all been paid on time. The eleven other people mentioned, or rather shown in your report are not our staff members. They are idlers that just wait around the main gate and waste their time talking with friends, reading the newspaper, and looking for small jobs. They are all poor people and since we have had enough to eat for the past two years, we make some more food and offer it to them.'

"The mzungus disagreed with me. The idlers told them that they open the main gate when a vehicle comes or leaves, or they help in the farm, or carry potatoes to the market. They complained that while they are given some food and potatoes, they have not received a salary from us while the rest of the staff is paid every month. The DC started laughing when he heard this. He saved me the trouble of explaining that if the idlers come and sit around our premises, it does not mean that they should be paid for it. I said, 'If we start paying idlers, there will be five million people waiting outside to collect their salary.' And that was it! This was the basis of their allegations and such a long report. I was not sure whether I should laugh or cry – whether I should be happy that this issue was resolved so quickly or sad about the damage done. I was not sure whether the report actually helped draw attention to our problems or gave a false impression of corruption. A person who understands how things work in Kenya will realize the silliness of the report, but will our mzungu donors understand?

"The DC looked at the mzungus and scolded them for the next ten minutes for not seeking clarifications from me and sending the inaccurate report to so many people. He threatened to prosecute them for tarnishing my reputation and hurting the home. After some more discussion and clarifications, the mzungus finally saw their mistake and apologized. The DC is a man of action. He ordered the mzungus to immediately send for his review another report providing detailed clarifications and evidence that the allegations were untrue. After his and my approval, the report was to be sent out to everyone that received the previous report. Right then, the DC called the non-profit and requested them to expedite the grant money. He recommended that I ask the idlers to leave immediately and stop giving them food. 'Since you like writing reports so much,' he told the mzungus, 'why don't you supervise all the repairs and write a detailed report about it.'

"As he got up to leave, he pointed to the newspaper-covered box and said that it was a gift of cornmeal and sugar for our residents. 'But don't feed it to the idlers,' he warned me. He finally looked at the mzungus, smiled and said, 'Make sure that there are more photos in your report on the repairs than the number of photos in the silly report you sent me yesterday. Also, now that the idlers are gone, why don't you spend some time in the shambaa learning how to grow potatoes?' Then he rushed out of the room leaving me face-to-face with the mzungu boys. We just sat down in silence.

"So," Sister Phoebe concluded, "I am not sure whether this incident helped us or hurt us. We actually got the grant funds in the following week and the repairs were carried out as planned. Some of the donors stopped sending money while the report prompted some others to contribute funds and food supplies."

"What about the idlers? Did they leave?" Okello asked.

"We were afraid that they would create a scene but I told them that we could not feed them anymore. They left without causing any problems," Sister Phoebe said.

"What about the mzungus? Did they also leave?"

"When the DC walked out, they could have left with him or stayed with me," Sister Phoebe replied. "They chose to stay. They apologized to me many times about the whole issue. They supervised the repairs so thoroughly that even the fundis complained to me that the mzungus made them work twice-as-hard. They did some fundraising and installed additional lights and painted our entire home. Six weeks later, we all went to meet the DC to brief him on the completion of the repairs. The DC was pleased with their colorful report and was very surprised to receive a bag of potatoes that they had harvested from the farm."

"So, did you finally forgive the boys?" Obongo asked.

"I forgave them as soon as I read the report because I realized that they were not acting with malice. They were trying to do what they considered was in the best interest of our residents. The deep concern for the residents' needs, and the desire to make their flailing lives better, was something we shared very deeply. I was upset that they approached their concerns very recklessly and irresponsibly. But they were young people and this is how young people everywhere learn their lessons. I forgave them immediately and when I saw them work very hard over the next six weeks, I developed a deep respect for them. Instead of calling me sister like the rest of the Kochia, they started calling me mama. I like that."

"Sister Phoebe, the German boys call you mama," Okello laughed, "and those mzungu girls are soon going to call Odhiambo, baba." Everyone burst out laughing as Odhiambo blushed and warned everyone not to joke about the mzungu girls.

"Odhiambo, didn't you say that they are coming back soon?" Obongo asked.

"Actually, they are already in Nairobi and will be coming here next week." Odhiambo smiled and looked at Okello. "But, I have instructed them that they need to seek approval from you for every thing they want to do at our toilets. Everything, besides using the toilet itself!"

"I remember those girls." Obongo nodded his head. "or I must say, everyone in Kochia remembers them. But Odhiambo, did you finally understand what they were trying to do?"

"Thanks to Okello, towards the end of their trip, we completely understood their project. But, by then, the damage had been done. It ended up costing me 5,000 Shillings that my wife still nags me about. I have not informed her yet that they are coming back next week."

"So what was their project?" Obongo asked, "and why did you end up spending so much money?"

Odhiambo hesitated a bit, took a big gulp of the busaa, gave an ear-to-ear grin and started the story in his inimitable style. "One afternoon, three mzungu girls and one mzee knocked on my door. They had found out about Moneymaker Toilets and wanted to talk to me about it. I advised them that the Moneymaker toilet was on the main road but if it was urgent, they could use my toilet. I took their silence for shyness and walked them to the toilet. They just stood there. I opened the door for them but they signaled to me that I should enter first. I refused. This was quite peculiar. Once again, I inquired how I could help them. They said they wanted to talk to me. At that point, I was very confused. Surely, I thought, the four mzungus, three of them girls, did not want to talk to me in the toilet. There is no way we would all fit. Then, I realized that since the toilet was on the backside of my home, and was not an independent structure, they thought that the door to the toilet was actually the door to my home. I quickly walked across to the other side, opened the door, and invited them into the main room. This tactic seemed to work – they followed me, entered the room and assumed seats on the sofa.

"The mzee was a professor and the three girls were his students. They came from an American university and had developed some technology that was related to toilets. I was very proud to have women engineers in my home. I called my wife and eldest daughter to greet them and listen to what they had to say. I want my children to become scientists and engineers. I thought my daughter would learn something from them. The mzee asked me very many questions about our toilets, their locations, costs, how the toilets worked, if there was a sewage system, if we did any waste management. He kept asking me questions for the next hour while the girls kept writing in their books. These mzungus really like to ask questions and write everything down. I think I answered most of the questions. They congratulated me many times about my business. I must admit that I was very pleased. Then they explained their project to me. They talked about generating gas. I found the conversation very uncomfortable, especially in front of all the women – my wife, daughter and the mzungu girls. I did not quite understand why one might want to generate more gas but I was not comfortable asking. The mzungu girls were very serious but my daughter could not stop giggling. I sent her inside but she came back again. The mzee talked a lot and he spoke so fast that I did not understand most of what he said.

"Then the professor asked me if it was okay for his students to stay here for two weeks. I agreed. He said the girls would stay at a hotel in Homa Bay. Every day, they would come to the toilets on the main road to do their project. My daughter was very amused that engineers do their projects inside toilets. I intervened to explain that engineers build very many things and toilets are just one example. This was my chance to outperform the professor and I did so by giving examples of very many technologies. The mzungus seemed impressed with my knowledge of engineering. I appreciated their kind words but little did I know that my explanation was going to cost me dearly. Once again, the professor talked a lot and asked me if I agreed. At this point, I just wanted to end his talk so I kept on saying that it is okay and there is no problem to all his questions. After all, who was I to disagree with the professor? Then they departed. While I did not hear from them for four more days, I was informed by the toilet attendant that the girls spent most of their day over there. My daughter joined them on several occasions and I liked that very much.

"Then next morning, as I was having tea and getting ready to visit Obongo, the toilet assistant called me. He sounded very nervous and extremely agitated. I was told that the girls had come with two well-built Kenyan men from Homa Bay. They had metal rods and picks and spades and were getting ready to tear down the toilet block. My heart just stopped. I didn't even bother to put on my shoes. I ran to the toilets as fast as I could. When I reached the toilets, the attendant was laughing and chatting with these two fundis and the mzungus. The first thing I did was slap the toilet assistant across his face. How dare he lie to me! I almost died during that ten-minute run and he was here, laughing! While I caught my breath and the man vigorously rubbed his face, the mzungu girls and fundis had retreated a few steps to get away from me. A few onlookers must have heard the slap for they came around to find out if another one was forthcoming. The toilet structure seemed intact and so I asked the man why he lied to me. When he recovered from his daze, he explained that when the fundis arrived with their tools and drove the metal rod into the ground next to the toilet, he assumed that they were here to take down the toilet. When they started talking, they discovered that they were in fact cousins. And just then, I ran towards them in my panicked state. The rest was history.

"I apologized to him for the violence and turned to the mzungus and fundis. The fundis retreated a few more steps while one of the mzungu girl started explaining that they were not going to harm the toilet structure. She indicated that they were digging a hole a little further from the toilet and it would not impact the structure or my business in any way. After a few minutes of her talking and assurances that they will not touch the toilets, I went back home to fetch my shoes and proceed to visit Obongo. I had not even reached Obongo's place when the toilet assistant called me again. He insisted that a very big problem was in the making and urged me to come back as soon as possible. He suggested that I call the police as well. Once again, I ran to the toilet trying my best to imagine what could have happened. Fortunately, I did not call the police. Over a hundred people had gathered around the toilet building. I had to push my way through them to reach the front. Let me tell you, it was not easy. The people were just not ready to move.

"The three mzungu girls seemed to be digging a hole in the ground behind the toilets. They were wearing short pants that failed to reach the ends of their backsides and their tiny blouses left little to the imagination. They were oblivious to the crowd that had gathered around them. They just kept digging and digging and digging. The toilet attendant ran up to me, his palms pressed against his cheeks. 'Did you see how many people have gathered here,' he said. I am afraid they might hurt our guests. It was surely an act of God that I did not slap him for the second time that day for I was very greatly angered. I said to him, 'Why did you not advise them to dress properly and ask our people to leave?' The man insisted that he was afraid that the people would lynch him for stopping the show. I ran over to the girls and asked them to stop digging and put on clothes immediately. They hesitated a little bit but when they realized how many people had gathered, they picked up their shirts from a heap and put them on. They pulled down the legs of their shorts but that did not seem to help much. Most of the spectators were just curious youth from the high school and local farmers. Within fifteen minutes, I succeeded in dispersing the crowd and averting any untoward incident.

"I took the girls home with me. My wife and I tried to explain to them the inappropriateness of their dress and how they had placed themselves in a very risky situation. Finally, they apologized and agreed to dress properly from the next day. They were just about the leave when I remembered to ask them the most basic question: why were they digging a hole and what became of the fundis? I was told that the hole was vital to their project and the fundis were sent home because they wanted too much money. So the mzungus started digging the hole themselves. They had rented the equipment for five days. I offered them help with digging but they turned it down saying that the toilet attendant had agreed to help them going forward. I didn't like the idea very much but I was too tired to object. It had been a very hectic day and I did not even meet Obongo. That night, I forbade my daughter from meeting the mzungu girls again. It is not safe, I told her. We will see their project after it is complete and then you can learn all about engineering. My only consolation for the day was an excited phone call from the toilet attendant to inform me that business had tripled for the day. My joy was tarnished when he inquired if the mzungus will be back the next day and if so, what will they be wearing. I warned him that if any people gathered at the toilet, he would lose his job. He insisted that I didn't know how to run a business and disconnected the line.

"The following day went smoothly. I was told that the girls' clothes got longer and the hole in the ground got bigger. I was really curious about this project but pressing issues at a new Moneymaker toilet location kept me from visiting the project site. When I finally went there two days later, the girls welcomed me and proudly led me to an enormous hole in the ground. It was at least eight feet in diameter and six feet deep. A few people could live in it. I stared at it for a few minutes and congratulated them on successfully digging such a big hole. Then, I insisted that I wanted to know right then and there exactly what would happen next inside this big hole. I was expecting them to put some kind of toilet there – maybe an advanced American pit latrine. Instead, I was told that they were going to put a big tank with its top cut off and then put another inverted tank inside this tank. There would be a big pipe at the bottom and another one on top. I was completely confused. I don't know how long she talked before I cut her off. Just tell me how does one use this toilet, I asked the girls. My imagination was failing me. Even the toilet attendant was getting curious to learn the answer.

"The quieter girl now spoke up. 'Mr. Odhiambo, didn't our professor explain to you the first time we met! This is not a toilet. We will take the waste from all your toilets and put it inside the tank. Then after a few weeks, it will start giving methane gas that you can use for cooking food.' I could not believe my ears. I made her explain it to me two more times. Finally, when I was convinced that I was hearing it right, I asked her, 'Who was going to take the waste and put it in the tank?' I must commend the toilet assistant's sixth sense. Even before she started talking, this man started nodding his head. 'Don't worry,' she told me, 'we will do it for now and then the toilet attendant can take over. It is a very easy job.' By now, the toilet assistant was wildly oscillating his head from side-to-side and gesticulating with his hands. 'I will leave my job immediately if you ask me to do such dirty things,' he declared. The mzungus looked at him in utter disbelief as if he had refused to baptize his children. The panicked toilet attendant went on a tirade announcing what his job responsibilities were and were not. I finally calmed him down by assuring him that I would not expect any such things from him. I gave him fifty bob and suggested that he should go and have a soda. He took the money but refused to move.

"Then I asked the girls, 'Let us assume that we solve this difficult problem of getting the human waste in the big tank. Who is going to use this gas and what will they do with it?' 'Anyone can use this gas and the simplest way to use it is for cooking,' they said very casually. 'Even your wife can use it to make ugali or sukumawiki or anything else.' Now, it was the toilet attendant's turn to watch me nod my head in disgust. He laughed hysterically but was wise enough to quiet down when I scowled at him. I said, 'Don't even think of saying such a thing to my wife, or anyone else for the matter. If people find out that you are proposing taking human waste and converting it into gas and then using it for cooking food, they will be shocked. It might work in your country, but I don't think it will fit into our culture.' The girls were a little distraught about my lack of enthusiasm about their project. They started arguing with me but I refused to entertain further discussion. As we know, encouragement is very important for students. So, I told them, let us meet tomorrow morning to talk to our engineer, Okello, and see what he has to say.

Mzungus Digging a Big Hole

"Okello knew everything about their technology and how it was supposed to work. He explained to me that the anaerobic digester that they were trying to build was the same as the biogas technology that we learned about in school long time back. Now, I understood everything. I asked them, 'Why not use cow manure instead of taking this radical step of using human waste?' The mzungus explained that we did not have enough cows in this area. They had come looking for me because a lot of organic waste would be generated at a commercial toilet. This constant supply of waste would keep producing methane gas. When I had intervened and talked about various technologies, they assumed that I knew a lot about technology and hence did not get into specific details.

"Okello said that the project would work if two problems were solved. First, the waste matter must automatically feed into the machine and not require a person to do it manually. More importantly, we need to find an application for the gas, other than cooking our daily meals. Okello suggested that we could convert the gas into electricity and use it to charge phones or use the gas to heat water, which can then be used for bathing. I liked the phone charging idea much more than hot water idea.

"I felt much better with Okello's support and advice on this project. I tried my best to build the girls' confidence and encourage them to complete the project. I was afraid that they would leave with this enormous hole in the ground. Unfortunately, that is exactly what happened. The big tank they needed was not available in Homa Bay and had to be ordered from Kisumu. We were told that it would take ten days to arrive. The mzungus had only three days left before the professor would come back to pick them up. So, they decided to perfect the hole and come back during their next vacation to build the digester. I knew exactly what was going to happen next. There is only one way to perfect a hole – and that is to make it wider and deeper. The mzungus spent the next three days digging further so that it was ten feet across and ten feet deep. They also dug a series of steps to go down to the bottom of this hole. I was informed that it would be helpful for maintenance purposes.

"When the professor returned, he was very pleased with the hole and congratulated all of us. He raised his hands in joy and shook my hands vigorously. We were all invited to have dinner with him. I invited Okello to the dinner meeting. The mzungus and Okello came up with a plan for the next year. I also made sure my daughter was present for this conversation so that she would not think that engineers just dig holes.

"Finally, the mzungus returned home leaving the hole behind for me. Okello insisted that it would be very valuable when it was completed. He insisted that I must respect it by calling it a project rather than a hole. I readily agreed. The project boosted our business a little because people would come by to see it, and then use our toilets. I asked my doctor if seeing a big hole encourages one to go to the toilet but he did not think so. Though I cannot claim to be particularly pleased with the project, it did not bother me either. It was one of these things that just happen. However, once it started raining and the project filled up with water, my opinion changed. People started falling into it and kids came around just to use it like a swimming pool. I was afraid that if someone drowned in it, there would be a police case and I would be in real trouble.

"Finally, one fine day, the project had filled up with rainwater and a cow decided to swim in it. Since there was no easy exit, she did not know how to come out of the pool. Fortunately, for the cow, some passersby alerted others and a small crowd gathered. They used bamboos to keep the cow afloat while, as the owner of the project, I was summoned to find a solution. I was forced to pay 500 Shillings to three men who literally pulled the cow out of the project. Next week, I paid 3,500 Shillings to a fundi to put three planks of wood on the project and seal it. I also made him build a fence around it for additional security until the rightful champions of the project would come back and complete it."

"Odhiambo," Okello assured his friend, "let me tell you. You are going to be so proud of that project once it is working. Then you can build these biogas plants with all your toilets and make much more money on the side. Just think of your 5,000 Shillings as an investment."

"The mzungus are doing the research for you and also building the first one for free," Obongo added. "That is very good for you."

"As long as they don't come back and leave me with a few more enormous holes, I mean projects, that attract incompetent cows, I don't have a problem," Odhiambo said. "Besides, as you know, I like those girls. They became good friends with my daughter and after they complete the project, they will also become good role models."

"I remember how much they cried on the last day they were here," Okello said. "They did not want to leave. All our children were crying – even some of the women. Our friend here wiped off some tears too."

"I was not crying," Odhiambo clarified, "but I admit that I was sad. In just two weeks they had formed such deep relationships with us. When they called me from Nairobi last week, I told them that, 'This is your house and your project. Everyone here is eagerly waiting for you. You are just like our children. Come home soon.'"

"Sometimes, I think that these mzungus are not able to find enough love where they live," Reverend Ndiege remarked. "So, when they find love and affection here, they get addicted. While they have their families at home, we become their extended families."

"There is no such thing as enough love," Okello said. "We, humans, are greedy. No matter how much love we get, we always want more."

"I completely agree," Sister Phoebe said. "The German mama told me a similar story. She said that she works every day from early morning to night. Her son is in college and busy with his own life. Her husband left her many years back. Now, she has no one to talk to. When she comes here, she says that she comes back home to her own family and so many people to talk to. One day, she said something that really moved me. She said that when she is here in Kenya, she feels human again."

"And at the same time," the Reverend added, "what I learned from my experience with the mzungus and the coffee farmers was that they did not understand the importance of relationships in all our personal and professional matters. I concluded that these mzungus keep their personal and professional circles separate. Whereas, for us, all our professional relationships are fundamentally personal in nature."

"All our relationships are based on trust and respect," Chief Achieng chimed in, "and that trust is more important than money or time...or any written document. These mzungus, on the other hand, love their written documents. If there is a problem, instead of meeting and talking about it for an hour to resolve it, they will spend sixty hours writing a report."

"I can speak about relationships from a different angle," Peter offered. "As you know, I work as a driver for a travel company in Nairobi. I take tourists and businessmen around Nairobi and Mombasa and Kisumu and Nyeri and wherever else they want to go. A few of my regular customers come to Kenya just to have physical relationships. Most of them are older mzungu men looking for young Kenyan women. Some prefer to find new women every day or every week while others have been visiting the same lady for many years. Sometimes they ask me where they can find women and I take them to the tourist bars and other places. It is not my job to preach or question them. If both sides are happy with the arrangement, who am I to intervene?

"There is one particular mzee I have been driving for many years now. We eat together and talk about everything. He tells me about his family and his children and grandchildren. So one time, I asked him why he had to come all the way to Kenya to find women. He told me that his wife passed away many years back and he was too old to find willing ladies in his own country. He was too old to chase younger women and the older ones were not interested in him. But in Kenya, no one cared. He had a Kenyan girlfriend and he paid some other women for sleeping with him. He was proud that he was not lying or cheating or making false promises to anyone for getting the intimacy he wanted.

"This mzee is almost 70 years old. Once I was very curious and so when I was driving his young girlfriend to his place, I asked her about their relationship. She said that the old man just wants someone to talk to and spend time with. Sometimes they sleep together but that is not why he keeps coming back to Kenya. She said that she was very happy with the relationship. She liked him very much. He insisted on paying her college fees and her sister's school fees. There are very many mzungus that come here just to get some love and sex. You might be surprised to know that there are also many women who come for the same reasons. I once drove an elderly mzungu woman around the coast for a week. Her boyfriend was 30 years younger than her but they got along very well. Once I took them to a club in Mombasa and, let me tell you, there were atleast 25 mzungu mamas and twice as many of our young men there. They were there to form short-term alliances just like what the men were seeking from the women. The young man said that in some cases, money and material benefits were changing hands, but other times, they were not. I consider these young people as social workers. I respect them just as much as I respect my parents and my pastor.

"Some of my customers say they are here to work on development projects and improve our people's lives and make our companies more efficient. But then, I see these mzees and mamas having to travel all the way here, thousands of miles away, to get physical and emotional intimacy. It leaves me very confused. When these people are not happy and satisfied with their own lives, I don't understand how they can improve our people's lives. How is their way of living more efficient if they have to spend so much money and travel so far for some company? I don't have much money, but I am satisfied with my life. I am not that young anymore. But wherever I go, I never have a problem finding women who love life as much as I do and want to share it with me."

"We all know about the legendary charming nature of Luos," Obongo intervened. "But please spare us the details, especially, in front of the Reverend and Sister Phoebe."

Everyone's gaze moved back and forth between the Reverend and Sister Phoebe, waiting to see who would speak up and scold Peter for his lifestyle and supporting extra-marital sexual relations. The Reverend just nodded in disapproval and gulped down the rest of his soda.

"You want me to scold Peter, but I will not," Sister Phoebe finally said. "My religious training does not conflict with my pragmatic thinking over such personal issues. Who am I to judge the mzungus, the young people, or Peter? I will just say – think carefully about your choices and be safe so you can live long and happy lives."

"I wish all our wives would take some lessons from Sister Phoebe and stop judging us," the fisheries officer laughed.

"However," Sister Phoebe continued, "I want to respond to Odhiambo. He suggested that busaa is a unique contribution from our culture to the world. I think that, it is not the busaa, but this spirit of togetherness and deep respect for each other that we can share with everyone. Whoever comes to visit us, we accept them with open arms. We make them part of our lives and share what little God has given us. Most of our visitors come to help us. By mistake, some of them might end up hurting our people and our communities. But that is okay. We just accept it as a part of the parcel."

"Amen, Sister. I wonder if they will accept us in their communities just like we accept them in ours?" Obongo mused.

"There are so many mzungus and muhindis[1] that have lived around here for many years," Okello said. "If you remove their skin color, they are just like us. When I lived on the coast, I had mzungu and Asian and Arab friends and once we started talking and working together, we built such deep relationships. At some point, you just stop thinking about tribe and religion and skin color. You don't see it. It becomes invisible and what remains is this fundamental human connection."

"I agree with you on all that," Obongo argued, "but that is in our country. The question is – will the mzungus welcome us with open arms if we go to their country?"

"I am sure they will," Sister Phoebe assured, "but we must not think too much about such things. We must do the very best we can to make our community and culture more welcoming. We must share our knowledge so we can all benefit."

"Someday, I want to go to their country and dig big holes," Odhiambo proclaimed, and then he turned to Peter and winked. "But for my other ambition, it might be more efficient just to go to Mombasa."

"Aye," Peter raised his chin and grinned. "We will all go together. I will arrange for transport."

"Yaai Yai Yaaai!" the Reverend sighed, "I warned you that the busaa transforms decent people into sinners. My friends, there are many types of Kenyans and many more types of mzungus. We must not generalize. Let us put our busaa aside and join the celebration with Phillip and Wambui. I can see that lunch is ready. Trust me, the fried Tilapia tastes best with warm soda."

---

[1] Muhindis = People from the Indian subcontinent (Kiswahili)